Networked Feminism

The publisher and the University of California Press Foundation gratefully acknowledge the generous support of the Anne G. Lipow Endowment Fund in Social Justice and Human Rights.

Networked Feminism

HOW DIGITAL MEDIA MAKERS TRANSFORMED GENDER JUSTICE MOVEMENTS

Rosemary Clark-Parsons

UNIVERSITY OF CALIFORNIA PRESS

University of California Press
Oakland, California

Library of Congress Cataloging-in-Publication Data

Names: Clark-Parsons, Rosemary, 1991- author.
Title: Networked feminism : how digital media makers transformed
    gender justice movements / Rosemary Clark-Parson.
Description: Oakland, California : University of California Press,
    [2022] | Includes bibliographical references and index.
Identifiers: LCCN 2021061683 (print) | LCCN 2021061684 (ebook) |
    ISBN 9780520383838 (cloth) | ISBN 9780520383845 (paperback) |
    ISBN 9780520383852 (epub)
Subjects: LCSH: Fourth-wave feminism—United States. | Internet and
    activism—United States—21st century. | BISAC: SOCIAL SCIENCE /
    Women's Studies | POLITICAL SCIENCE / Political Process / Media &
    Internet
Classification: LCC HQ1155 .C58 2022 (print) | LCC HQ1155 (ebook) |
    DDC 305.42—dc23/eng/20220107
LC record available at https://lccn.loc.gov/2021061683
LC ebook record available at https://lccn.loc.gov/2021061684

30   29   28   27   26   25   24   23   22
10   9   8   7   6   5   4   3   2   1

To our Robyn, and to Alice, Josephine, Emanuela, Theresa, and Clara, who every day give me hope for a more feminist future

Contents

Acknowledgments

In the fall of 2013, my first semester in graduate school, I began considering the kernel of an idea that would grow into this book. Well-intentioned faculty and colleagues questioned whether feminism was a relevant topic. Later that year, I watched, at times in disbelief, as Beyoncé put the word "FEMINIST" in lights on the Video Music Awards stage, as viral feminist campaigns took over social media, and as "femvertising" became the cutting edge of commercial marketing messages. In the years since, so much has changed across the political and cultural landscape of the United States. While we often find ourselves grappling with major losses and hurdles for civil rights, it is at the same time nearly impossible to go a week without hearing the word *feminism* mentioned in a mainstream news outlet or hashtagged on a social media platform.

This book emerged from my own desire as an activist to make sense of this complicated moment for feminist social movements. But it would not have grown from a kernel into a manuscript if it had not been for feminist organizers in Philadelphia, who so generously gave me the opportunity to work alongside them and share their stories. I am especially grateful to the members of three groups: the March to End Rape Culture, Permanent Wave Philly, and Girl Army. The persistent audacity and creativity of your "do-it-ourselves" spirit are at the heart of this book. Thank you for sharing your time and energy with me and for giving me an activist home in Philly.

I completed this book with the support of a long list of people who believed in me and this project from the very start. Guobin Yang, my doctoral advisor at the University of Pennsylvania's Annenberg School for Communication, is at the top of that list. Guobin champions and believes fiercely in his students, even when they might not believe in themselves. This book would not exist without his mentorship and guidance. I cannot thank him enough for his generosity of time and spirit. I am also deeply grateful for the insights and encouragement of my dissertation committee members: Sarah Banet-Weiser, Jessa Lingel, and Victor Pickard. Most of the book's manuscript was prepared while I was a postdoctoral fellow at the Annenberg School's Center on Digital Culture and Society. I am grateful for the support of Annenberg faculty, staff, and alumni, especially John Jackson, Michael X. Delli Carpini, Litty Paxton, Jasmine Erdener, Elisabetta Ferrari, Emily Hund, Elena Maris, Lee McGuigan, Samantha Oliver, and Christin Scholz. After my time at Annenberg, I was fortunate enough to join the stellar team at the Center for Social Impact Strategy at Penn's School of Social Policy and Practice. Thank you, Peter Frumkin and Ariel Schwartz, for providing me with the time and resources necessary to complete the manuscript.

Parts of this book began as feverish notes jotted down after inspiring conversations with students. I am especially grateful to the high school and undergraduate students whom I had the great pleasure of teaching at Penn and Saint Joseph's University, as well as the master's students in Social Policy and Nonprofit Leadership at Penn's School of Social Policy and Practice. Your commitment to activism and social justice gives me hope for the future, even on the most difficult days.

Michelle Lipinsky, my editor at University of California Press, made the experience of publishing a book an empowering one. I am so thankful for Michelle's patient, unwavering support of my vision for this manuscript. Special thanks are also due to Laura Portwood-Stacer, whose wisdom and insights demystified the book proposal process. I am grateful to the conference groups that helped nurture this book, especially the Feminist Scholarship Division and the Activism, Communication, and Social Justice Interest Group of the International Communication Association.

Portions of chapters 3 and 4 were previously published in *Feminist Media Studies, Communication, Culture & Critique,* and *New Media & Society.* I appreciate these journals for supporting my scholarship and allowing me to reprint previously published work here.

The clearest path to this book starts with my family. My parents, Susan and Paul Clark, have always supported my love for reading and writing as powerful tools for creating a better world. Together with my sisters, Catherine Reimer and Elizabeth Palumbo, they are my best friends and biggest cheerleaders. Their humor and constant presence in my life saw me through the highs and lows of developing a book project. My husband, Ryan Parsons, has done everything he could possibly do to support me on this journey, from driving me all over Philadelphia to feminist meetings, to volunteering at feminist protests and fundraisers, to talking through early iterations of the book's central ideas. "Thank you" is simply not enough to acknowledge your tireless love and support, but it will have to do here. Linda and Thomas Parsons, my parents-in-law, have rooted for me as if I was their own daughter and have been there for both of us through it all.

This book is dedicated to our daughter, Robyn, and to my five nieces, Alice, Josephine, Emanuela, Theresa, and Clara. You are my sunshine and my guiding lights. I hope someday that the activists whose stories I tell here inspire you to fight for what is right and to be yourselves, even in the face of adversity.

1 Hope for a Feminist Future

In 2017, the first year of Donald Trump's presidency, journalists and commentators in the United States heralded the dawning of "The Year of Women." A contributor for the *Huffington Post*, for example, confidently explained "Why 2017 Will Be the Year of Women," assuring her readers in March that "while recent events are a constant reminder of the challenges facing women in today's world, I am more convinced than ever that 2017 will be our year" (Jain, 2017). Year-in-review headlines published in December 2017 implied that these earlier prognostications had been correct: "2017: The Unexpected (and Inspiring) Year of Women" (Dvorak, 2017); "The Year of Women, in Policy and Politics" (Epstein, 2017); "A Timeline of the Year of Women" (*Boston Globe*, 2018); "Did You Hear Her Roar? 2017 was Unquestionably the Year of the Woman" (Shamus, 2017).

A similar rash of trend stories surfaced twenty-five years earlier when, after a handful of women were elected to the heavily male-dominated Senate in 1992, headline writers widely touted the arrival of the "Year of the Woman" (Zhou, 2018). But the more recent "Year of Women" extended beyond the walls of political institutions. While record numbers of women were once again running for office, analysts also pointed to the Women's March on Washington following Trump's inauguration and the viral #MeToo movement against sexual violence as indicators that conditions were ripe for a feminist reckoning. Some highlighted a relationship between women's improbable ascendance and a recent surge in women-centric television, film, and digital content, describing 2017 as "the year of women's anger, onscreen and off" (Grady, 2017). The pattern would continue into the future. A year-end piece published on CNN's website guaranteed that "2018 Will be the Year of Women" (Schnall, 2017), while a cover story for *Politico* looked further into the unknown, eyeing the next presidential election: "Why 2020 Will be the Year of the Woman" (Scher, 2017). Everywhere you looked, headlines indicated that women were having a "moment" across politics and popular culture despite the odds they faced.

And the odds were undeniably against women. The same news outlets that heralded "The Year of Women" made it clear that, under President Trump, women and marginalized groups, including people of color, immigrants, queer and trans people, Muslims, people with disabilities, and laborers, were under attack. Within hours of being signed in as president of the United States, Trump began dismantling the Affordable Care Act, President Barrack Obama's signature legislation, which aimed to make health care accessible and affordable to all, even those with preexisting conditions (Luhby, 2018). Later, Trump halted Obama's Equal Pay Rule, ending the requirement that large companies report how much they pay workers by race and gender (Khimm, 2017). He also proposed budget cuts to the National Domestic Violence Hotline and programs under the Violence against Women Act (Planned Parenthood Action Fund, 2017). That summer, the U.S. government, under Trump's orders, began separating families seeking asylum at the U.S.-Mexico border, even going so far as to remove nursing infants from their mothers (Kirby, 2018). Meanwhile, the Supreme Court, weighted toward conservative opinions thanks to the Trump-appointed Justice Neil Gorsuch, voted to allow pro-life "crisis pregnancy centers" to masquerade as abortion clinics (Liptak, 2018), to uphold the president's travel ban on Muslims (Liptak and Shear, 2018), and to end the practice of mandatory union dues, delivering a sharp blow to organized labor in the process. With Justice Anthony Kennedy's retirement and the appointment of Justice Brett Kavanaugh, a conservative judge facing multiple sexual violence accusations, the Supreme Court was positioned to destroy the 1973 landmark *Roe v. Wade* decision legalizing abortion in the United States (Litman, 2018).

How could 2017, 2018, or even 2020 be "The Year of Women" against this backdrop of institutionalized white male supremacy? Why could commentators envision a feminist future, precisely at a moment when *women's* futures, especially the futures of women of color, queer and trans women, and working-class women, seemed so bleak? The answer lies, at least in part, in the creativity, resilience, and audacity of contemporary *feminist media activism*, or collective communication practices directed toward ending misogyny and oppression.[1]

At the same time that feminists' values and hard-won legislative victories were under siege, hope for a feminist future grew out of the steady revitalization of U.S. feminist movements, spearheaded by media-savvy activists. After a period of anti-feminist backlash throughout the 1980s (Faludi, 1991), media activists produced *zines*, or mini-magazines, to breathe new life into feminist politics throughout the 1990s, before moving their work online as early feminist "e-zines" and, later, the feminist blogosphere. Digital activism brought feminists an unprecedented degree of visibility, pushing feminist politics into the mainstream spotlight. The Women's March, which began with a single Facebook post, exploded into one of the largest protest events in U.S. history; activists used the #MeToo hashtag more than nineteen million times in the campaign's first year, making sexual violence a trending topic nationally and globally (Brown, 2018); commercial outlets have featured feminist issues, ideas, and figures, once erased and maligned in mainstream media, prominently and positively (Banet-Weiser, 2018a, 2018b). With feminism in the streets and on our screens, hope for a feminist future in the United States has felt plausible, even in moments of intense reactionary politics.

In print and digital media and across popular culture, media activists have driven the steady growth of what some have referred to as feminism's "fourth wave" (e.g., Munro, 2013; Schulte, 2011; Solomon, 2009), riffing on the oceanic metaphor long used to periodize U.S. feminisms' ebbs and flows.[2] But while the current "wave" has descended from the tides of previous generations, a key feature distinguishes this cohort from its antecedents. Formal organizations and grassroots collectives with clear leaders and distinct voices and luminaries structured the second-wave feminism of the 1960s and the third-wave feminism of the 1990s (Reger, 2012). Historical accounts of these feminist eras are punctuated by well-known groups and figures. Narratives of 1960s "second-wave" feminism tell the stories of the National Organization for Women, Gloria Steinem, Betty Friedan, the Combahee River Collective, Angela Davis, and others. The "third wave" highlighted the insights of visionary thinkers like bell hooks, Audre Lorde, and Gloria Anzaldúa, who pushed against the second wave's failure to account for how race, class, and sexuality intersect with gender. Nineties feminism also brought us the insurgent politics of young writers and artists like Rebecca Walker, Jennifer Baumgardner, and Kathleen Hanna, who opened up creative spaces to redefine what "feminism" meant to their generation. As new waves rise, however, it has become increasingly difficult to name leaders or organizations at the center of feminist movements. Instead, descriptions of the "fourth wave" underscore communication technologies and highly mediated flashpoints that, like the Women's March and #MeToo, ignited global action and discussion. Pioneering feminist blogger Jessica Valenti, when asked if she considers herself a fourth-wave feminist, captured the increasing centrality of media for feminism in a 2009 *New York Times* interview: "Maybe the fourth wave is online." Contemporary U.S. feminist movements revolve, not around singular leaders or big-name organizations, but around *media* and everyday media makers, users, and consumers.

This book tells the story of how activists have used media to reconfigure the face and reach of feminist politics. Against a vibrant backdrop of existing scholarship on the structures of political opportunities and constraints surrounding feminist media activism, it centers the perspectives of feminist activists, draws connections across feminist media campaigns, and sheds light on consistencies across feminists' media activism. It asks, how have contemporary feminists used media to craft an activist praxis that reflects their values *and* responds to the challenges of their political context? And what are the implications of their media activism for feminist movements in particular, and social movements more generally? If any year is to be the "Year of Women," we need a better understanding of how feminist activists are navigating this contradictory political context and complex media landscape.

Through years spent participating in grassroots communities and observing viral campaigns, I found that contemporary feminists engage in a *do-it-ourselves* feminism (DIOF), a feminism that is characterized by the use of everyday media technologies and platforms. Faced with an electoral system and a history of collective organizing that have failed to address complex systems of oppression, do-it-ourselves feminists do not rely on existing political organizations, institutions, authorities, or experts. Instead, they use digitally networked media to build movements from the ground up that reflect their values and meet the challenges of the current political climate, all the while juggling the affordances and limitations of their media tools. It is this tactical creativity and resilience that fuels the power, potential, and *hope* of the "fourth wave." This chapter sets the scene of our story by describing feminists' shift to networked activism. I delineate the social and technological conditions that led to this shift and outline the opportunities and challenges facing networked feminists. It concludes by turning to what feminist activists are doing with media and how their media practices are reshaping social justice work for the digital age.

FEMINISMS ACROSS THE U.S. MEDIA LANDSCAPE

The current media landscape is marked by a plurality of feminism*s*. A convergence of often contradictory discourses has swirled around the concept of feminism across U.S. media over the past several decades, creating a complicated social and political backdrop for feminist media activists. This section maps a series of feminist media histories, each of which overlap with and feed into one another, through a synthesis of existing feminist media studies scholarship. Together, they recount how feminists' status within the United States has shifted since the rise and fall of second-wave feminism and the role that media—including mainstream commercial media, activist-produced media, and digital media platforms—have played in this process. In turn, they also tell the story of networked feminism's evolution and historicize contemporary feminists' media practices. While a growing body of scholarship offers case studies of individual feminist media campaigns, less clear is *why networked media have become* *so central to the U.S. feminist repertoire* at this particular juncture. U.S. feminists' turn toward networked activism and away from highly structured organizations cannot be explained through the availability of digital media tools alone. Rather, their practices stem from a precarious sociopolitical context for feminist discourse, a desire to reimagine a more inclusive feminist politics, and a long tradition of feminist media making.

Media and the Undoing of Feminism

Starting in the mid- to late 1980s, feminism took on a precarious position in the United States, and media were partly to blame. The activism of feminists throughout the 1960s and 1970s had fundamentally altered the social, political, and economic fabric of society, troubling patriarchal norms and creating new possibilities for women in the workplace, in the home, and in the public sphere. Following this period of revolutionary change, however, a "postfeminist sensibility" (Gill, 2007, p. 5) flooded U.S. media, framing feminist movements as unnecessary, undesirable, and out of touch with young women's lives (McRobbie, 2004). Some scholars have pointed to the 1980s rise of the religious right's conservative "family values" platform under President Ronald Reagan and have described this era as a concerted backlash aimed at undermining leftist movements' achievements (Faludi, 1991; Whelehan, 2000). But while the backlash thesis tells a compelling narrative of America's political pendulum swinging from left to right, theorists of postfeminist media culture argue that the reality was not so straightforward. The postfeminist sensibility did not offer a flat-out rejection of feminism. Rather, postfeminism selectively took *some* feminist ideas and values into account (McRobbie, 2004) as commonsense thinking, while simultaneously dismissing feminist politics. As Rosalind Gill (2007) puts it, within postfeminist culture, "Feminist ideas are at the same time articulated and repudiated, expressed and disavowed" (p. 163). Much like feminist media, *post*feminist media produced throughout the 1990s and early 2000s emphasized "educational and professional opportunities for women and girls; freedom of choice with respect to work, domesticity, and parenting; and physical and particularly sexual empowerment" (Tasker and Negra, 2007, p. 2). At the same time, however, postfeminist media suggested that feminism had already achieved these goals, that those who continued to perform feminist activism were extremists, and that participation in feminist politics deprived women of some essential feminine fulfillment in the domestic sphere. As Angela McRobbie argues (2004), postfeminism engages in a "double entanglement" with both neo-conservative values and the liberalization of choice in domestic relationships and professional aspirations.

Postfeminist culture's subtle disavowal of feminist politics cut across 1990s and 2000s film, television, print media, and music. While '90s pop culture staples like the Spice Girls, *Xena: Warrior Princess*, and sex-positive *Cosmopolitan* headlines heralded the age of "girl power," their marketing and production sold women's agency in traditionally feminine packages. Powerful women and girls exhibited strength at work, in school, and in their personal lives, but they also adhered to traditional standards for beauty and feminine sexuality. The postfeminist subject was also at the center of the "makeover paradigm" (Gill, 2007, p. 156) that dominated television throughout this period. Viewers of reality television staples like *What Not to Wear*, *Extreme Makeover*, and *The Swan* followed women contestants as they found personal empowerment and fulfillment through new wardrobes, beauty routines, cosmetic surgery, and weight loss. The ideal postfeminist subject achieved empowerment through self-surveillance, self-discipline, and self-improvement via participation in consumer culture, *not* collective action. The postfeminist sensibility refused to acknowledge the role systems of power like sexism or racism play in shaping individuals' personal lives, instead positioning "women as autonomous agents no longer constrained by any inequalities or imbalances whatsoever" (Gill, 2007, p. 153). With structural inequities erased from view and empowerment framed as a matter of choice, the collective politics of a social movement were no longer necessary. The result was a generation of women who, by some accounts, refused to identify as feminists, even as they acknowledged their debts to past feminist movements and the persistence of sexism at home and in the workplace (Scharff, 2016). Postfeminism's double entanglements left feminism to exist, in sociologist Jo Reger's (2012) words, "everywhere but nowhere," a distilled version of feminist ideas and identities "diffused into the culture and structure of society" (p. 3) but without the organized support of a social movement.[3]

From the 1980s through the early 2000s, the rise of postfeminism mainstreamed a flattened, one-dimensional, individualistic understanding of agency, erasing from view the systems of power that structure everyday life and making collective action seem unnecessary. Theorists of postfeminism describe this era as an impasse for feminist activists, as the possibility for widespread social, political, and cultural transformations informed by feminist politics appeared increasingly improbable. Combined with growing internal discord over the marginalization of women of color, queer women, and working-class women within feminist movements, these conditions made feminist work especially precarious (Reger, 2012). This, McRobbie (2004) argues, was the "undoing of feminism" (p. 255).

Media and the Popularization of Feminism

But, by the mid-2010s, the tide of popular culture shifted. In the words of Andi Zeisler (2016), founder of feminist outlet *Bitch Media*, "feminism got *cool*" (p. x). Across the U.S. media landscape, the repudiation of the postfeminist sensibility gave way to *celebration*, and a new era of "popular feminism" began (Banet-Weiser, 2015b, 2018a, 2018b).

The shift from postfeminism to popular feminism reached a fever pitch in August 2014. More than eight million viewers watched Beyoncé close out the MTV Video Music Awards while standing defiantly in front of a giant screen emblazoned with the word "FEMINIST." Her girl-power anthem "Flawless," which samples a recording of Nigerian author Chimimanda Ngozi Adichie paraphrasing a dictionary definition of "feminism," blared in the background. But while she created a breathtaking moment in feminist media history, Beyoncé was not the only celebrity aligning herself with the feminist label. A number of other stars "came out" as feminists, including Miley Cyrus, Lady Gaga, Lorde, Lena Dunham, Elliot Page, Emma Watson, and Taylor Swift, and media outlets even began curating lists of "top" celebrity feminists.

This "celebrity feminism" emerged against the backdrop of an undeniably feminist "moment" in U.S. media. In 2013 and 2014 "hashtag feminism" emerged through some of the first feminist hashtag campaigns, including #YesAllWomen, #NotYourAsianSidekick, #SolidarityIsForWhiteWomen, #WhyIStayed, #BringBackOurGirls, #YouOkSis, and

#RapeCultureIsWhen, among others. During those same years, feminist nonprofit The Representation Project launched the #NotBuyingIt campaign and mobile app, inviting Super Bowl viewers to take to Twitter, call out the big game's traditionally sexist commercials, and harness the power of women consumers through threats of brand boycotts (Clark, 2014). Their efforts went viral, ushering in a new era of what commentators have alternatively referred to as "femvertising," "empowertising," or "go-girl marketing" (Ciambriello, 2014; Zeisler, 2016; Zmuda and Diaz, 2014). In 2015, women's lifestyle company SheKnows Media launched their annual Femvertising Awards. From Always feminine hygiene products to Bud Light beer, socially conscious advertisements featuring positive representations of women and girls breaking down gender roles and barriers became the new norm (SheKnows Media, 2018). Meanwhile, successful women entrepreneurs, like Facebook chief operating officer Sheryl Sandberg and Nasty Gal founder Sophia Amoruso, penned best-selling feminist books, drawing on their own life experiences to advise women on how to *Lean In* and become a *#Girlboss*. And while gender gaps still plagued the television and film industries, these years also brought an increase in the presence of trans women in popular culture through television series like *Transparent*, *Orange Is the New Black* , and *I Am Cait* and through the activism of celebrity actors and advocates like Laverne Cox and Janet Mock. Feminist ideas and rhetoric popped up in even the most unexpected places. Women's magazines such as *Cosmopolitan, Elle, InStyle,* and *Teen Vogue* shifted away from the genre's emphasis on beauty and fashion and traditional representations of gender and sexuality and started running explicitly feminist content (Groetzinger, 2016). Even *Playboy*, the men's "lifestyle" magazine known for its pornographic centerfolds and long derided by feminists (temporarily) stopped printing nude photos and began publishing stories with headlines like, "You Can't Have Feminist Liberation without Choice."

These are just a fraction of the media sites, figures, products, and trends that have embraced feminism in recent years. By 2017, Merriam-Webster declared *feminism* its "Word of the Year," citing the Women's March and the #MeToo movement alongside film and television offerings like the *Wonder Woman* reboot and *The Handmaid's Tale* as evidence for the term's comeback. Suddenly, in a clear reversal of Reger's (2012) prognosis, feminism, with a big, capital *F*, was absolutely *everywhere*, loud, proud, and clear as day.

It is difficult to isolate any one variable that triggered feminism's ascent in U.S. media. But while the exact cause of feminism's popularization remains unknown, as Valenti (2014a) argues, one thing is for certain: "The zeitgeist is irrefutably feminist." We are living in a moment that Sarah Banet-Weiser and Laura Portwood-Stacer (2017) describe as "decidedly not postfeminist" (p. 886). Rather than casting feminism as unnecessary or outmoded, advertisers, celebrities, and corporate leaders have adopted the feminist label and its associated rhetoric of empowerment. In a dramatic shift from the "backlash media" (Faludi, 1991, p. 94) of the postfeminist era, the current media landscape has given feminism a "new luminosity in popular culture" (Gill, 2016, p. 614). As Banet-Weiser and Portwood-Stacer (2017) put it, "For us as feminist media scholars, feminism has always been a useful lens through which to *understand* popular culture. However, we are now living in a moment when feminism has undeniably *become* popular culture" (p. 884).

Media and the Traffic in Feminism

The popularization of feminism through its commercial and digital media diffusion has made feminism accessible and even admired, a remarkable feat when compared with the postfeminist sensibility that infused media markets in the 1990s and early 2000s. Feminism's unprecedented degree of visibility has offered gender justice advocates a variety of new political opportunities and affordances, as feminist ideas and rhetoric reach wider audiences than ever before. Feminism's hypervisibility, however, has also created three major challenges for feminist activists. To borrow McRobbie's language for describing postfeminism, popular feminism has become *doubly entangled* in both the resurgence and the undermining of feminist collective politics.

First, popular feminism's emphases on identity, representation, and empowerment are easily co-opted and commodified. Banet-Weiser and Portwood-Stacer (2017) argue that "the terrain of popular feminism is currently occupied in large part by the individualist-feminism of neoliberal consumer culture" (p. 884). The most popular forms of feminist media are inflected with a discourse of self-improvement and individual choice. From the inspirational self-care messages that circulate on social media to feminist-branded clothing to the girl power marketing of femvertisements, popular feminism often celebrates feminism in name only while simultaneously upholding marketplace values. Zeisler (2016) argues that these manifestations of popular feminism, however alluring they may be for activists who could once hardly imagine a culture that celebrates feminism, are merely "facsimiles" of feminist "ideas, objects, and narratives that are, on closer inspection, almost exclusively about personal identity and consumption" (p. 74). This "marketplace feminism" (Zeisler, 2016, p. xiii) is necessarily decoupled from analyses of structural inequities, which would undermine the capitalist systems of exchange that enable it to exist. The most popular forms of feminism only go so far as to recognize that feminism is necessary and that inequities exists, but stop short of actually disrupting the systems of oppression that justify feminist politics in the first place. Instead, they point to consumption and the marketplace as solutions to social injustices (Banet-Weiser and Portwood-Stacer, 2017). Drawing on anthropologist Gayle Rubin's (1997) analysis of the "traffic in women" within capitalism, Banet-Weiser and Portwood-Stacer (2017) refer to this phenomenon as the "traffic in feminism" (p. 886); just as capitalism depends upon and reproduces gendered oppression, today, capitalism depends upon and reproduces a particular version of feminism that supports individualist marketplace values. Popular feminism *enables* the gendered, racial, sexual, and economic oppressions of capitalism by linking empowerment with consumption and work on the self, masking persistent inequities, and creating the illusion that we live in a feminist society (Banet-Weiser, 2015b; Banet-Weiser and Portwood-Stacer, 2017; Gill, 2016; Zeisler, 2016). The traffic in feminism produces and reproduces a more palatable, depoliticized version of feminist ideas and rhetoric, shoring up capitalist ideologies and benefitting only those most privileged "feminists"—the celebrities, CEOs, and marketers—best positioned to profit from marketplace visibility (Banet-Weiser and Portwood-Stacer, 2017).

Second and relatedly, popular feminism's linking of empowerment to consumption and choice implies that feminism is an individual enterprise, one open to interpretation and uncommitted to a particular political agenda. Perhaps nowhere does this dynamic play out more clearly than in the media frenzy over celebrity feminism. Entertainment media's obsession with exposing which actors and pop artists identify as feminists and which do not has produced a full roster of celebrity activists. What being a "feminist" actually *means*, however, has gotten lost in the f-word's surge in popularity, leaving feminism to be treated as a label rather than an action, a movement, or a set of values (Valenti, 2014b). This has opened the door for celebrities and politicians whose beliefs and platforms contradict basic feminist ideals, including conservative figures like Sarah Palin and Ivanka Trump, to brand themselves as feminists (Filipovic, 2017; Valenti, 2014b). Celebrity feminism and other forms of popular feminism make the movement more accessible to a broader base, offering a gateway to feminist politics for the otherwise uninitiated. Even so, when feminism is boiled down to a label, a soundbite, or a headline, it is left, in Gill's (2016) words, "contentless" (p. 618), an identity that can be taken on or off like a trendy T-shirt, unencumbered by the weight of a specific set of politics or positions. Whether it takes the form of Beyoncé putting the word FEMINIST in lights on the VMA's stage or Super Bowl advertisers promoting girl power, popular feminism is not equipped to confront ongoing systemic inequities. The large amount of media attention given to *identifying* as a feminist rather than *engaging* in feminism makes activism appear as easy as proclaiming yourself an activist.

Third, popular feminism has been met in equal measure with "popular misogyny," a "misogynistic political and economic culture, where rape culture is normative, violent threats against women are validated, and rights of the body for women are either under threat or being formally retracted" (Banet-Weiser and Miltner, 2016, p. 172). The hypervisibility of feminist cultures, Banet-Weiser and Miltner (2016) argue, has triggered an anti-feminist backlash, ushering in "a new era of the gender wars" (p. 171). The same digital platforms feminists have used to launch viral campaigns against sexual violence have been complicit in the perpetuation of violent harassment against feminist activists, as misogynist and racist users face few consequences for their actions. Offline, the backlash of popular misogyny has taken the form of attacks on the policy gains of previous feminist generations. The Trump administration, for example, undermined access to safe abortions and reproductive health care, anti-domestic violence programs, and workplace discrimination laws (Planned

Parenthood Action Fund, 2017). Despite the veneer of popular feminism, whose media takeover creates the perception that feminist values have won the day, women's rights and the rights of marginalized communities have never been more at risk.

While we are living in a moment that is "decidedly not postfeminist" (Banet-Weiser and Portwood-Stacer, 2017, p. 886), the challenges popular feminism presents to activists are similar to those of postfeminism: commodification and co-optation, depoliticized individualism, anti-feminist backlash. There remains a key difference between the postfeminist era and the current context of popular feminism. The undeniable commercial media market for explicitly feminist content combined with the sociotechnical affordances of digital media platforms have enabled feminist activists to mobilize highly visible campaigns, reach new audiences, amplify ignored voices, and build their own communities, all with little or no resources. Scholars and activists must remain critically ambivalent about popular feminist media content.[4] The hashtag campaign or girl power advertisement might encourage a user to express herself or introduce a young viewer to feminist ideas, but it also supports a capitalist system of exchange and marketplace individualism, exploitative ideologies that run counter to feminist collective politics. Within the "double entanglement" of popular feminism lies a generative potential, the possibility for creative resistance and subversive meaning making even as capitalist white male supremacy works to subsume it. This offers a reason, I argue throughout this book, to *hope*.

Media and the Redoing of Feminism

At the same time that postfeminism threatened to "undo" U.S. feminism in the late twentieth and early twenty-first centuries, a new generation of feminist activists began making their own media to "redo" (Baer, 2016, p. 29) feminism for this precarious political climate. These most recent waves of U.S. feminism have taken on the form of *networked activism*, a protest paradigm that replaces the leaders, finances, and people power of formal, big-name organizations with a variety of media practices, digital and otherwise. Here, "networked" refers to the communication tools these feminists draw on, from the production and circulation of alternative print media to the participatory web of social media platforms. "Networked" captures both the technological affordances and social affordances of feminists' media tools. Technological affordances allow one to communicate and receive messages through a distributed transmission system; social affordances provide an experience of a sense of connection with others across time and space. A "network" may also mean a "socio-technical assemblage" (Lingel, 2017, p. 15) of feminist activists, their technologies, and their technological practices that encompass print media, in-person spaces, face-to-face actions, as well as digital media. Feminist media studies scholar Aristea Fotopoulou (2016) pulls these elements together in her definition of *networked feminism* as "a form of contemporary political action that is characterised by complex connectivity and which operates at the intersections of online and offline, and across campaigning activities, feelings, and people" (p. 49). This complex connectivity is further underscored by careful negotiations, as feminists navigate the strengths and limitations of their networked media tools.

Contemporary feminists' shift toward networked activism was motivated by two factors. The first involves the political climate. The origins of networked feminism emerged in part from the conventions, challenges, and needs of practitioners' context. This generation of feminists turned toward networked media to fill the void of discursive spaces for feminism in the United States and to correct postfeminist media representations of feminism as unnecessary or outmoded.

The second, and more important, factor involves contemporary feminists' political *values*. Dissatisfied with the second wave's centering of white women, marginalization of women of color, and essentializing conceptualization of womanhood and women's condition, this generation of feminists drew on critiques authored by feminists of color to aspire toward more *intersectional* gender justice platforms. An intersectional approach to analyzing privilege and oppression rejects one-dimensional views of power and instead aims to account for differences and inequities between and within groups. Intersectionality is not just a theoretical tool for describing and analyzing oppression. Developed within the context of social justice struggles, intersectionality is an activist praxis for building inclusive movements (May, 2015). Kimberlé Crenshaw's (1989, 1991) theory of intersectionality directs feminists to evaluate and redress organizing practices (e.g., when and where meetings are held, who takes on leadership positions) and political visions (e.g., what problems and solutions are considered "feminist" ones, whose voices and concerns are prioritized) that collude with systems of oppression by excluding those who are of color, queer, and/or poor. In the nearly thirty years since Crenshaw (1989) defined the term, intersectionality has become the "gold standard" (Nash, 2008, p. 2) within both academic disciplines and activist communities for analyzing oppression and practicing inclusive politics. Networked feminism, which unfolds through media rather than formally structured and thereby potentially exclusive organizations, offers a more inclusive, participatory mode of feminist organizing and protest (Brown, Ray, Summers, and Fraistat, 2017; Daniels, 2016; Kendall, 2013; Kuo, 2016; Loza, 2014; Rodino-Colocino, 2014; Tynes, Schuschke, and Noble, 2016).

What scholars have alternatively referred to as the "redoing," "resurgence," "reclaiming," "renewing," and even "rebranding" of feminism (Baer, 2015; Dean and Aune, 2015; Evans, 2015; Lewis and Marine, 2015; Thornham and Weissmann 2013) as an intersectional, modern, and sorely needed movement began quietly at first, tucked between the pages of young feminists' handcrafted zines, before exploding into a vibrant network of feminist blogs, message boards, online communities, and more.

During the 1980s decline of leftist politics, disaffected youth began building alternative spaces that offered what Stephen Duncombe (2008) describes as "a way of understanding and acting in the world that operates with different rules and upon different values than those of consumer-capitalism" (p. 10). It is within this context that punk zines, descended from the science fiction "fanzines" of the 1930s and the underground press of the 1960s and 1970s, emerged (Duncombe, 2008). While the genre eludes precise definition, Duncombe identifies several key features of zines: "Zines are noncommercial, nonprofessional, small-circulation magazines which their creators produce, publish, and distribute by themselves" (p. 11). Throughout the 1980s and early 1990s, their production, circulation, and exchange cultivated the network ties of a counterculture where alternative politics ruled.

The punk scene at the center of this alternative underground culture, however, was male dominated; women were not viewed as legitimate contributors to the traditional masculine space and were often sidelined, their voices marginalized and their activist labor made invisible (Piep-meier, 2009). Confronted with a variety of factors—a political climate where collective action was no longer seen as viable but severe inequalities persisted, a feminist movement that seemed too distant and exclusive, an alternative arena that, like the New Left and the abolition movement before it, claimed to challenge power dynamics and yet did not fully recognize the contributions and concerns of women—young women drew on the long tradition of alternative media making among U.S. feminist movements and began creating their own zines (Piepmeier, 2009). Starting in the Pacific Northwest and spreading through different cities across the country, the Riot Grrrl movement exploded against the backdrop of an emerging "third-wave" feminism that emphasized the politics of everyday life and identified culture as a site of both oppression and resistance (Duncombe, 2008; Piepmeier, 2009). Like zinesters within the broader punk scene, grrrl zinesters' handmade publications followed a do-it-yourself ethics. Their zines were printed cheaply, poached from commercial print outlets, exchanged at low cost or free of charge, created activist networks, and often focused on music, artists, celebrities, and culture. Unlike other zine genres, however, grrrl zines also served as important sites for feminist theory building and knowledge production for a cohort of activists that was largely dissatisfied with their antecedents' treatment of femininity, sexuality, and difference across the overlapping intersections of identity (Duncombe, 2008; Eichhorn, 2014; Piepmeier, 2009). Drawing on their everyday personal experiences, third-wave media makers explored identity and oppression, talked back to mainstream media, meditated on both the burdens and the pleasures of gender performance, and reimagined feminism for a new generation.

Commercial access to the internet emerged precisely at the moment that legacy feminist media institutions were struggling to survive and young feminists were eagerly developing alternative media platforms from which to theorize their experiences, share knowledge, deconstruct popular discourse, and build communities while also including as many voices as possible. Digital media's destabilization of the producer/consumer binary and participatory nature paralleled the do-it-yourself ethos and intersectional politics of the third-wave generation (Lievrouw, 2011). Some zinesters created online *distros* (distributors) for their print zines, while others produced "ezines," a genre that closely mirrored grrrl zines and laid the groundwork for feminist bloggers (Piepmeier, 2009). By the early 2000s, the feminist blogosphere was a thriving network composed of countless nodes and growing every day, as the work of pioneering sites like TheFBomb.org, Feministing.com, Feministe.us, CrunkFeminist Collective.com, Scarleteen.com, and Shakesville.com, among others, inspired readers to take part.

This budding feminist blogosphere helped mobilize one of, if not *the*, earliest instances of networked feminist activism. The 1997 Million Woman March in Philadelphia, the original namesake of the Women's March on Washington, is among the largest protest marches in U.S. history. Like the Women's March, the Million Woman March was *not* organized by high-profile leaders or big-name organizations, but by two local women, Phile Chionesu and Asia Coney, who found their particular concerns as Black women unrepresented in either anti-racist or feminist movements (Everett, 2004). Without the support or resources of a movement organization, Chionesu and Coney created their own network of websites to promote the event and its mission statement. Women of color in homes and offices across the country printed the websites' pages to share with computerless friends and family members (Everett, 2004). On October 25, 1997, their digitally networked grassroots efforts brought, by some estimates, *1.5 million people* to Philadelphia's Benjamin Franklin Parkway to demand social, political, and economic empowerment for Black women, their families, and their communities (Everett, 2004). The accessible, participatory nature of networked media helped Chionesu and Coney create an intersectional protest action to uplift Black women, who were often marginalized within movements that focused on gender *or* race but that overlooked their intersections.

In the two decades between the Million Woman March and the Women's March on Washington, networked feminism flourished, with activists developing new protest forms as new platforms became available. Feminist bloggers initiated the dialogues that led to the 2011 international SlutWalk movement and to the recent rise in activism against sexual violence on college campuses (Mendes, 2015). Social media users developed hashtag feminism, pairing viral campaigns with traditional protest actions like street protests and boycotts (Bonilla and Rosa, 2015; Clark, 2014).

Beyond direct action, networked feminism has created countless spaces for feminist dialogue and critique, which have spilled over into mainstream commercial media. The success of the feminist blogosphere, for example, demonstrated a demand for feminist content, leading mainstream outlets to hire feminist voices and cover feminist topics (Groetzinger, 2016; Keller, 2016). Several bloggers responsible for the early growth of the feminist blogosphere, including Jessica Valenti (Feministing), Jill Filipovic (Feministe), and Brittney Cooper (Crunk Feminist Collective), landed gigs at commercial media outlets the likes of the *Guardian*, *Cosmopolitan*, and *Salon*. And while online platforms continue to inspire new, highly visible forms of resistance, feminists have also used digital networks to facilitate older tactics for internal community building, including the production and circulation of paper-based zines and the cultivation of safe spaces.

Like feminism more generally, networked feminism is complex; multiple; diverse; and often messy, contradictory, and filled with inner tensions. Any attempt to trace its growth over time is bound to be incomplete and to oversimplify its history and nature. While it may be too expansive to define or historicize with exact precision, one thing remains certain— networked feminist activism and discourse are, against all odds, thriving.

THE POWER AND CONTRADICTIONS OF NETWORKED FEMINISM

Feminists' turn toward networked activism reflects the broader digital reconfiguration of social and political life. Like the communication technologies that preceded it, the internet has transformed the public sphere, from the macrosocial systems of state politics, global economies, and civil society to the microsocial interactions among family, friends, neighbors, and coworkers (Benkler, 2006; Castells, 1996; boyd, 2008; Friedland, Hove, and Rojas, 2006; Tufekci, 2017). Digital networks, rather than formal and informal organizations, have become the organizing principles and building blocks of society (Castells, 1996; Friedland, Hove, and Rojas, 2006). The twenty-first-century public sphere is, as danah boyd (2011) puts it, a collection of *networked publics*: "They are simultaneously (1) the space constructed through networked technologies and (2) the imagined collective that emerges as a result of the intersection of people, technology, and practice" (p. 39). While digital networks are altering the technical means through which we communicate within the public sphere, they are also recasting our understanding of social connection and community in network terms, and with it, the "logic of how and where we can interact; with whom, and at what scale and visibility" (Tufekci, 2017, p. 11). This networked "logic" extends well beyond digital platforms to permeate life "offline," as the internet becomes more and more embedded in everyday experiences of the world (Hine, 2015; Lingel, 2017).

Social movements take on new forms, tactics, and trajectories within the networked public sphere. Sociologists Jeff Goodwin and James Jasper (2015) define *social movements* as "conscious, concerted, and sustained efforts by ordinary people to change some aspect of their society by using extra-institutional means" (p. 3). Digital media platforms have radically expanded the extra-institutional means available to social movement participants. Across the political spectrum, the networked logic of digital media is changing how movements mobilize and whom they reach. Lance Bennett and Alexandra Segerberg (2013) described the digital reconfiguration of activism as the shift from *collective* to *connective* action. Whereas "the logic of collective action" involves strong organizational coordination of actions and messages, "the logic of connective action" involves little or no organizational coordination. Within the logic of connective action, *networked activism* becomes the tactic of choice and communication networks become key organizing structures. Among contemporary social movements, diffuse assemblages of digital media users and outlets have taken on roles comparable to activist leaders and organizations.

Existing research highlights the many affordances of networked activism for feminists. For one, networked feminists have gained access to large audiences at low cost. Drawing on an assemblage of media platforms, sites, and practices, networked feminists have mobilized global protest actions, inspired viral conversations about sexual violence (Rodino-Colocino, 2014), initiated national boycotts against sexist media representations (Clark, 2014), and more, all without the resources of formally structured organizations. Previous feminist generations struggled to shoulder their way into the spotlight of commercial media attention (Steiner, 1992). But through the highly public nature of social media platforms, networked feminist campaigns gain visibility quickly, their political dissent converging with news and entertainment media outlets and spilling over onto the popular culture stage (Banet-Weiser, 2015b).

Beyond mainstream visibility, self-produced feminist media offer outlets for challenging restrictive gender norms, especially those promulgated through commercial media representations. Piepmeier (2009) and Zobl (2009) describe feminist zinesters' practice of cutting and pasting images from commercial print media to critique them and offer alternatives as a vital form of countercultural production. In recent years, Twitter hashtags have become central to feminist media critique; feminists have initiated hashtag campaigns to intervene on degrading or oppressive representations of gender and sexuality in advertisements (Clark, 2014), news media (Meyer, 2014), and the entertainment industry (Horeck, 2014). Feminist hashtag campaigns have been especially effective in debunking the victim-blaming myths that characterize news coverage of sexual assault and domestic violence (Clark, 2016; Rentschler, 2015; Rodino-Colocino, 2014; Thrift, 2014) as in the case of #MeToo and #WhyIStayed, and in challenging stereotypical or offensive representations in advertisements, as in the case of #NotBuyingIt (Clark, 2014).

Feminist media also make visible oppressive, everyday experiences normalized into invisibility. Carrie Rentschler (2015), for example. Highlights how visibility and recognition play key roles in feminists' use of social media responses to individual experiences of sexual violence. Regardless of the exact form their networked activism takes, as Kaitlynn Mendes, Jessica Ringrose, and Jessalynn Keller (2019) argue, "girls and women are using participatory digital media as activist tools to dialogue, network, and organize to challenge contemporary sexism, misogyny, and rape culture" (p. 2). Feminist media have also functioned as key spaces for confronting tensions and shortcomings within feminist movements. Steele (2016) argues that blogs offer Black feminists outlets to "talk back" to not only the systems of power that marginalize people of color, but to feminist and anti-racist activist communities that have historically excluded Black women's voices and concerns. Susana Loza (2014) makes a similar argument in her analysis of the 2013 hashtag campaign, #SolidarityIsForWhiteWomen, as a watershed moment for reflecting on who is and is not included in U.S. feminism. As outlets for free expression, feminist media are critical spaces for developing feminist actions, identities, politics, theories, and histories.

Lastly, scholars have documented how the webs of networked feminism lay the groundwork for new feminist social formations and communities. Harris (2003), for example, argues that the exchange of zines, often for free, barter, or trade, forges communal bonds that encourage the collective formation of critical feminist subjectivities. Others have highlighted similar social processes unfolding online. Keller (2016), in her ethnographic study of girl feminist bloggers, explores how blogs function as a "discursive space" (p. 14) where young women develop feminist identities and alternative feminist histories through personal reflections and interactions with one another, forming "networked counterpublics" (p. 80). According to Kaitlyn Mendes (2015), the networked counterpublics of the feminist blogosphere were crucial for sparking SlutWalk, a global street protest movement that began in 2011; these same networks later became critical spaces for feminists to debate the movement's tactics and messages. Carrie Rentschler and Samantha Thrift (2015) argued that "networked community building" (p. 330) has also unfolded through the viral spread of feminist memes, like the 2012 Mitt Romney–inspired "Binders Full of Women" meme; by constructing and circulating memes, feminists not only engage in collective acts of political critique, they also foster communal ties through shared humor that cut across differences. Importantly, pointing to their open, low-cost, participatory nature, feminist media studies scholars have also described these networked communities as more inclusive than traditional, face-to-face spaces and organizations (Brown, Ray, Summers, and Fraistat, 2017; Daniels, 2016; Jackson, Bailey, and Welles, 2020; Kendall, 2013; Kuo, 2016; Loza, 2014; Rodino-Colocino, 2014; Tynes, Schuschke, and Noble, 2016).

While this review is not exhaustive, it highlights five key goals scholars consistently identify as motivating contemporary feminists' orientation toward media: critiquing dominant discourse, promoting free expression, making oppression visible, negotiating feminist principles, and fostering collective solidarity. These are long-standing priorities for U.S. feminism and continue to shape contemporary gender justice activists' definitions of progress. Today's feminist media activism carries on a long tradition of feminist struggles for recognition, voice, and community. Researchers have likened contemporary feminist zines, blogs, hashtags, memes, and mobile apps to the 1960s consciousness-raising circles, protests, speak-outs, and alternative presses and bookstores of the second wave, recogniz-ing the urgency with which U.S. feminists have always taken up media and communication as necessary forms of activism (Keller, 2015; Kennedy, 2007; Shaw, 2012; Wood, 2008). Stacey Young (1997) calls this tradition *discursive activism*, a repertoire of collective action directed at "promot-ing new grammars, new social paradigms through which individuals, collectivities, and institutions interpret social circumstances and devise responses to them" (p. 3). For decades, U.S. feminist activists have pro-duced their own media to deconstruct the discourses upholding patriar-chy and white supremacy. In their place, generations of feminist media activists have built new discursive frameworks for representing margin-alized identities, interpreting oppressive experiences, and responding to systemic injustices.

What sets the current generation apart is the high degree of media-tion that characterizes feminist tactics, discourses, identities, communi-ties, and organizational structures. The activism of second-wave feminism unfolded primarily through in-person meetings and actions coordinated, mobilized, and framed by organizations with a distinct membership and, often, a central leadership. Reger (2012) describes the second-wave genera-tion as composed of two "strands," each with differing organizational structures (p. 12). One strand consisted of formalized women's rights organizations with national and regional offices and bureaucratic mem-bership structures, such as NOW, the Women's Equity Action League, and the National Women's Political Caucus. The other strand included more radical women's liberation groups like the New York Radical Women and the Redstockings. Formed in response to frustrations with the hier-archical, top-down leadership structures of women's rights organiza-tions, these groups instead encouraged horizontal, collectivist approaches that allowed every participant equal say. Despite these key differences in organizing philosophies, both strands of second-wave feminism followed a logic of *collective action*, with organizations and groups coordinating actions and messages. Similarly, feminist social movement scholar Nancy Whittier (1995) traces a history of feminist generations from the 1960s to the 1990s, punctuated by formal membership organizations, radical grassroots collectives, rape crisis centers, women's shelters, feminist bookstores, and women's studies departments. The same collective action organizing logic characterized the work of older feminist generations. In *Survival in the Doldrums,* Leila Rupp and Verta Taylor (1987) identify the National Women's Party, a women's rights organization formed in 1916 with a formal staff and board, as essential to maintaining feminist communities, dialogues, and actions throughout the 1940s and 1950s, after the peak of the suffrage movement and before the dawning of the second wave. These historical accounts paint a portrait of U.S. feminist movements as far too varied and complex to fit neatly into the traditional "wave" metaphor. At the same time, they reveal a U.S. feminist landscape punctuated by a network of named organizations, groups, collectives, and spaces, composed of dedicated membership bodies and distinct leading voices.

In stark contrast, contemporary feminist activism in the United States unfolds primarily through *media,* not organizations or groups. Of course, media production and critique were important political priorities for previous feminist generations. The second-wave feminist underground press, composed of hundreds of self-published newspapers, magazines, and newsletters that cropped up across the country throughout the 1960s and 1970s, stands as an important precursor to today's feminist media networks (Steiner, 1992; Stevenson, 2020). A key difference, however, separates these two generations of feminist media activists. Following the logic of collective action, second-wave organizations, collectives, and leaders structured movement communications, actions, and participation. But today, as feminists shift toward *connective* action, media and communication networks have become organizing structures, in and of themselves. For contemporary feminists, participation in feminist movements and campaigns is structured through blogs, hashtags, memes, email listservs, and zines, among other media genres and outlets. These channels mediate political discourse, direct action campaigns, collective identity formation, community building, coordination of street protests, and more, to the point that contemporary feminist movements have become nearly inseparable from digital media. As Fotopulou (2016) puts it, *"doing feminism* and *being feminism* implies enacting ourselves primarily as embodied and social subjects through media practices and imaginaries of technologies and the internet" (p. 2). For previous generations of U.S. feminism, media helped support the movement. In the age of networked feminism, media *are* the movement.

Networked activism can be found across a variety of social movements and activist campaigns. But as ongoing scholarly and popular debates demonstrate, the digital reconfiguration of protest and the public sphere presents particular opportunities and challenges for feminists. On the one hand, digital platforms reduce barriers to entry, making it easier not only for diverse constituents to participate in an activist campaign, but to play a meaningful role in shaping its core messages and tactics. Social movement scholars have demonstrated the role digital networks play in informing activists of protest logistics (Gerbaudo, 2012; Tufekci and Wilson, 2012), sharing collective feelings of outrage and hope (Castells, 2012), decentralizing movement leadership (Bennett and Segerberg, 2013), and decreasing the costs of organizing and joining a movement (Earl and Kimport, 2011). The accessible, participatory nature of networked activism is of special importance to feminists committed to intersectional frameworks for social justice. Feminist media scholars have argued that networked activism enables more inclusive, intersectional feminist spaces than traditional, in-person modes of collective action. In digital spaces, a diversity of activists can articulate experiences of difference, collectively produce intersectional analyses of power, and develop political actions and theories (Keller, 2016; Mendes, 2015; Rentschler and Thrift, 2015; Brown, Ray, Summers, and Fraistat, 2017; Daniels, 2016; Kendall, 2013; Kuo, 2016; Loza, 2014; Rodino-Colocino, 2014; Tynes, Schuschke, and Noble, 2016). Networked feminists share and identify linkages between personal experiences of injustice, updating the 1960s-era feminist slogan, "the personal is political," for the digital age. But unlike the most prominent organizations of 1960s feminism, which were often dominated by white college-educated women, social media platforms offer new opportunities for activists standing at the intersection of multiple, overlapping oppressions to build coalitions, deconstruct interlocking systems of power, and critique exclusionary activist practices (Noble and Tynes, 2016). Digital media platforms, in other words, are easily adapted to contemporary feminists' political goals and values. They offer new spaces for political engagement at a time when marginalized communities are increasingly disillusioned with conventional political institutions and channels (Baer,

2016; Tufekci, 2017). When successful, the networked diffusion of activist campaigns pushes these diverse voices into the mainstream media spotlight, where they may alter and shape public responses to social justice issues (Shaw, 2013; Young, 1997).

But while digital media users have increased movements' accessibility, diversity, and visibility, networked activism has simultaneously left feminists vulnerable to backlash, repression, and co-optation. Social media may have given U.S. feminists a more prominent national profile, but these platforms have also provided an outlet for networked misogyny, online gender-based harassment that includes harmful silencing practices like hate speech, revenge porn, doxxing, and threats of violence (Banet-Weiser and Miltner, 2016). Feminism's networked hypervisibility also leaves feminist politics open to co-optation. When feminist rhetoric and ideas become "popular" and circulate through commercial media, activist messages of empowerment are often repackaged to support capitalist values of individualism, choice, and consumption, rather than collective politics (Banet-Weiser and Portwood-Stacer, 2017). This reduction of the political to the personal has led critics to question the efficacy and staying power of feminist movements. Feminists' shift toward networked activism and away from more traditionally organized collective action spearheaded by leaders with well-defined goals and messages may come at the cost of achieving long-term institutional changes (Banet-Weiser, 2015a; Fraser, 2013). While digital networks enable movements to quickly mobilize viral actions, activists are at times left without the collective solidarities, leadership structures, decision-making capabilities, and capacities for tactical innovation necessary for sustained struggle (Tufekci, 2017).

Networked activists must navigate the structural constraints of corporately owned social media platforms. Social media may offer useful organizing and outreach tools, but services like Facebook and Twitter profit from activists' digital labor and make their personal data available to third parties (Youmans and York, 2012). For feminist activists concerned with empowerment and liberation, this raises concerns about consent, agency, and surveillance. What's more, as feminist political scientist and media scholar Jodi Dean (2005, 2009) argues, the pitfalls of adopting commercial internet spaces as arenas for political participation extend far beyond individual privacy concerns. In our age of "communicative capitalism"

(Dean, 2005), the content and meaning of our digital messages matter far less than their exchange value within the networked circulation of information. Social media companies profit from users' contributions to streams of content and, in turn, personal data. Consequently, social media companies promote circulation above all else. They frame digital communications as meaningful forms of social participation and expression to encourage users to participate in the abundance of messages that flood these platforms on a daily basis. In the realm of activism and social movements, the framing of digital media as outlets for political participation risks a disconnect between the digital circulation of political messages and the institutional enactment of official policy. In other words, when circulation is valued above all else, response and engagement with activists' digital messages are not guaranteed. Networked activists may feel like they are contributing to meaningful action, but their primary contribution is to the circulation flow. What's more, by contributing to the circulation flow, activists support social media companies with profit-driven political agendas that run counter to feminist politics.[5] Do-it-ourselves feminists may work outside of political institutions as we typically imagine them, but like all social media users, their reliance on sites like Twitter and Facebook means that they are always embedded in the political machinations of "Big Tech." Communicative capitalism, the marketplace values of popular feminism, and the often fleeting nature of digital activism snowball into an avalanche of obstacles, blocking any one clear path toward sustainable, effective, and values-aligned movements for gender justice.

Networked feminism, then, is a double-edged sword. For feminists, to be networked is to be *both* politically empowered *and* vulnerable (Fotopoulou, 2016). On the one hand, networked media grant activists access to global audiences at little or no cost and enable more inclusive and participatory modes of protest. On the other, the turn toward digital media has left activists open to harassment, co-optation, and burnout without the support of a traditionally organized movement. Perhaps nowhere is this clearer than in the contradictions of "The Year of Women" coinciding with Trump's first years in office. Paradoxically, digital networks are, to again borrow McRobbie's (2004) phrase from her study of feminist media cultures, *doubly entangled* in the rejuvenation *and* suppression of feminist politics.

Understanding the power of networked feminism for gender justice movements requires us to look beyond the sword and consider the goals, values, and experiences of the people wielding it. The internet presents a complex spectrum of exciting possibilities and dangerous pitfalls for feminists locked in decades-long struggles for recognition, voice, and community. Through their careful and creative negotiations with these affordances and limitations, networked feminist activists shine a light on the generative potential of media activism for dismantling systems of oppression and creating new pathways for collective strength. Theirs is not a straightforward story of an internet revolution, but an ongoing, imperfect practice in building feminist movements and spaces online and off.

STUDYING THE PRACTICE OF NETWORKED FEMINISM

This book examines how feminist activists have navigated the paradoxes of networked feminism. Feminist media are not merely texts or tools, but also *practices*. I draw on Nick Couldry's (2012) media-as-practices framework, which directs attention toward "the specific regularities in our actions related to media and the regularities of context and resources that make certain types of media-related actions possible or impossible, likely or unlikely" (p. 78). Couldry frames media as *actions* that emerge from and are shaped by media practitioners' values, goals, needs, and resources. Rather than beginning with content and ask how media messages affect consumers, the media-as-practices framework begins with *people* and asks what people actually do with media, how people understand what they do with media, and how contexts inform media practices. This framework centers activists' voices and highlights the connections among their goals, environment, and communication strategies, opening possibilities for engaged scholarship that supports social justice projects.

In this book, I specifically examine how U.S. feminists use networked media to organize resistance, stage protests, and build communities in ways that reflect their values and respond to the challenges of their environment. Focusing on U.S. feminism narrows the global plurality of feminist movements, philosophies, histories, and tactics to a particular geographic region and allows me, a feminist researcher living and working in the United States, to more easily connect with feminist activists. U.S. feminists have been key pioneers in the practice of networked feminism; they were among the first to use blogs as vehicles for fostering internal dialogue and mobilizing street protests (Everett, 2004). Through the Western domination of global media flows, their voices and actions have often, for better or worse, risen to prominence as models for activists organizing in other national contexts. At the same time, the geographic boundaries on this study bring into view a wide range of different practices across a variegated political spectrum that extends well beyond the scope of this book. Feminist scholars and activists have identified a whole typology of U.S. feminisms, whose values include "liberal," "Marxist," "cultural," "eco-," and "intersectional" feminisms, alongside the "popular," "marketplace," and "celebrity" feminisms that have pervaded consumer culture and co-opted feminist politics (see Tong and Botts, 2018). I am specifically invested in studying U.S.-based feminist movements and communities that appropriate networked media in an effort to create *sociopolitical transformations* in both institutional and everyday life. The feminist activists whose voices are at the heart of this book share an explicit commitment to dismantling misogyny, racism, heterosexism, and other identity-based systems of oppression. Taken together, their stories create opportunities to reflect on best practices in feminists' ongoing struggles for social justice.

Case Studies

Approaching feminist *media* as feminist *practices* calls for a methodology that prioritizes feminist media *practitioners*. I employed a multimodal qualitative methodology that centers feminist media practitioners' voices, perspectives, and actions. My research process revolved around a three-year, multi-sited, ethnographic analysis of feminist media activism in the city of Philadelphia. Each of the chapters begins with one or more vignettes from this fieldwork to ground my analysis in the experiences of my participants. To supplement this fieldwork, I also conducted textual analyses of national and transnational feminist media campaigns, in-depth interviews with feminists, and digitally archived reflections from activists. In all, this book focuses on six case studies: (1) the 2017 Women's March on Washington, which inspired a global wave of protests on Trump's inauguration day; (2) Philadelphia's annual March to End Rape Culture, the city's local chapter of the international SlutWalk movement; (3) the #MeToo campaign, whose message against sexual violence went viral in 2017; (4) Girl Army, a Philly-based feminist Facebook group; (5) the U.S. feminist zine community, a nationally dispersed network of print media makers; and (6) Permanent Wave Philly, a grassroots feminist music and arts collective. In my analyses of each, I bring together existing feminist, social movement, and communication theories with feminist media practitioners' insights and experiences to develop a theoretical framework that sheds light on U.S. feminists' relationships with media.

The six cases represent a set of what Jessa Lingel (2017a) calls *networked field studies*, linked not only "by a shared interest in addressing a particular set of questions" (Lingel, 2017a, p. 13), but through participant overlap. Activists in each field site participate or have participated in *at least* one of the other five field sites. For example, during my ethnographic fieldwork with Philly's March to End Rape Culture, the organizers participated in the city's local Women's March, used social media accounts to amplify the #MeToo campaign, connected with other area feminists through the Girl Army Facebook group, created zines, and attended or even helped organize the Permanent Wave collective's events. My study of feminist activism began with the March to End Rape Culture. In the spirit of anthropologist George Marcus's (1995) view of multi-sited ethnography, I "followed the people" (p. 106) from one site to the next, mapping a web of networked feminist practices that scale up from the hyperlocal to the global. I joined the MTERC team after speaking with Chelsea, a key MTERC organizer, at the 2014 march about my research. Another MTERC organizer later invited me to join the Girl Army group, a communications hub for Philly feminist happenings, via Facebook. I became involved with Permanent Wave Philly (PWP) after signing up for the collective's listserv at an information and merchandise table they hosted at MTERC. These three network connections opened doors to others. PWP members, who collaborate on an annual zine, introduced me to the handmade paper booklets and the broader circuit of feminist zine festivals, distributers, and websites. And it was through Girl Army members that I first learned about the earliest rumblings of the Women's March and, later, the #MeToo movement.

I do not claim to offer a representative or generalizable view of all U.S. feminist media. Rather, this multi-sited approach has produced a detailed and situated account of a variety of practices that, as evidenced by the overlap in my field studies, are central to the networked feminist repertoire. These networked field studies allow me to develop a theoretical framework that illuminates connections and similarities across U.S. feminist media practices. By taking a *networked* approach to studying *networked* feminism, I allowed my participants to guide my analytical attention, thereby centering activist-practitioners in the scaffolding of my project.

Data Collection and Analysis

For each case study, I drew on at least two of three different qualitative methods: participant observations, in-depth, semi-structured interviews, and textual analysis. In every case, I deployed a particular set of methods with the goal of understanding, from multiple angles, the relationship between feminists' politics and their media practices.

Data collection for the three sites localized in Philadelphia—MTERC, Girl Army, and PWP—involved extensive ethnographic observations. I spent three years within the networked field of grassroots feminist media activism in Philly, from September 2014 through September 2017. During that time, I was actively involved in the planning and execution of MTERC's annual protest event and of PWP's music shows, arts events, and annual zines. For nine months during that three-year period—from January to October 2015—I conducted an ethnographic analysis of Girl Army, a secret feminist Facebook group whose members are primarily from the greater Philadelphia area. Over the course of those nine months, I interacted with Girl Army throughout the day via the Facebook mobile app, and I also set aside one hour per week dedicated to browsing, posting, and lurking in group discussions. I estimate that I spent approximately 120 hours, 300 hours, and 100 hours working and interacting with the MTERC organizing team, the PWP collective, and Girl Army members, respectively.

The three remaining translocal case studies—WMOW, #MeToo, and feminist zines—involved more episodic participant observations. I watched the Women's March grow in the fall of 2016 from a Facebook event to a globally networked protest movement through my own social media accounts and later joined the local march in Philadelphia. When

#MeToo went viral the following year, I watched as important conversations about sexual violence began popping up all around the world and joined in activist discussions on Twitter about the promise and perils of a media campaign that asked survivors to tell their stories on a public stage. A similar mix of casual and formal observations informs my analysis of feminist zines. As a participant observer in PWP, I contributed to and edited one annual zine and helped produce and sell copies of others. I also participated in local zine festivals; distributed copies of PWP zines to local bookstores, where I connected with other zinesters; and contributed to another collaborative zine published by a different feminist grassroots collective. In all three cases, these episodic observations give my analysis more contextual details. Whether extensive and ethnographic or casual and episodic, participant observations of networked feminism gave me the opportunity to study activists' practices firsthand.

For three of my case studies—Girl Army, PWP, and the feminist zine community—I conducted in-depth, semi-structured interviews with participants. To develop a deeper understanding of Girl Army members' practices, I supplemented my ethnographic observations with interviews with seven members, each of whom represented a different level or type of experience in the group, from highly active moderators to lurkers. I took a similar approach to studying PWP, using interviews with the collective's three most active members to explore themes that emerged throughout my fieldwork in greater depth. In my analysis of the feminist zine community, interviews constitute the bulk of my data. I interviewed twelve zinesters who had exhibited work at the Philly Feminist Zine Fest to consider the role paper-based goods play in the digitally networked feminist media repertoire. In total, I interviewed twenty-two feminist activist practitioners. All interviews had a semi-structured agenda that incorporated scripted but flexible, open-ended questions and encouraged participants to take the conversation in the direction of their choosing. While participant observations allowed me to study feminists' actions, in-depth interviews gave participants a chance to reflect on their practices, offering new insights into the behind-the-scenes negotiations feminist perform between their politics and their media tactics.

For all six case studies, I used textual analysis in conjunction with observations and/or interviews to study the media texts participants produced, news media coverage related to the activism in question, and activists' written reflections regarding feminist movements and their tactics. To understand activists' public outreach work as well as public opinion about their tactics, I archived and studied the public-facing websites and social media accounts as well as news coverage of WMOW, MTERC, and PWP. Data collection for the other three case studies—#MeToo, Girl Army, and zines—involved developing more targeted archives of a particular feminist media practice: tweeting hashtags, posting in Facebook groups, and circulating print zines. For both WMOW and #MeToo, I also collected activists' reflections on the movements' tactics that were published in editorial pages or on public platforms like Twitter. In existing scholarship on networked activism, researchers often use textual analysis to conduct studies focused on campaigns' content. This work has yielded a wealth of rich descriptions of feminist media but has also resulted in an under-theorization of the politics and philosophies that inform feminists' media practices. While I, too, use textual analysis to study feminist media content, this material functions primarily as contextual information for my case studies. To refocus attention on the feminist activist-practitioners behind the content, I paired my study of feminist media content with observational and interview data and conducted archival analyses of activists' published reflections.

The combination of all three qualitative methods across this project highlights activists' actions, voices, and perspectives from a variety of different angles. Throughout this book, I offer analyses that are simultaneously rooted in activist-practitioners' experiences and informed by existing feminist, social movement, and communication theories. In each chapter, I bring theories of power and resistance to bear on my interpretation of feminists' media politics and tactics. It is this combination of theoretical resources born out of social justice projects and practitioner-focused data that brings do-it-ourselves feminism to light as an organizational paradigm guiding contemporary feminist movements and communities.

Feminist Research Ethics and Reflexivity

While any research done with human subjects raises ethical concerns, studying social movements requires unique considerations. Stefania Milan (2014) outlines four special ethical considerations that social movement scholars must take, all of which apply to my study of networked feminism. First, because social movements are knowledge projects in and of themselves, social movement researchers must treat this knowledge with the same respect granted to academic scholarship and strive to incorporate knowledge "from below" into their own work. Second, activism in any context is often risky, and disclosing the dynamics of activism through scholarly work might expose activists to surveillance, repression, and personal threats. Researchers must incorporate an awareness of these potential consequences into their project designs. Third, activists are, of course, highly invested in their movements and may likely expect movement scholars to at least be politically aligned, if not politically *involved*, in their dissident work, leaving the researcher to strike a balance between personal activist and academic work. Fourth and finally, practitioner-centered scholarship in any context requires research subjects to perform labor for the researcher. In the case of social movements, the researcher takes from practitioners' limited time and energy, which might be otherwise invested in activist projects. The researcher, then, must interrogate this power imbalance and develop strategies for compensating for it. When read alongside Couldry's work, Milan's concerns indicate that a research approach that truly centers activist media practitioners must include an "ethically informed positioning of the researcher in relation to the values and practices of the movement" (p. 447) under study.

To address these ethical concerns and further prioritize feminist media makers in my analysis, I drew inspiration from the field of feminist ethnography to develop a project informed and driven by feminist values. Since the 1980s, feminist ethnographers have launched important challenges to the norms and assumptions underpinning knowledge-building projects across multiple disciplines within social science. Whereas, in decades prior, feminist social scientists invested ample energy into correcting the androcentric biases of their fields by adding women to research samples and preexisting theoretical frameworks, this more radical generation of researchers advanced a fundamental line of questioning that shook the very foundations of their fields: What is the nature of social reality? Who can know? What can be known (Hesse-Biber, 2007)? For decades, they have endeavored to deconstruct the researcher/researched binary and center marginalized subjects as legitimate authorities on social life.[6]

Feminist ethnographers typically do not identify as unbiased scientists capable of producing universal theory, but instead view their methods as situated and subjective, their representations as incomplete and constructed, and their research as explicitly political projects that contribute to social change (Hesse-Biber, 2007; Schlock, 2013). They attempt to destabilize the hierarchy between the researcher and the researched by validating participants' situated experiences as knowledge, grounding their claims in their participants' experiences, engaging in research that is of use and relevance to their participants, and seeking participants' feedback throughout the research process (Hesse-Biber, 2007; Schlock, 2013). Reflexivity is central to this process; at every stage, feminist ethnographers must "recognize, examine, and understand how their social background, location, and assumptions affect their research practices" (Hesse-Biber, 2007, p. 17). The feminist ethnographic project offers an instructive guiding framework for researchers studying the media practices of social movements. Politically motivated, partial, and reflexive, feminist ethnographers, working closely with their participants, attempt to produce social science that honors difference and advances justice.

Throughout the course of conducting the research for this book, I have attempted to the best of my ability to do the same. This has involved a range of pragmatic steps, such as using pseudonyms to protect participants' identities, compensating interviewees for their time, making careful choices about which tactics and personal stories to bring to light through my scholarship, and sharing what I learn with the activists who might use it. My research approach has also included more complex processes, such as asking participants for feedback on my findings and developing methods for highlighting activists' voices without also asking them to perform extra labor on my behalf. Most importantly, I have tried, at every opportunity, to contribute to participants' social justice projects. Sometimes, this has entailed "borrowing" reams of printer paper from the department office for zine-making or using local university connections to promote a protest. Other times, it has meant utilizing my privilege as an academic to procure campus event spaces for film screenings or panel discussions. Still elsewhere, I have taken up the everyday grunt work known to all activists deep in the struggle, from screen-printing T-shirts, stapling flyers on telephone poles, and taking meeting minutes to drafting press releases, fielding emails, and fundraising. And in its most exciting moments, doing research that centers the needs, well-being, and work of activist-practitioners has meant being an *accomplice*, not an ally (Indigenous Action Media, 2014), and talking back to the sexist cop who made fun of an anti-rape protest chant or using a megaphone to rally a crowd against a group of misogynist counterprotesters. While my participants and I share certain marginalizing identity markers—many of the voices that fill these chapters are, like me, women from working-class backgrounds—I recognize that my status as a white, educated, cisgender woman not only shapes my subjective understanding of power and oppression, but also enables me to push where less privileged activists might face pushback.

If the vitality of feminist politics and activism is, as the scholarship reviewed throughout this book suggests, bound up with the growth of networked feminism, then identifying and meditating on shared struggles, successes, and tactics across networked feminist projects is key to building stronger feminist movements over time. This is where academic researchers studying feminist social movements and their media practices can directly support activists. Those embedded in the daily struggle of mobilizing and sustaining protest actions and movement communities often do not have the time or ability to take a step back and reflect on common threads that cut across the broad spectrum of U.S. feminist activism. I have written this book as an accomplice, in hopes that the space it creates for reflecting on networked feminism might function as a social justice project, in and of itself, and help activists craft tactics for pushing forward, even in the face of incredible odds, until every year is our year

OVERVIEW OF FINDINGS AND CHAPTERS

Feminists' negotiations among their media tools, political contexts, and intersectional values produce a particular activist *praxis*, or embodied relationship between their political goals and media practices. I call this praxis *do-it-ourselves feminism (DIOF)*, an organizing paradigm in which activists use networked media to build feminist politics, actions, and spaces. The bottom-up resilience and creativity embedded in this praxis open up space for more inclusive and, in turn, more impactful feminist movements.

While networked feminist campaigns vary in form and content, from hashtags and zines to street protests and online communities, they share a do-it-yourself ethos, a common orientation toward crafting new solutions regardless of experience levels or available assets. But unlike do-it-*yourself* home projects or crafty Pinterest hacks, do-it-*ourselves* feminism is not an individualistic or self-serving endeavor (Dawkins, 2011; Lee, 2014; Luvaas, 2013). By contrast, while campaigns may sometimes start with the actions of one person, DIOF is a fundamentally *collective* endeavor. It grows *not* through the aspirations and enterprising of a single leader, but through the energy and solidarity of a group. Its practitioners possess a rebellious spirit. Frustrated with the failures of government channels and earlier movements to address intersecting systems of oppression, do-it-ourselves feminists have appropriated media to carve their own paths toward social justice. Over time, feminist activists have exercised and sharpened the DIOF praxis to build movements and spaces that reflect their goals and values. The do-it-ourselves organizational logic can be found at work in networked feminist protest actions that, like the Women's March, the March to End Rape Culture, and the #MeToo campaign, enable the open expression of personal narratives, unfiltered by the purview of any one movement leader or institutional gatekeeper. Its self-starting nature also characterizes networked feminist communities like Girl Army, the feminist zine scene, and Permanent Wave, whose members come together online and off to build safe spaces that center marginalized voices.

Taking up the media-as-practice approach described above, the following three chapters identify the activist praxis guiding networked feminism and demonstrate how this paradigm has shaped U.S. feminist movements, actions, and spaces. Chapter 2 traces the history and contours of a new feminist organizational logic and identifies the relationship between contemporary feminists' political visions and their networked mobilization tactics. Against the backdrop of this broad sketch, chapters 3 and 4 offer detailed analysis of how feminists put this organizational logic into practice to launch networked visibility campaigns and build networked community safe spaces. Each of these three chapters focuses on a particular dimension of networked feminist activism: networked feminist organizing, networked feminist visibility, and networked feminist communities. These three categories are not mutually exclusive; an organizing team or a protest event can, for example, feel like a community. But they represent long-standing core objectives of U.S. feminism, the pursuit of which has shifted alongside activists' turn toward highly mediated modes of collective action and away from formally structured organizations. Together, these three empirical chapters tell the story of the rise of *do-it-ourselves feminism*, the possibilities and challenges this activist media praxis creates, and the strategies feminists are using to navigate both.

Drawing on two case studies of contemporary feminist protest—Philadelphia's March to End Rape Culture (MTERC) and the Women's March on Washington (WMOW)—chapter 2 identifies do-it-ourselves feminism as the emergent organizational logic underpinning networked feminist actions, from local, grassroots initiatives to global waves of protest. Citing examples from each, I describe the three key features of DIOF: it is an *everyday*, highly *mediated* activist praxis, whose practitioners aspire toward *intersectional* feminism.

Following this general overview of do-it-ourselves feminism, chapters 3 and 4 trace how activists take up this feminist praxis in pursuit of different movement goals. Chapter 3 focuses on a feminist protest tactic that has become a central component of the contemporary feminist repertoire—*networked visibility campaigns*, or digitally networked protest actions aimed at drawing attention to a particular issue. Taking up a highly visible recent campaign—the global #MeToo movement against sexual assault and harassment—this chapter considers practitioners' perspectives on hashtag feminism and highlights the processes through which activists develop their tactics within the social and technological constraints of both the current context and the Twitter platform.

While chapter 3 focuses on public-facing protest actions, in chapter 4, I turn my attention toward feminists' practices for building *networked safe space communities*. In this chapter, I apply the media-as-practice approach to three case studies: a secret feminist Facebook group, the feminist zine community, and a feminist grassroots collective; with these I identify the connections between feminists' goals and their mediated community-building tactics. More specifically, I argue that feminists in each site use media to construct community boundaries that prioritize marginalized voices and foster open expression among members, who otherwise lack safe outlets to share their experiences of oppression.

In the final chapter, I review the core findings of the book and discuss the implications of do-it-ourselves feminists' media practices for scholars invested in the study of social movements and digital media and for practitioners navigating the world of networked activism. Feminists' turn toward diffuse, decentralized media networks and away from more formally structured organizations has led, in equal measure, to both opportunities and challenges for feminist movements. At the same time that digital platforms and technologies offer new possibilities for building movements, raising awareness, and cultivating communities, they have added new complexities to long-standing challenges for feminists, including harassment, co-optation, and burnout. As activists navigate these tradeoffs, their do-it-ourselves ethos models a distinctly *feminist* form of networked activism and, in the process, reimagines collective action and social transformation for the digital age.

2 Networked Feminist Organizing

In the weeks leading up to the 2017 Women's March on Philadelphia, one of nearly seven hundred marches planned around the world to demand support for women's rights on President Donald Trump's first day in office (Women's March on Washington, 2017b), organizers predicted that approximately twenty thousand people would join the Center City protest (6abc, 2017). When I arrived at Logan Square on the morning of January 21, I waded into a sea of picket signs and iconic pink "pussyhats" bottle-necking slowly toward the Benjamin Franklin Parkway. It quickly became apparent that our numbers were much bigger, too big even to truly march down the half-mile strip between City Hall and the Art Museum. Local news outlets later reported that some fifty thousand people from the Philadelphia area and beyond inched, shoulder-to-shoulder, down the Parkway over the course of the afternoon (6abc, 2017).

By all accounts, Election Day 2016 had been a dark one for U.S. feminists. Hillary Clinton, the first woman candidate for president nominated by a major party, a lifelong public servant, and a fervent supporter of women's rights, had lost to Trump, a businessman who had never held office and whose campaign frequently degraded or threatened marginalized groups. But the mood that morning on the Parkway was one of jubilant defiance.

A dozen women and girls led the procession to the rhythm of drums, keeping spirits high even as the temperature dropped and the massive protest occasionally ground to a halt. Nearby, a portable Bluetooth speaker belted out Beyoncé at one moment, Aretha Franklin at another. In a different section of the crowd, call-and-response chants let passersby know that "This is what democracy looks like!" Still elsewhere, a group of protesters from a local synagogue directed a makeshift choir to the familiar tune of "This Little Light of Mine," improvising lyrics for the occasion: "All the way to the White House, I'm gonna let it shine. All the way to Trump Tower, I'm gonna let it shine." Birds-eye photos shared on social media would depict the protest as a single, pink-spotted mass moving in unison, but on the ground, individual protesters represented a multiplicity of personal identities, experiences, and concerns. Their colorful posters addressed reproductive justice, sexual violence, immigrants' rights, queer and trans rights, Islamophobia, white supremacy, ableism, climate change, public education, affordable health care, and voter suppression, among other issues.

Commentators and activists critiqued the inclusivity of the global protest movement, particularly the original Women's March on Washington's emphasis on white, cisgender women throughout its early stages of development (Stockman, 2017). In Philadelphia, however, *intersectionality* emerged as a key organizing principle among protesters (Crenshaw, 1989; 1991). Their signs and chants pointed toward capacious definitions of womanhood, women's rights, and women's issues. They captured personal experiences of gender and gender-based injustices across the overlapping axes of race, sexuality, class, faith, and ability. One protester's sign articulated in rainbow-colored marker what Crenshaw (1989) calls the "multidimensionality" (p. 139) of gender: "I am Black, Latina, LGBT, Muslim, Jew, all of these and WOMAN, too!" The Women's March on Philadelphia, and the hundreds of local protests like it, expressed a collective message of dissent from a broad spectrum of subject positions that grew into the single largest demonstration in U.S. history (Chenoweth and Pressman, 2017).

Eight months after the Women's March, on September 30, 2017, I joined a decidedly smaller crowd of several hundred people. We had converged on Thomas Paine Plaza in Center City to participate in Philadelphia's seventh annual March to End Rape Culture (MTERC), formerly known as SlutWalk Philadelphia. MTERC protesters filled the streets surrounding City Hall, waving signs and chanting loudly, their unified voices breaking into laughter at one corner and erupting with righteous indignation at another. Following a tradition established by the international SlutWalk movement in 2011, some participants wore lingerie or protested nude, a symbolic declaration of their right to move through public space without facing harassment, regardless of their state of dress. Picket signs and banners, ranging dramatically from hilarious to heartbreaking, called out a myriad of issues: sexual violence, sexual consent, intimate partner violence, victim blaming, street harassment, homophobia, transphobia, racism, police brutality, slut shaming, fat shaming, reproductive health rights, restrictive gender roles, the erasure of male survivors, the concept of "friend-zoning," sexist media, and more.

While protesters marched for two and a half miles under these seemingly disparate rally cries, volunteers gave bystanders postcards that defined the umbrella term under which their grievances fell: "*Rape culture* is a term used to describe a culture in which sexual violence is accepted as a part of everyday life." Marching under this broad framework, protesters held signs that told stories of surviving a range of violent experiences, from sexual harassment to sexual assault. For some, the violence was emotional or psychological, as in the case of protestors demanding an end to shaming people based on their sexuality, gender identity, or body type. In most cases, the violence was doubly inflicted, once by the perpetrator—the rapist or the harasser—and then again by the discourses that enable the violence to persist—the victim-blaming tropes or the ineffectual legislation. With a sense of painful irony, we witnessed this system manifest itself as a group of men seated at a sidewalk cafe catcalled at protestors. An organizer on a bullhorn led our response: "Wherever we go, however we dress, 'no' means no and 'yes' means yes!" Following the march, protestors reassembled in the plaza and speakers connected sexual violence to the rights of transgender people, people with disabilities, immigrants and refugees, and the homeless, as well as to the Black Lives Matter movement, labor movements, movements for the decriminalization of sex work, and movements against mass incarceration. This intersecting system of violence represented collectively through protestors' signs, chants, speeches, and bodies constituted what MTERC organizers call *rape culture*.

These two protest events vary drastically in scale. The record-breaking turnout for Women's Marches held across the globe stands in sharp contrast to the small but mighty crowd that gathers annually for Phila-delphia's March to End Rape Culture. They share, however, what social movement scholars have termed a common *organizational logic* (Bennett and Segerberg, 2013), a similar methodological approach for organizing collective action that sets them apart from previous generations of U.S. feminists.

Both the Women's March and the SlutWalk movement, of which MTERC is a critical offshoot, have inevitably drawn comparisons to the Women's Liberation Movement of the 1960s and 1970s (e.g., Dow and Wood, 2014; Hess, 2017a). Like this earlier "wave" of U.S. feminist activism, both pro-test events emphasize that *the personal is political*, that structures of power circumscribe individual actions and experiences, that seemingly private concerns and situations are symptomatic of systemic injustices (Butler, 1988; Hanisch, 1969). And, like their foremothers, the protesters at both marches were galvanized in part by the notion that the inverse is also true, that individual actions can reshape configurations of power, that choosing to protest could rewrite the scripts that marginalize some bodies while privileging others (Butler, 1988).

But *unlike* the protests of previous generations, neither the Women's March nor the March to End Rape Culture emerged from the political vision of a formally structured organization or a high-profile feminist leader. Their global and local expressions of dissent were *not* fueled by the membership or finances of a nonprofit like the National Organiza-tion for Women (NOW), nor were they spearheaded by luminaries the likes of Gloria Steinem or Angela Davis, though all three 1960s icons made appearances at the Women's March on Washington. Instead, both protests stemmed from the digital media practices and the resilient creativity of dispersed networks of activists who, working with little or no institutional resources, sought to transform intersecting systems of oppression. It was a Facebook event organized by one person that ultimately led an estimated *five million people* to take to the streets worldwide the day after Trump's inauguration (Stein and Somashekhar, 2017). Meanwhile, a crew of about ten stalwart volunteers operating on spare time, crowdsourced funds, and digital media savvy launch MTERC every year to protest sexual violence and the sociocultural norms that enable it. Both movements are self-starting, extra-institutional, participatory, and above all, mediated and networked. Their participants tactically appropriate the technological and social affordances of digital media platforms for the purposes of dissent.

I call this new organizational logic *do-it-ourselves feminism* (DIOF), an activist praxis that draws on digital media tools to mobilize protests and build communities from the ground up that, in process and product, reflect feminists' values. In naming this praxis, I am borrowing from the language of MTERC organizers who participate in and draw resources from the "do-it-yourself" or DIY community in Philly, the city's underground arts and music scene. The DIY community thrives on offbeat venues, independent bookers and outlets, and an economy of sliding-scale admission fees and handmade goods (Lingel, 2017; Silberling, 2015). The same emphasis on creativity, collectivity, resourcefulness, accessibility, and freedom from institutional restraints characterizes the organizational logic behind recent feminist protest actions like the Women's March and MTERC. Recognizing this connection, researchers have used the terms "do-it-yourself" (DIY) feminism (Bail, 1996) and "do-it-together" (DIT) feminism (Mann, 2014, p. 23) to describe various tactics within the contemporary feminist repertoire. Throughout this book, I use the term *do-it-ourselves* (DIO) feminism because the plural reflexive pronoun best captures the networked and collective, though not always communal or collaborative, nature of feminist media activism. DIO feminism includes both the collaborative work of organizing a feminist protest and the individually produced but collectively networked expressions of feminist discourse on social media. Moreover, some do-it-*yourself* modes of civic and cultural engagement have been critiqued for their emphasis on the marketplace value of individualism (Dawkins, 2011; Lee, 2014; Luvaas, 2013). Do-it-*ourselves* feminism is a distinctly collective praxis aimed at social transformation.

The Women's March and the March to End Rape Culture are not the only examples of do-it-ourselves feminism. Rather, the turn toward DIOF constitutes a major paradigm shift for contemporary U.S. feminism in general. Throughout the 1960s and 1970s, U.S. feminist movements unfolded within a web of closely tied, highly structured organizations like NOW, the Women's Equity Action League, and the National Women's Political Caucus, alongside more radical but still formally structured groups like the New York Radical Women and the Redstockings (Reger, 2012). Over the past decade, however, *networked feminism*, from the feminist blogosphere to hashtag feminism, has outpaced movement organizations and institutional politics. With access to wide audiences just a few keyboard strokes away, feminist social media users have mobilized direct action campaigns and sparked transnational movements, despite lacking infrastructural support and despite, as in the case of the Women's March, initially acting alone. Networked feminist campaigns vary widely in form, scale, and agenda. They share, however, a common *do-it-ourselves* ethos, a central orientation toward rebellious, bottom-up cultural production fostered through the participatory nature of digital media networks. Their tenacity and ingenuity have reenergized feminist politics precisely at a moment when women's rights and the rights of marginalized communities are under siege in the United States.

This chapter offers an in-depth exploration of do-it-ourselves feminism as an emerging organizational paradigm for networked feminism. In doing so, it begins to unpack the question at the heart of this book: How are U.S. feminists using media to craft an activist praxis that reflects their values *and* responds to the challenges of their political context? Taking a case study approach grounded in three years of ethnographic fieldwork with the MTERC organizing team, participant observations of the Women's March on Philadelphia, and textual analyses of media associated with both movements, I identify three key features of do-it-ourselves feminism. First, DIOF is *everyday*. Its practitioners pay close attention to how power manifests in everyday life. Second, DIOF is highly *mediated*. It is fueled by a network of media tools, digital and otherwise, and the users behind them. These two core features give rise to the third: do-it-ourselves feminism aspires to be *intersectional*. The everyday, mediated nature of DIOF makes it an accessible, participatory mode of activism. It is open to anyone with time, interest, and digital media literacy, and it is personalizable according to participants' experiences and concerns, paving the path toward more diverse feminist discourses and spaces. DIO feminists also practice intersectional reflexivity, engaging in careful self-critique to build movements that reflect their values of difference and inclusion.

Do-it-ourselves feminism is difficult but fulfilling. Without the resources of a formally structured organization or an experienced political leader, DIOF's amateur practitioners often must improvise responses to obstacles like cooptation and backlash. Crafting movements from scratch in line with their values takes a lot of hard work, even more perseverance, and a fair share of audacity. It is a precarious endeavor, and one that can come with both personal and political costs. But for activists organizing protests like the Women's March and the March to End Rape Culture, engaging in resistance on their own terms is worth it.

DIOF IS EVERYDAY

A defining feature of do-it-ourselves feminism is its *everydayness*. The activists behind both the Women's March and the March to End Rape Culture work from a conceptualization of power as diffuse, everyday, everywhere—suffused through all aspects of personal life. Their political visions extend what Stacey Young (1997) describes as U.S. feminists' "longstanding focus on domination and resistance at the level of daily life" (p. 14), as captured in the second-wave slogan, *the personal is political*. This approach to understanding power parallels Michel Foucault's (1991) concept of *disciplinary power*. In contrast to a top-down model of control in which a single authority wields absolute power over the population, disciplinary power is enacted through a bottom-up model of control in which power is dispersed throughout the social fabric and enacted between people through the everyday performance and enforcement of behavioral norms. According to Foucault, *discourse*, dominant interpretive frameworks for thinking, taking about, and responding to particular topics, is the primary vehicle for the diffusion and wide acceptance of a particular set of norms at a given time and place. In her work on Black feminist thought, Patricia Hill Collins (2000) describes disciplinary power manifesting as a discursive "matrix of domination" (p. 18), a composite of intersecting oppressions along multiple axes of race, gender, sexuality, and class and the particular sociopolitical practices, from government policies to mass media imagery, used to maintain those oppressions at a given point in history. Contemporary activists continue U.S. feminists' decades-long work of uncovering these quotidian experiences of oppression so that they might become sites for resistance.

This expansive conceptualization of power as an everyday phenomenon is at the heart of the Women's March's public platform. The march's

Unity Principles, a guiding vision for the movement authored by the ad hoc "National Committee" that initially launched the Women's March on Washington (2017a), offers an "ambitious, fundamental, and comprehensive agenda" (p. 1) that links laws, rights, and policies with everyday life. The document includes demands for legislative and policy changes, including an end to police brutality and mass incarceration, equal pay for equal work, paid family leave, workplace protections for undocumented laborers, voting rights, environmental protections, and the passage of an Equal Rights Amendment. Its authors also argue, however, that these changes must take place alongside transformations in daily life. The committee calls for respect for women's right to live free from everyday forms of physical violence, such as domestic abuse and sexual assault. They link this freedom to the end of discursive forms of violence, such as oppressive "gender norms, expectations, and stereotypes" (p. 3) and the awarding of power "disproportionately to masculinity to the exclusion of others" (p. 3), both of which take away from the "power to control our bodies" (p. 3). The document goes on to name specific everyday sites where this matrix of domination plays out, like the devaluation of women of color who work in the care and service industries, discrimination against non-heteronormative families and families of color in the housing market, and prejudice in health care facilities against individuals in the LGBTQIA community. When the Committee refers throughout the Unity Principles to "women's rights," they are pointing toward this multidimensional platform for social, legislative, and economic empowerment.

The March to End Rape Culture mobilizes around an equally expansive conceptualization of power, one that captures both everyday and institutional systems of oppression, summed up in the event's title—*rape culture*. The annual event, however, began under a different name as Slut-Walk Philadelphia, the city's local chapter of an international movement sparked in January 2011 after a Canadian police officer told an assembly of York University students that "women should avoid dressing like sluts" to prevent rape (Mendes, 2015). Around the world, SlutWalk organizers used social media to call for protests, inviting participants to dress "like sluts" in order to both challenge the discourse surrounding sexual violence victims' clothing choices and to reclaim the word "slut" to support women's sexual agency (Mendes, 2015). In 2013, SlutWalk Philadelphia changed their annual protest's name to the March to End Rape Culture in solidarity with women of color activists who, noting that reclaiming oppressive language requires a certain degree of privilege, found SlutWalk's mission to be negligent of Black women's historical experiences with norms regulating gender and sexuality (Murtha, 2013).[1] The "slut" in SlutWalk, the organizers argued, centered the sexual agency of white cisgender women, who had privileged access to the term's binary and correlative opposite—the pure virgin. The virgin/slut double bind did not resonate with Black women, whose marginalization under white male supremacy depends in large part on their wholesale classification as sexually amoral and available. "Rape culture," the organizers explained in an open letter published on their Facebook page, captures a more intersectional vision of oppression beyond white women's experiences: "the concept of 'rape culture' has been one that has been identified in many forums and communities to describe the cultural forces which conspire to make it so that sexual violence occurs so often, and with so few of the perpetrators being held accountable for their actions" (qtd. in Murtha, 2013). The bystander card organizers distribute to onlookers every year throughout the protest includes a litany of these cultural forces: "There are many different aspects of society that contribute to rape culture including victim blaming, rape jokes, transphobia, slut shaming, keeping survivors in silence, racism, the use of bodies as sexual objects, the sexualization of violence, lack of education around consent, intimate partner violence, homophobia, sexist media message, the list is never ending." As an entry point for analyzing oppression, the term *rape culture* suggests that "rape" and "culture" are inseparable and visualizes an interlocking system of physical and discursive violence that manifests in both everyday and institutional life.

The definition of "rape culture" MTERC organizers advance is broad, encompassing a spectrum of violent experiences and an expansive matrix of interlocking oppressions. This creates space for protesters to incorporate their own personal expressions of dissent into the march. Every year, many of the protesters who gather in Thomas Paine Plaza use posters, clothing, and their bodies to share their experiences with sexual violence. At every march that I attended, several participants carried signs stating that they were wearing the same clothes they wore when they were raped, undermining news media's and litigators' tendency to blame sexual violence on victims' choices and behaviors. Others reenacted the victim-blaming discourses they were confronted with following their assaults. A protestor at the 2016 march carried a poster that included the question people posed to her when she spoke out about her sexual assault: "Why didn't you just push him off?" Yet another poster listed common excuses for assailants' actions: "He was just a 'nice guy' who was 'hot and bothered.'" Still others used their bodies to make explicit the dominant discourses that normalize and excuse sexual violence, writing phrases like, "I am not asking for it," in paint or marker across their chests, legs, and arms while waiting in the plaza for the march to begin. The similarities across these protesters' everyday experiences of violence, connected through their expression at the annual protest, shed light on rape culture as a matrix of domination otherwise normalized into invisibility.

In both sites, feminists' understanding of power is everyday, everywhere, and *networked*. Rather than being centralized within the state or a set of institutions, for these feminist activists, power reaches indefinitely in all directions across an array of interconnected nodes. This same webbed image of power is at the heart of Foucault's (1991) "carceral network" (p. 298) and Collins's (2000) "matrix of domination" (p. 18). It follows that do-it-ourselves feminists mobilize networked modes of activism in a struggle to meet this everywhere, everyday networked form of power step for step. While contemporary feminists share their antecedents' understanding of power as diffuse and personal, their networked tactics of resistance set them apart.

DIOF IS MEDIATED

Neither the Women's March nor the March to End Rape Culture followed the trajectories of previous feminist generations' movements and protest actions. In past generations, as Tufekci (2017) argues, a large, organized march or protest would typically "be seen as the chief outcome of previous capacity building by a movement" (p. xiv). In "the networked era," however, the march or protest "should be looked at as the initial moment of the movement's bursting on the scene . . . the first stage in a potentially long journey" (p. xiv). Activists no longer require the capacities or resources of a formally structured movement organization, which can take months to build, to launch direct actions. Instead, as in the case of both the Women's March and MTERC, a handful of people using social media platforms can ignite global dissent within a matter of hours. The affordances of networked technologies combined with users' creativity and resourcefulness lay the groundwork for the second key feature of do-it-ourselves feminism—its highly *mediated* nature. Just as DIOF practitioners politicize everyday life, they appropriate everyday media tools and resources to mobilize political actions. In January 2011, Toronto resident Heather Jarvis was browsing Facebook when she stumbled upon a link to an article published in the *Excalibur*, York University's student newspaper, recounting the campus assembly on sexual violence in which a police officer blamed rape on women's clothing choices (Mendes, 2015). Infuriated at the officer's perpetuation of dangerous rape myths, Jarvis shared the article on her personal Facebook page, which in turn initiated a conversation among friends about what steps they could take in response (Mendes, 2015). Jarvis and her friend, Sonya Barnett, decided that a protest was necessary and, after one of Barnett's colleagues joked that they should call their march a "slut walk," the global movement was born (Mendes, 2015). Jarvis and Barnett created a website, Facebook page, and Twitter account, calling on supporters to join them for a "Slut-Walk" from Queen's Park in Toronto to the city's police headquarters (Mendes, 2015). Several thousand protesters, some dressed provocatively to challenge the discourse surrounding sexual violence victims' clothing choices, joined SlutWalk Toronto three months later on April 3, 2011 (Mendes, 2015). In the lead-up to and following the march, SlutWalk went viral; popular feminist blogs covered the event and word continued to spread through international news media. By the end of the year, Slut-Walks popped up in more than two hundred cities and forty nations, from North America to Asia (Carr, 2013). While the global movement eventually slowed, annual marches would gather in many cities for years to come, including Philadelphia.

The first SlutWalk Philadelphia took place in August 2011 and would convene yearly until 2013, when organizers changed the event's name to the March to End Rape Culture and continued the annual protest tradition under a revamped mission. Over time, in the aftermath of SlutWalk's

initial bursting onto the scene, MTERC has gathered some of the organizational "capacities" (p. xi) Tufekci (2017) describes. They have learned
through trial and error, for example, how to manage a budget and track
expenses, how to file a permit for a rally in a public square that includes
performers and merchants, how to secure a certified ASL interpreter to
translate speeches, and how to write a press release and land news coverage. While the planning committee's membership changes from march to
march, and even from meeting to meeting, a small group of steady volunteers has developed the specialized set of skills and knowledge required to
get a public event of this scale off the ground in Philly.

Even so, the march remains, at its core, a networked, do-it-ourselves
effort, fueled by organizers' commitment, makeshift creativity, and digital
media savvy. Throughout my fieldwork, the committee would start off each
planning year with little or no budget to cover what typically amounted to
approximately $3,000 worth of expenses, including rental fees for tables,
chairs, audio equipment, and accessibility ramps, honoraria for speakers
and artists, upfront costs for producing T-shirts and other merchandise,
and printed promotional materials. Organizers set up crowdfunding websites and tapped into their personal and professional connections to link
up with organizations and businesses willing to donate money, supplies, or
venues for fundraising events. The same improvisational approach characterized their recruitment practices. A small group of about ten people
consistently showed up to march meetings, but a much larger team was
necessary to make the event a reality. Every year, open calls for volunteers
were spread online through Facebook and in person, at any relevant local
event whose host granted us a bit of table space, until the committee had
enough people power to work through its overwhelming to-do list. Like
the broader SlutWalk movement, MTERC organizers also relied on social
media to spread the word about the protest. While organizers would tape
or tack printed flyers to light poles and cafe community boards across the
city, it was their Facebook profile and event page, along with their official
website, that drew the largest numbers to the march. Digital media also
functioned as the planning committee's core structure. Without an official
membership, a formal leadership structure, or a central meeting place, the
planning committee effectively consisted of whoever joined the MTERC
listserv, private Facebook group, or Slack, where in-person meetings were

scheduled and where discussions and decision-making between meetings took place. Just as MTERC mobilizes around a conceptualization of power as diffuse and everyday, it also mobilizes *through* a diffuse network of volunteers and supporters, connected through everyday media tools and platforms. SlutWalk in many ways pioneered networked feminist activism, emerging at a moment when other movements, including the Arab Spring, Indignados, and Occupy, were using social media platforms to reach global audiences.

Five years later, the Women's March would follow SlutWalk's model of highly mediated feminist organizing. After watching Trump win the presidency, Theresa Shook, a retired grandmother living in Hawaii, created a Facebook event on election night, November 8, 2016, inviting her friends to a protest in Washington, D.C., scheduled for the day after the inauguration (Stein and Somashekhar, 2017). The next morning, Shook woke to more than ten thousand RSVPs (Stein and Somashekhar, 2017). The event quickly spread to Pantsuit Nation, a Facebook group where Hillary Clinton's supporters connect, share stories, and plan actions (Women's March on Washington, 2016). Similar events started appearing across Facebook and thousands of users began making plans to attend protests in Washington (Women's March on Washington, 2016). New York–based fashion designer Bob Bland, who recently had risen to prominence through her anti-Trump T-shirt line, proposed a "Million Pussy March on Washington" in a Facebook post dated November 10 (Bland, 2016). Once Bland discovered that she was not alone in her desire to march, she worked with others to consolidate the events into a unified effort, represented by a single Facebook page (Women's March on Washington, 2016). Initially, the protest was organized under the name, Million Woman March, a reference to a 1997 Philadelphia protest organized by and for Black women. At the time, however, Bland's organizing team for the 2017 march was composed entirely of white women, leading women of color and their allies to raise concerns on social media about appropriation and inclusivity (Women's March on Washington, 2016). In response to these critiques, Bland and her team recruited three women of color activists to serve as cochairs of the march on Washington—Tamika Mallory, Carmen Perez, and Linda Sarsour—who, together in 2015, led a march from New York City to D.C., walking for 250 miles to demand an end to mass incarceration

(Women's March on Washington, 2016). By December, their team grew into a National Committee of nearly ninety organizers, intentionally recruited for their leadership within diverse communities (Women's March on Washington, 2016; 2017a). The Committee changed the protest's name to the Women's March on Washington, in homage to the 1963 March on Washington, where Martin Luther King delivered his "I Have a Dream" speech, with the blessing of King's daughter (Felsenthal, 2017). As Bland wrote in a post to the official Facebook event page, "Now voices including Asian and Pacific Islanders, trans women, Native Americans, disabled women, men, children, and many others, can be centered in the evolving expression of this grassroots movement" (Women's March on Washington, 2016).

Word of the march spread globally through Facebook, Twitter, and the official Women's March on Washington website. By the eve of Trump's inauguration, at least one march was planned on all seven continents, most with a Facebook event page directing participants to their nearest town square and a localized Twitter hashtag providing updates on logistics and speaker lineups. A march even took place on Antarctica, where an international group of about thirty people hosted a small demonstration on an expedition ship off the coast of the Antarctic Peninsula (Bowerman, 2017). Although dispersed geographically, protesters around the world were connected through a digitally networked communications infrastructure established by the National Committee, consisting of Twitter lists, aggregated social media streams, photo and video archives, and a collection of hashtags active before, during, and after Inauguration Day, including #WhyIMarch, #WomensMarch, and #WomensMarchGlobal (Women's March on Washington, 2018a). Following Inauguration Day, the National Committee would continue to grow and even formalize into an official "Board," led by co-presidents Tamika Mallory and Bob Bland, and a "National Team," composed of nonprofit directors, entrepreneurs, field and communications strategists, and web developers, who would go on to launch other resistance projects (Women's March on Washington, 2018b). But it was ultimately a dispersed network of passionate activists improvising with social media tools, not a formally structured movement or organization, that sparked a global day of protest in January 2017.

Many social movements in the networked era are characterized by a high degree of mediation, but for do-it-ourselves feminists, using media tools to practice resistance stems from U.S. feminists' unique historical emphasis on the everyday as a site of power. DIO feminists make the personal political by using common media tools to expose and transform the everyday, everywhere systems of gender-based oppression. In his work on mass culture and everyday life, Michel de Certeau (1984) referred to such practices as *tactics*. Drawing on a wide array of everyday tactics, ordinary "individuals already caught in the nets of 'discipline'" (p. xiv) can "make do" (p. 66) with materials at hand and circumvent seemingly all-encompassing systems of power. DIO feminists tactically make do with everyday networked media platforms and tools, finding creative ways to resist institutionalized and everyday forms of white male supremacy, often while operating with little organizing experience and few resources. DIOF is a rebellious, bottom-up media practice that draws on everyday tools, rejects the authority and slow grind of bureaucratic organizations and institutions, and encourages even the most amateur activists to take action (Ratto and Boler, 2014).

DIOF ASPIRES FOR INTERSECTIONALITY

The everyday, mediated qualities of do-it-ourselves feminism make the praxis available to anyone with the time, interest, access to, and basic literacy in the technologies and platforms that fuel it. Through its use of everyday tools like Facebook and Twitter and its emphasis on extra-institutional voices and engagement, DIOF shares what is often referred to as the "DIY ethos" (Ratto and Boler, 2014, p. 10) that underlies other creative amateur practices. DIOF prioritizes open accessibility and participation, regardless of one's previous experiences or financial resources. Teresa Shook, the retiree whose Facebook event eventually grew into the Women's March on Washington, had no prior experience in activist organizing, had not been politically active before Trump's campaign, and had none of the financial backing or people power of a traditional movement organization (Stein, 2017). *But* she had a Facebook account with broad network connections extended through the Pantsuit Nation group, which at the time had nearly three million members (Collins, 2016), and some friends had taught her how to make and share a Facebook event (Stein, 2017). Similarly, while

Heather Jarvis and Sonya Barnett had participated in political activism before, they only needed a few social media accounts to launch the international SlutWalk movement (Mendes, 2015); the March to End Rape Culture continues this do-it-ourselves tradition every year in Philadelphia. The result of this feminist generation's DIY ethos is an activist praxis that is more inclusive and participatory, open to nearly anyone looking to channel political outrage into a social movement.

Scholars have documented a similar degree of accessibility and participation in other movements' shift from traditionally organized collective action toward what Bennett and Segerberg (2013) call *connective action*. Connective action unfolds when *personal action frames*, or "easily personalized ideas" (p. 37) are linked together through digital networks, as exemplified in the case of hashtag activism (Clark, 2016). Without a formal organization keeping a firm grip on a movement's message framing, connective action allows protesters to express themselves more freely and personalize their participation according to their specific experiences and concerns, all while still taking part in a collective solidary action. Ratto and Boler (2014) observe the participatory nature of connective action at work in other types of DIY political projects, and researchers have cited Bennett and Segerberg's work to theorize protesters' involvement in the Arab Spring (Howard & Hussain, 2013), Indignados (Anduiza, Cristancho, and Sabucedo, 2014) and Occupy movements (Theocharis, Lowe, van Deth, and Albacete, 2013), among many others. Less clear, however, is how the participatory nature of connective action might map onto a movement's politics. While new media platforms facilitate connective action and make this organizing logic available to activists, their existence alone does not guarantee that activists will choose to engage in networked activism over traditionally organized campaigns by default. Rather, following the media-as-practice approach, connective action likely emerges from a combination of activists' goals, values, needs, resources, and contexts.

For contemporary U.S. feminists, *intersectionality* is a driving factor in their turn toward networked activism. Within the traditional collective organizing more characteristic of second-wave feminism, movement leaders performed a gatekeeping function, choosing whose voices and concerns shaped feminist public platforms. While the movement claimed to fight for the rights of all women, this filtering process often privileged white women, whose stories and experiences were more likely to resonate with the mainstream press (Rothenberg, 2002). DIOF's networked organizing logic eliminates gatekeepers, creating space for activists standing at various intersections of difference to participate in and shape feminist politics.

As critiques of the whiteness of the Women's March and SlutWalk suggest, this does not mean that all DIOF movements, actions, and communities always feel welcoming and inclusive to all marginalized people. Rather, they are characterized by an *aspirational intersectionality*, a named commitment to prioritizing difference and equity, to admitting when they have failed to do so, and to repairing harm. For DIO feminists, intersectionality is not a quality of a movement but a foundational organizing practice that includes a genuine openness to critique and a deep emphasis on reflexivity. The mediated and participatory nature of do-it-ourselves feminism enables a feedback loop of intersectional critique and reflexivity between activist organizers and the communities they rally.

The aspirational, reflexive quality of DIOF's intersectionality became most apparent in the lead-up to the Women's March when the National Committee began drafting the movement's Unity Principles. While the National Committee was tasked with coordinating the logistics of the march on Washington and developing an infrastructure of support for sister marches around the world, the Women's March was largely decentralized, its expression of dissent shaped and refined through constant feedback from activists via social media. Critiques circulated through Facebook, Twitter, and the feminist blogosphere about the composition of the organizing team and the event's name had altered who the marches represented and would later influence what message the marches communicated. The National Committee published an initial draft of the Unity Principles on January 12, 2017: "Recognizing that women have intersecting identities and are therefore impacted by a multitude of social justice and human rights issues, we have outlined a representative vision for a government that is based on the principles of liberty and justice for all" (Women's March on Washington 2017a, p. 1). Soon after its publication, activist bloggers and Twitter users highlighted major gaps in the document, including support for the rights of sex workers (Rowntree, 2017) and people with disabilities (Ladau, 2017), while others critiqued the organizers for not taking a clear stance in support of access to safe and affordable abortion services (Graham, 2017). By inauguration weekend, the Unity Principles were updated to include an expression of solidarity with sex workers' rights movement, multiple references to disability as a social justice issue, and a clear demand for reproductive freedom for all. National Committee members combined their commitment to intersectionality and openness to critique with the participatory nature of social media platforms to foster an expression of dissent unfiltered by any one leader or organization. As march organizers wrote on Twitter, "The leadership of the Women's March on Washington are not experts on every issue—but we are committed to being bridge-builders and amplifiers of shared values" (womensmarch, 2017).

The MTERC team's organizing practices also centered reflexivity as it aspired toward intersectional organizing practices. Throughout the planning process for the 2016 march, a number of in-group disputes made it evident that the planning committee members' politics were not completely in line with one another. One particularly heated debate focused on whether white people in the group should, whenever possible, take a step back from responsibilities to better center the perspectives and interests of people of color. After several organizers on both sides of the debate left MTERC, committee members came together to draft what they refer to as their "Points of Unity," a mission statement explicitly laying out the group's shared values, beliefs, and goals. Two organizers wrote an initial draft of the statement with guidance from other Philadelphia-based feminist collectives who had recently authored similar documents. The draft was then posted on the committee's Slack, where members could comment on it and suggest revisions, which were incorporated into the document through a consensus-based process. The final version, which was shared publicly through the MTERC website, outlines a vision for intersectional organizing, including an explicit statement in support of prioritizing participants of color, among other practices:

> This organizing committee is guided by principles of intersectionality, anti-oppression and combating rape culture. All members must be open to learning about these ideas and reflecting on their own biases. We understand that unpacking and unlearning our own biases and privileges allows us to create space for the various experiences of survivors of all different

backgrounds & narratives and the ways they experience rape culture and other violence.

The Points of Unity document became a touchstone for navigating debates in any decision-making process. One such debate arose when a committee member used the official MTERC Facebook page to share a letter calling out cisgender people who expect trans people to disclose their identities during dates and romantic encounters. Some members expressed concerns that the letter's language was too radical and would alienate more moderate supporters. The Facebook post had sparked a heated exchange in the comments section, which included transphobic language, raising concerns that, in addition to potentially offending followers, it may have also hurt trans supporters of MTERC. For the planning committee, the question became whether or not the post should be deleted. After reviewing our Points of Unity, the committee collectively decided that the post was in keeping with MTERC's mission to support trans people and that its tone and language mapped onto the march's own radical politics. Members then went about responding to or deleting comments that did not reflect MTERC's values. For the MTERC planning committee, the Points Unity document offered a way for members to systematically make decisions in keeping with their intersectional values, while also maintaining their emphasis on open participation.

The "DIY ethos" (Ratto and Boler, 2014, p. 10) of networked activism— its open, participatory nature—shares a unique resonance with aspirational intersectionality. The same logic of connective action that undergirds DIOF characterizes a number of other contemporary movements and campaigns. My case studies suggest, however, that feminists' turn away from traditionally organized collective action and toward networked activist campaigns emerges from a particular set of concerns, including a desire for more intersectional movements and an ongoing search for protest forms that allow the open expression of everyday experiences with injustice. This generation's use of digitally mediated tactics represents a particular feminist *praxis*, an ever-expanding repertoire of practices informed by a specific set of goals, values, and needs that can scale up from grassroots projects like MTERC to global movements like the Women's March.

DOING IT OURSELVES, NO MATTER WHAT

The praxis of do-it-ourselves feminism has, in many ways, revolutionized gender justice activism for the twenty-first century. Pairing media tools and platforms with their personal politics and intersectional values, contemporary feminists have spearheaded movements and campaigns that include a diversity of experiences while still fostering the solidarity necessary to transform systems of power. But some of the same features that grant DIOF its social and technical affordances—its everyday and mediated nature—have also left it vulnerable to burnout, backlash, and co-optation.

Unlike previous generations of activists, do-it-ourselves feminists often launch actions without first building the capacities of a formal organization. This allows a more diverse range of actors, who may not have access to organizational resources or public platforms, to make their voices heard. At the same time, however, DIOF's lack of a strong infrastructure raises concerns about long-term sustainability. While rebellious and artful, without the financial support or reliable people power of a big-name or nonprofit organization, feminists' tactical improvisation can become a drain on their time, energy, and, eventually, their mental health.

This activist "burnout" was apparent among MTERC organizers, particularly toward the end of my fieldwork, as they struggled to maintain the energy and commitment required to fund and launch the event year after year. Often, at the beginning of MTERC's planning year, I would watch as dozens of interested activists would show up to the first meeting to begin laying the groundwork for that year's march. Then, as months passed, attendance would dwindle and important tasks would fall to Chelsea, an activist involved in multiple feminist projects throughout the city and the march's unofficial lead organizer.[2] When, after volunteers failed to follow through on key day-of responsibilities for MTERC 2015, Chelsea kicked off the planning year for MTERC 2016 with a speech about accountability:

> You know, it's great that so many of you are here and that so many people want to volunteer every year, but it is incredibly frustrating when people who volunteered to take on particular tasks at the march just don't show up. You might think your job is small, like directing protestors along the march route, but if no one shows up to do that job, then I have to scramble to find

someone else to do it or else everything goes to shit. If you're gonna sign up, you need to show up, that's all I'm saying.

But showing up is often easier said than done. Making time not only for scheduled monthly meetings but for on-the-fly problem-solving and crisis response took its toll on many MTERC organizers, who also worked full-time or multiple part-time jobs and who, in many cases, were also struggling to cope with their own trauma related to sexual violence. Even Chelsea, who had been a key figure on the planning committee since the protest's name change in 2013, announced her plans to take a step back after MTERC 2016, following a particularly difficult year balancing personal life issues with her growing list of march responsibilities. Others stopped attending meetings following internal disagreements. Without a formalized structure for leadership and decision-making, the planning committee lacked the means to address infighting and disputes.

If, as Tufekci (2017) argues, the trajectory of networked social movements begins with, rather than culminates in, a large protest action, the question becomes how to create a support system for keeping activists engaged in the struggle while also maintaining their energy and building capacity for tactical innovation in response to new obstacles. Without one in place, DIO feminists risk limiting their political engagement to attention-grabbing actions such as global street protests or viral hashtag campaigns that do not grow into sustainable movements. The Women's March offers a potentially helpful counterexample, as the National Committee pooled resources to formalize the protest into an ongoing struggle for women's rights that took the form of national voter registration tours and campaigns for progressive women candidates for office (Power to the Polls, 2018). But with its formalization and growing profile came critiques that the National Committee had fallen out of touch with its support base's intersectional values (e.g., Pagano, 2018). Do-it-ourselves feminists must juggle the competing goals of fostering open, accessible, intersectional movements and establishing the infrastructure necessary to carry movements forward.

The participatory nature of DIOF enables protesters to express their own perspectives, experiences, and concerns without having their voices filtered by a centralized gatekeeper. But the openness and flexibility of the praxis can make articulating a clear platform with definitive political values and commitments difficult. This challenge came to the fore in the debates concerning white women's overwhelming presence at women's marches across the United States. While the National Committee had, in collaboration with activists voicing their concerns over social media, authored a set of Unity Principles with intersectionality at its core, women of color described feeling uncomfortable or unwelcome around white, liberal, feminists who had not turned out in equal numbers to support anti-racist efforts like the Black Lives Matter movement or condemn state violence against Black and Brown bodies (Dupuy, 2018). Others expressed a feeling of distrust for white women, the majority of whom (53%) voted for Trump in 2016, and a disappointment in their failure to mobilize friends and family members against his racist campaign (Dupuy, 2018). Reports from local protests of white women thanking police officers for safeguarding the march (Chen, 2017), chanting loudly over Black feminists' speeches (Xiao, 2017), or spending more time taking selfies with friends in pussyhats than engaging in speakers' calls to action (Obie, 2017) only exacerbated these frustrations. Following the 2017 marches, participants and commentators struggled to balance the desire to offer the uninitiated a gateway to more radical activism through the Women's March with their frustration with "white feminism's" complicity in systems of violence. In opening its arms to anyone, from the liberal center to the far left, who wanted to participate, the National Committee behind the Women's Marches brought massive turnouts for protests held around the world. But, at the same time, they also laid the groundwork for a movement whose politics, particularly when it comes to racial justice, were less clear in practice than in writing, leaving feminists of color feeling unheard and unsupported. Moreover, when paired with DIO feminists' focus on everyday life, the lack of a definitive platform can make the path toward creating long-lasting institutional change, such as policy reform, unclear.

Lastly, DIO feminism's politicization of everyday life and emphasis on open participation leaves movements vulnerable to co-optation and backlash. As Banet-Weiser and Portwood-Stacer (2017) argue, the personalized, individual aspects of networked feminism are easily transmuted into "marketplace feminism" (Goldman, Heath, and Smith, 1991; Zeisler, 2016). When, for example, the Women's March captured the world's attention, marketers used rhetoric associated with the global movement and the broader anti-Trump resistance to sell their products. Popular clothing brands even mass-produced T-shirts with march slogans (Hess, 2017b). While the practice might have further amplified the movement's messaging, it also risked, as feminist journalist Amanda Hess (2017b) put it in an article for the *New York Times*, "leading audiences away from the hard work of political action and civic organization and toward the easy comfort of a consumer choice." The same media tools that led the Women's March to become both a worldwide political action and a pop culture phenomenon also opened activists up to harassment. Two days before inauguration, the hashtag #RenameMillionWomenMarch began trending on Twitter, flooding the platform with sexist messages targeting feminists' appearance and intelligence (Harvard, 2017). Without a tightly structured organization with the capacity for issuing collective or innovating tactics, DIOF movements can struggle to issue collective responses to co-optation, backlash, and other obstacles.

At the same time, the do-it-ourselves praxis creates a variety of new affordances for feminist organizing, it also poses a unique set of challenges, the solutions for which seem out of reach without a more traditional, structured approach to collective action. Feminist activists are, however, aware of the pitfalls and continue to navigate the shortcomings of networked activism in order to make the most out of its strengths. For contemporary feminists, the benefits of "doing it ourselves" outweigh the risks enough to make the difficult balancing act worth it.

This became particularly evident during the planning year for MTERC 2016, when the pros and cons of shifting toward a more formalized approach to collective organizing became a key talking point among the organizing team. Having struggled for several years to fund the event, organizers briefly considered applying to the IRS to obtain 501(c)(3) status and incorporate the group as a formal nonprofit organization. In addition to potentially increased credibility, becoming a nonprofit offered a number of potential benefits, including the ability to apply for grants restricted to 501(c)(3) organizations and give donors tax deductions when they make charitable gifts. But after some exploratory research, the idea was squashed. Incorporating as a 501(c)(3) would make the group accountable to the government and legally restrict their ability to engage in partisan politics at any level or speak out against candidates with oppressive agendas.[3] Organizers were also concerned that incorporating would shift the group's focus toward professionalization; they feared they would become more caught up in the bureaucratic ins and outs of keeping a nonprofit organization afloat and lose sight of their mission to dismantle rape culture and support local survivors. Plus, organizers worried that as a nonprofit organization, they would have to tone down the march's radical politics and generally "edgy" nature in an effort to maintain a professional public appearance. "But," I asked Chelsea once at a meeting, "wouldn't incorporating make fundraising much easier?" She just smiled at me and said, "We will raise our own funds. We always get people to donate supplies even without the tax deduction. We'll just keep doing it ourselves, and then the march can keep being what we want it to be."

For these activists, DIOF's precarity was at times a hazard, but it was also a strength and even a source of pride. Starting the march every year from scratch was strenuous. The committee's struggle to retain more than ten members at one time has been a testament to that fact. But the flexible, improvisational nature of do-it-ourselves feminism enabled MTERC organizers to craft a protest event that, in process and product, reflected their values and the concerns of their supporters. The intersectional reflexivity activists build into this praxis allows them to recognize and grapple with both the political possibilities and limitations of networked feminist organizing.

A NEW IMAGE OF FEMINISM

The Women's March on Washington and the March to End Rape Culture evidence a paradigm shift in U.S. feminist organizing. Feminist movements no longer orbit around highly structured organizations, with clearly defined leaders and tightly controlled messages. Instead, feminist media makers and platform users stand at the center of the complex, multifaceted terrain that is U.S. feminism. Their creative, extra-institutional activism constitutes a new organizing logic that I call *do-it-ourselves feminism (DIOF)*.

In many ways, the pink pussyhat, which became the signature look of the Women's March, offers the perfect metaphor for DIOF. Riffing on

Trump's leaked 2005 conversation with *Access Hollywood* host Billy Bush, in which he claimed his celebrity status allowed him to "do anything to women," including "grab them by the pussy" (Fahrenthold, 2016), friends and artists Krista Suh and Jayna Zweiman shared the pattern for a cat-eared hat online (Walker, 2017). Countless feminist knitters soon joined the Pussyhat Project (Walker, 2017). While each individual hat carried the personal touches of its creator, making, wearing, and exchanging pussy-hats became collective acts of protest and community building. Feminists hosted virtual and in-person knitting circles, shared photos of their hats alongside their particular political concerns via social media under the hashtag #PussyHatGlobal, and distributed hats to fellow protesters (Pussyhat Project, 2017). Hundreds of thousands of handmade pussyhats appeared at marches around the world, each a visually striking signifier for the movement and, as the *New Yorker* put it, "a personalized act of labor dedicated to communal protest" (Walker, 2017).

Like the pussyhat, contemporary feminism in the United States is a network of self-starting, participatory, open-access movements, tactically appropriating everyday media tools and resources to create protest actions. Channeling their dissent through the social media platforms we browse on a daily basis, this generation of activists has built movements and campaigns open to anyone with internet access and some spare time. Importantly, without the gatekeepers of formally structured organizations, networked feminist activism allows participants to express themselves freely, play a role in directly shaping movements' messages, and even launch campaigns around their personal experiences of oppression. The pussyhat offered an outlet for self-expression while simultaneously linking participants in shared acts of protest. Similarly, feminists' rebellious, bottom-up approach to political action enables an activism that is both personal and collective, that both honors the particularities of individual experiences and fosters solidarity across intersections of difference. While U.S. feminism's history of exclusions haunted the Women's March, its organizational style enabled a set of Unity Principles built around women as a complex, multifaceted class, rather than a monolith defined solely by gender. As one journalist quipped, "A new image of feminism—intersectional, DIY, unapologetically pink—was solidified" (Brooks, 2017). Above all, like the pussyhat, today's feminist movements have gained a striking degree of visibility across U.S. media culture, offering a bright glimmer of hope in a dark political moment.

But the pussyhat protest tactic was not without its shortcomings. Trans women and women of color critiqued the hat for centering through its symbolism the bodies of white cisgender women (Compton, 2017). The hat was also easily mass-produced and sold for profit, turning feminist dissent into a commodity and upholding capitalist values that run counter to feminist collective politics. As a low-risk personal fashion statement, some critics charged that the pussyhat gave participants a false sense of accomplishment, as if, by donning the hat, they had done *something* to affect the status quo, which could in turn lull them into complacency. Perhaps more than any other action taken at Women's Marches around the world, the pink, cat-eared caps sparked a flurry of internal discord within feminist communities.

The *do-it-ourselves* activist media praxis behind contemporary feminist movements faces similar problems. Without clear movement structures, DIO feminists lack a means through which to hold one another accountable for following through on their intersectional principles. Their turn away from a centralized leadership and toward open, personalizable participation can make establishing a specific set of political values and commitments difficult. The individualized nature of DIOF also leaves it vulnerable to commercial co-optation, and when its message is distorted or commodified or activists face backlash, it is often missing the organizational capacity necessary to issue a collective response. The networked media praxis also faces a sustainability problem. Millions of marchers may have made and worn pussyhats, but what happens after the viral protest action's media attention comes to an end? Networked feminist actions can disperse just as quickly as they come together. A key question for today's feminist organizers is how to keep activists engaged in long-term struggles for social justice, even when feminism is not making headlines.

But the pussyhat controversy illustrates a key feature of do-it-ourselves feminism. In the weeks leading up to and following the Women's March, feminists' critiques of the tactic flooded social media platforms and editorial pages. These discussions and debates stand as a testament to the intersectional reflexivity of today's feminist activists, who consistently evaluate whether their actions align with their politics and revamp their tactics accordingly. Through their reflexive praxis, DIO feminists actively confront the double-edged nature of networked activism and negotiate between their political goals and media resources.

The following two chapters trace how activists, drawing on the DIOF praxis, use media to pursue two long-standing goals of U.S. feminism: bringing visibility to personal experiences of oppression and cultivating safe, inclusive communities. Against the backdrop of their challenging political context and the structural constraints of media platforms, they build new feminist protests and spaces, all without the capacities or resources of formal organizations. Their choice to "do it ourselves," no matter what and against all odds, has changed the face of U.S. feminism.

3 Networked Feminist Visibility

In 1997, Tarana Burke was working as a counselor at a youth summer camp, when a young camper asked to speak to her in private. The camper disclosed to Burke that she had been sexually abused. Heartbroken and caught off guard, Burke sent the camper to another counselor. The exchange haunted Burke, who is also a sexual violence survivor: "I didn't have a response or a way to help her in that moment, and I couldn't even say 'me, too,'" Burke told the *New York Times* (Garcia, 2017). In 2006, Burke founded Just Be Inc., a Philadelphia-based nonprofit organization focused on the well-being and growth of young women of color. Remembering that camper, Burke used the organization to launch the "me too movement," aimed at creating "empowerment through empathy" (Just Be Inc., 2013) for girls and young women who have endured sexual abuse, assault, or exploitation.[1]

More than a decade later, those two simple words—"me too"—spread like wildfire across social media. On the evening of October 15, 2017, actor Alyssa Milano tweeted, "If you've been sexually harassed or assaulted, write 'me too' as a reply to this tweet."[2] Inspired and infuriated by the wave of allegations against Hollywood producer Harvey Weinstein, which had emerged in the weeks prior, Milano sought to expose the pervasiveness of sexual violence beyond the film industry (Sayej, 2017). The hashtag #MeToo quickly went viral, creating an outlet for survivors to tell their stories and sparking a global conversation about harassment and assault.

#MeToo was not the first instance of *hashtag feminism*. This form of networked feminist activism appropriates Twitter's metadata tags for organizing posts to draw visibility to a particular cause or experience and has become a core component of the do-it-ourselves feminist repertoire. While feminist hashtags appear on other platforms like Instagram and Facebook, Twitter's highly visible, public-by-default nature makes it especially fertile grounds for viral campaigns.[3] The tactic has allowed individual activists with both small and large followings to mobilize national and even global discussions and direct actions. Given their ease of participation, wide reach, and participatory nature, feminist hashtags embody the DIO ethos and dozens of feminist hashtags concerning gender justice issues have taken off in recent years.[4] #MeToo's diffusion, however, exponentially outpaced many of its predecessors. Prior to #MeToo, 2014 campaigns #WhyIStayed and #YesAllWomen, two of the earliest feminist hashtags, were the most visible Twitter campaigns against sexual violence; in one day, they were tweeted more than 46,000 times and 61,000 times, respectively (Grinberg, 2014; Main, 2017). By comparison, within twenty-four hours, #MeToo was used in 109,451 tweets (Main, 2017) and referenced in more than 12 million posts and comments on Facebook (Park, 2017).

At the time of her original tweet, Milano was unaware of Burke's grassroots "me too" movement. Women of color journalists and activists, wary of white women appropriating Black women's labor and dominating the conversation surrounding sexual violence, quickly took to Twitter to call out the erasure of Burke's work (Hill, 2017). Two days after the hashtag went viral, Milano publicly credited Burke with having founded the movement and the two joined forces, taking media interviews together to promote the movement's message (Hill, 2017).

In the weeks after the campaign first went viral, #MeToo outlived the fleeting temporality of most hashtags and grew into a powerful, transnational movement against sexual violence. The hashtag was quickly translated into its French (#BalanceTonPorc/"call out your pig"), Spanish (#YoTambien/"me too"), Italian (#QuellaVoltaChe/"that time"), Hebrew (#גםאנחנו/"us too"), and Arabic (#AnaKaman/"me too") counterparts, among others (Lekach, 2017; Levy, 2017); the Chinese equivalent, #MiTu, translated into the seemingly innocuous nonsensical phrase, "rice bunny," to circumvent government censorship of internet platforms (Lake, 2018). Variants of the original hashtag, including #MosqueMeToo, #ChurchToo, #MeTooPhD, #MeTooK12, #MeTooCongress, #MeTooMilitary, and #Aid-Too, soon took off, calling attention to sexual misconduct across multiple sites and industries within and beyond the U.S. context. By the end of 2017, the still-active hashtag had been used on Twitter in eighty-five countries and posted on Facebook nearly ninety million times (Sayej, 2017).

The hashtag campaign had a number of ripple effects online and off. The same month the hashtag went viral, journalist Moira Donegan anonymously created and circulated the "Shitty Media Men" list, a shared Google spreadsheet that allowed anyone to document warnings about men in media industries who had allegedly committed sexual misconduct. While Donegan deleted the spreadsheet after it went viral, copies spread across the internet, naming more than seventy men as perpetrators of sexual assault and harassment (Grady, 2018). Olympic gymnast McKayla Maroney used the hashtag to publicly disclose that USA Gymnastics team doctor Larry Nassar had molested her while she was in his care; following Maroney's lead, *156* other victims came forward and Nassar was sentenced to life in prison (Correa, 2018; Park and Perrigo, 2017). In November 2017, Congresswoman Jackie Speier, herself a survivor of sexual assault as a young congressional staffer, introduced a bill to streamline the process for reporting sexual harassment on Capitol Hill (Serfaty, 2017).

The following month, *Time* magazine named the movement's "Silence Breakers," from celebrities like Milano to grassroots organizers like Burke, as its 2017 Person of the Year (Zacharek, Dockterman, and Edwards, 2017). After the hashtag opened an affirming public outlet for survivors, allegations of sexual misconduct were made against dozens of high-profile men in entertainment, politics, journalism, sports, the arts, and more (Almukhtar, Gold, and Buchanan, 2018). On January 1, 2018, inspired by #MeToo, three hundred actors, agents, writers, directors, producers, executives, and lawyers published an open letter in the *New York Times* announcing the launch of Time's Up. The initiative included a $13 million legal defense fund for underprivileged survivors, a call for new legislation against sexual harassment, and a formal effort to reach gender parity at film and TV studios and talent agencies by 2020 (Buckley, 2018). One week later, at the 2018 Golden Globe Awards, Time's Up mobilized its first symbolic action as celebrity supporters dressed in all black, donned pins bearing the initiative's name, addressed sexual violence in interviews, and brought grassroots activists as their guests to draw attention to gender justice issues beyond Hollywood (Weaver, 2018). Similar forms of red-carpet activism would punctuate the rest of the 2018 awards season (North, 2018).

As it became increasingly visible, a commercial market sprang up around #MeToo and the campaign's slogan was used to brand not only celebrities, but also clothing, accessories, makeup, and even a spate of mobile applications and start-up companies (Dwoskin and McGregor, 2018; Hampton, 2018; Salo, 2017). Once #MeToo became almost inescapable across social media, news outlets, and consumer culture, dozens of think pieces concerning gender, sex, and power emerged and some, like the hashtag, went viral, further extending the campaign's relevance beyond any one news cycle.[5] Perhaps most importantly, #MeToo sparked everyday conversations about consent at dinner tables, in classrooms, and on college campuses (Bennett, 2017; Crowley, 2018) and emboldened record numbers of individual survivors to seek support through crisis centers and hotlines (Koerth-Baker, 2018; Lambert, 2018; McCammon, 2017). What started out as a grassroots initiative and, later, a tweet exploded into a global, multimedia movement against sexual violence.

In the aftermath of its meteoric rise, #MeToo faced two diametrically opposed critiques. Conservative critics charged that the campaign had gone *too far*, destroying the lives of the accused and straining personal and professional relationships between men and women (e.g., Chattopadhyay, 2018; Kipnis, 2018; Richardson, 2018). But others wondered whether #MeToo had gone *far enough*, or if the hashtag was merely a media spectacle incapable of dismantling a system of oppression (e.g., Banet-Weiser, 2018a; Faludi, 2017; Kipnis, 2018). Both critiques echo a set of questions at the center of debates concerning networked activism: can hashtags cause "real" social change? What happens *after* the hashtag takes over news media? Or, as a PBS docuseries inspired by the campaign asked, *#MeToo, Now What?*

From early activist hashtags like the 2009 #IranElection or the 2011 #OccupyWallStreet campaigns to more contemporary movements like #BlackLivesMatter and #MeToo, discourse surrounding networked activism has circled around these questions, with polarizing results. So-called "techno-optimists" have argued that social media can indeed create real change by democratizing access to the tools and information required to build movements and stage protests, thereby lowering the cost of participation and, in the process, revolutionizing the public sphere (e.g., Benkler, 2006; Castells, 2011, 2012; Shirky, 2008). "Techno-pessimists," however, have made the case that networked activism is merely "slacktivism," a risk-free performance of virtue-signaling that *feels* satisfying but has little impact, that distracts from "real" activism, that opens activists up to surveillance, and that is incapable of building sustainable movements (e.g., Gladwell, 2010; Morozov, 2011). Viewed through the lens of these bifurcated debates, #MeToo seems to offer a case study for testing whether or not networked activism is an effective tool for social change.

The instrumentalist approach of the "activism vs. slacktivism" debate, however, lacks the capacity to hold at once both the possibilities and limitations of hashtag feminism and oversimplifies the multiple dimensions of a case like #MeToo. The campaign has simultaneously taken the forms of a grassroots organization, a hashtagged support network, a community conversation, a personal revelation, a coalition of actors and media makers, and a push for stronger legislation, *as well as* an individualistic celebrity self-branding mechanism, a capitalist marketing campaign, a superficial fashion statement, and more. The social, cultural, and political lives of #MeToo are numerous, and the campaign's impact can be neither wholly dismissed nor uncritically celebrated. Asking either/or questions of activist hashtags overlooks the possibility that the answer might be *both/and*, that hashtag feminism, like networked feminism more broadly, might be *both* politically transformative *and* politically problematic. In fact, that such polarizing tensions exist in empirical research and popular discourse concerning hashtag activism suggests that each side of this debate may be telling one part of a far more complex story. To borrow McRobbie's (2004) phrase, competing opinions on hashtag activism suggest that the tactic is *doubly entangled* in both liberatory politics and systems of oppression. Research questions that reject false dichotomies and embrace this complexity are needed to develop a fuller understanding of hashtag activism (Tufekci, 2017)

Moreover, the *techno-determinist* assumptions behind these debates—the notion that technology alone drives social change—leave little room for feminists' voices and agency and the complex negotiations they have historically made between their political goals and contexts when developing tactics. Though digital platforms may be new, for U.S. feminists, the struggle to balance both the compelling, highly visible drama of protesting personal experiences of injustice with the difficult, backstage work of collective organizing is not. Susan Faludi (2017) argues that feminist activism in the United States has, dating back to the nineteenth-century temperance movement, taken two forms: one is expressions of anger at the abuses of individual men, who provide unambiguous targets for activists' righteous outrage, and the other is the "less spectacular but essential" work of dismantling structures of inequality and building more equitable systems in their places. These two forms of protest can productively intersect, but "fighting the patriarch" is easier and often far more electrifying than "fighting the patriarchy," making the former more widely practiced and more easily digestible within mainstream media. Historical accounts of U.S. feminist activism like Faludi's (2017), in other words, suggest that digital media have intensified and complicated, rather than caused, feminists' struggles to sustain strong and effective movements over time.

In this chapter, instead of approaching social media as tools, I work from an understanding of social media as *practices* to develop a more expansive look at hashtag feminism through the lens of activists, themselves (Couldry, 2010). When digital media platforms are framed not as tools but as spaces for political participation, the contradictions of networked activism and the strategies practitioners use to navigate them come into view. Instead of asking about hashtag feminism's effects, a line of inquiry that demands definitive answers to what are in reality complex questions, I ask about feminists' hashtag *practices*, starting with the political values that inform them. How do activists view the political affordances and limitations of hashtag feminism and how do they juggle both? My goal is to illuminate the processes through which activists develop their tactics while working within sociotechnical constraints. This grounded, processual approach toward understanding hashtag feminism is especially key as do-it-ourselves feminists work to build a feminist praxis that reflects their values and responds to the challenges of the current political context and media landscape.

To explore these questions, I analyzed a large sample of *meta-tweets*—tweets in which activists use a hashtag to reflect on or call attention to it—from the #MeToo campaign. Drawing on theories of visibility, performance, and discourse, I argue that hashtag feminism is a type of contentious performance that enables activists to politicize the personal—a long-standing goal of feminist movements in the United States—by making it *visible*. #MeToo aggregated personal stories into a networked visibility campaign, illustrating the systemic nature of sexual violence. Making the personal visible on a globally networked media stage, however, posed a variety of challenges for both individual participants and the movement as a whole. To negotiate between the affordances and limitations of hashtag activism, #MeToo participants developed *performance maintenance practices* through which they evaluated the campaign's shortcomings, advanced solutions informed by their goals and values, and moved toward a specifically feminist approach to hashtag activism. Their efforts point toward do-it-ourselves feminism as a complex, interactional, recursive process aimed at achieving a transformative politics of visibility.

HASHTAG FEMINISM AND MAKING THE PERSONAL *VISIBLE*

Existing research on hashtag feminism largely leans toward one of two sides. Some scholars frame hashtag feminism as a powerful practice in the *politics of visibility*, a form of activism focused on shifting how we represent, interpret, and respond to social injustices through public performances. But others have argued that while the tactic is helpful for raising awareness, hashtag feminism is often complicit in what Sarah Banet-Weiser (2015a; 2018a; 2018b) calls an *economy of visibility*, a form of activism that begins and ends with performance and does little to transform structures of inequality. With the polarized reactions to #MeToo as a reference point, I consider each side of this tension in the literature below, before moving toward a practitioner-centered exploration of what it means to grapple with *both* the affordances and limitations of hashtag feminism.

Hashtag Feminism, a Politics of Visibility

Conservative #MeToo critics frequently referred to the hashtag campaign as a "witch hunt" (e.g., Collective 2018; Magness 2018; Walsh and Blackwell 2018), a "hysterical" rush to judgment that risked ruining lives and careers fueled by, in one director's words, a "new man-hating puritanism" (Nyren, 2018).[6] Beyond irreparable damage to the accused's reputation, others argued that #MeToo, as the *New York Post* put it, "lumped the trivial in with legitimate sexual assault" (Peyser, 2017). The hashtag, in other words, triggered a "sex panic" that could sap the fun out of workplace banter, flirting, romance, dating, and casual hookups for men and women alike (Merkin, 2018; Sommers, 2017), an ironic reversal of the feminist Sexual Revolution of the 1960s and 1970s (Gessen, 2017). Still others ridiculed #MeToo supporters for enabling a "culture of victimhood," which casts women as helpless and irresponsible for their individual actions or personal successes and silences anyone who challenges its logic (Phillips, 2018; Roiphe, 2018).

Embedded in these critics' fears about the campaign's long-term effects on everyday life was the tacit understanding that #MeToo engages in a *politics of visibility*, a representational struggle aimed at exposing power so that it might be transformed (Banet-Weiser 2015a). Within a politics of visibility, the collective articulation of oppressive experiences, such as sexual violence, challenges social norms that silence and excuse such experiences and, when successful, undermines the structures of inequality those norms support. As Banet-Weiser (2015a) explains, identity-political movements have long practiced tactics geared toward making historically marginalized political categories like gender visible. The demand to be seen, recognized, and valued has been a key component of feminist, antiracist, queer and trans, labor, and humanitarian movements' fights for the expansion of rights for underprivileged communities (Chouliaraki, 2006; Hall, Evans, and Nixon, 2013; Taylor, 1997). For U.S. feminist movements dating back to the 1960s, engaging in a politics of visibility has often involved *making the personal political*, or calling attention to the taken-for-granted gender norms that constrain everyday life so that they might be denaturalized and deconstructed (Carol Hanisch 1969). Put differently, U.S. feminists have historically drawn on tactics that make the personal *visible*, from street protests to alternative media making.

Theories of discourse and performance shed light on the political implications of making the personal visible. Drawing on tactics of discursive activism, feminists have endeavored to make visible and deconstruct the discourses that shape our expectations for appropriately feminine and masculine roles and behaviors (Young, 1997). In their place, feminists collectively construct and broadcast new interpretive frameworks for understanding and responding to gender-based oppression. As Patricia Hill Collins (2000) argues, this process of feminist "rearticulation" (p. 32) speaks power into visibility so that its very foundation can be challenged, deconstructed, and replaced with alternative ways of knowing, formed from a feminist standpoint. Here, speech is *performative*, but not in the colloquial sense of being inauthentic or superficial, a critique some commentators have leveled against hashtag activism. Rather, speech is performative in the sense that Judith Butler (1990) deploys the term to describe gender as a "stylized repetition of acts," which "founds and consolidates the subject" (p. 140). Speech, in other words, is *productive*, creating material effects for the speaker and listener beyond its transmission. Feminist politics of visibility are a *performative politics*, with the potential to produce change by destabilizing the dominant discourses shaping everyday actions and modeling alternative ways of being. Movements engaged in performative politics develop repertoires of "contentious performances" (Tilly and Tarrow 2015, p. 11), through which they "display for others the meaning of their social situation" (Alexander 2004, p. 529). Effective performances convince onlookers that the meanings actors convey are true and foster solidarity between actors and their audiences, thereby facilitating the type of discursive activism Young (1997) describes.

Do-it-ourselves feminists take the contentious performances of discursive activism to new levels with hashtag feminism. While the virality of a hashtag is typically short-lived, scholars have argued that hashtag campaigns can have major long-lasting effects. Hashtag networks create opportunities for people standing at the intersection of multiple, overlapping oppressions to build coalitions and deconstruct interlocking systems of power (Brown et al., 2017; Daniels, 2016; Kuo, 2016; Loza, 2014; Rodino-Colocino, 2014; Tynes, Schuschke, and Noble, 2016). The interpretive frameworks they advance can inform responses to social injustices long after an individual campaign has reached peak visibility. Samantha Thrift (2014) argues that hyper-visible hashtags take on the qualities of a "feminist meme event" (p. 1091), or a widely shared reference point for "how we conceptualize and choose to narrate misogynist aggression and gender violence in American culture" (p. 1091). Beyond conceptualizing gender violence, highly visible feminist hashtags like #MeToo can also influence how we respond to it, creating a lasting material impact on participants and their audiences (Keller, Mendes, and Ringrose, 2018; Rentschler, 2017).

Hashtag Feminism, an Economy of Visibility

But feminist #MeToo critics questioned whether the hashtag's unprecedented visibility did more to harm the movement than to strengthen it. #MeToo and its spinoffs exposed the prevalence of sexual misconduct across a variety of different sectors and industries and, in the process, took down a number of offenders. As Faludi (2017) lamented, however, the hashtag and its accompanying media coverage overemphasized the stories of *individual* survivors and perpetrators, which, while important, undermined the campaign's ability to create *systemic* transformations. Rather than framing sexual violence as embedded in an intersecting system of oppression, the #MeToo media frenzy focused more on stories of predominantly white celebrities' experiences and activism. Coverage of celebrities donning all black or wearing special pins in support of #MeToo at red carpet events, for example, dominated the 2018 awards season (North, 2018). This overemphasis on white celebrities limited engagement with the issue of sexual violence to performance alone (Hess, 2018; St. Félix, 2017; Faludi, 2017) and erased the experiences of women of color and women in low-wage jobs, who face disproportionately high rates of assault (Lockhart, 2017). For these critics, the most visible strands of #MeToo—the viral hashtag, the celebrity activists, the news cycles dedicated to the latest exposure of a high-profile perpetrator—limited engagement with these complicated issues to performance *alone*. Doreen

St. Félix (2017), for example, describes the "theatre of accountability" that emerged within the television news industry following the viral diffusion of #MeToo. When perpetrators like Matt Lauer and Charlie Rose were exposed, the accused's female coanchors were tasked with publicly embodying networks' shock, grief, and shame, an emotional performance with the power to distract audiences from the structural inequalities that have plagued the industry for decades (St. Félix, 2017). Amanda Hess (2018) argues that the film industry has similarly transmuted #MeToo's politics of visibility through performance, using celebrity spokeswomen's red-carpet activism to skirt "a conversation about its culture of harassment in favor of one about what an amazing job it is doing combating that harassment." Still other feminist commentators weighed the negative consequences of #MeToo's hyper-visible performance of feminist politics against any possible benefits. Rather than turning attention exclusively toward perpetrators, the campaign placed the burden of visibility on survivors, who relived traumatic experiences as they shared and read stories through the hashtag (LaMotte, 2017) and who faced harassment and trolling with the onslaught of "the #MeToo backlash" (Gianino, 2017; Tolentino, 2018).

For these critics, #MeToo's politics of visibility too often slip into what Banet-Weiser (2015a; 2018a; 2018b) calls *economies of visibility*, individualistic systems of exchange in which representation in consumer culture is positioned as the height of empowerment. Whereas, within a *politics* of visibility, representation is part of a collective struggle to achieve political goals, within an *economy* of visibility, political action begins and ends with representation. Economies of visibility dovetail neatly with U.S. feminists' long-standing demands to be *seen* and *recognized* in laws, media, the workplace, and other institutions, making feminist movements particularly vulnerable to absorption within them. As Nancy Fraser (1995), in her critique of Butler's work, argues, feminists' emphasis on the symbolic power of discourse and performance leaves them highly susceptible "to commodification, recuperation, and depoliticization—especially in the absence of strong social movements struggling for social justice" (p. 163). The DIO feminist Twitter hashtag, which promises easy access to large audiences without the resources of an organized movement but which is simultaneously embedded in a corporately owned platform, appears especially open to this co-optation. The most visible forms of #MeToo flow through the attention economy of commercial media, where clicks, likes, ratings, and ad revenues are the primary goals and where experiences as complex as sexual violence are easily simplified and commodified. Economies of visibility turn the feminist politics of visibility on its head; rather than making the personal political, economies of visibility constrain political action to an individual's performance of self in consumer culture. In this way, economies of visibility are like a funhouse mirror, reflecting and warping the do-it-ourselves ethos of contemporary feminist actions and movements. Rather than encouraging the collective, extra-institutional actions of do-it-ourselves feminism, economies of visibility emphasize individually focused and enacted performances. If feminist *politics* of visibility are performative in the sense of being productive, *economies* of visibility are performative in the sense of being individualistic, superficial, and politically ineffectual.

Critical feminist media studies scholarship identifies economies of visibility at work in Twitter campaigns. Hashtags trade on short but compelling narratives, which risk, as some scholars have argued, oversimplifying and even replicating structural inequalities (Berents, 2016; Loken, 2014; Maxfield, 2016). Others have argued that the hyper-visibility of hashtag feminism inevitably leads to backlash in the form of online harassment (Banet-Weiser, 2015b; Ganzer, 2014; Woods, 2014). U.S. feminist movements have historically faced backlash, but hashtag campaigns, due to their emphasis on viral performances rather than sustained organizing, do not possess the capacity to collectively address harassment and the Twitter platform's reporting mechanisms often fail to cut harassment off at the source. Scholars have also expressed concerns that hyper-visible hashtag campaigns can mask the need for offline organizing (Maxfield, 2016) or become co-opted for non-feminist purposes, such as merchandising and self-branding (Pruchniewska, 2017). Lastly, hashtag feminism can exclude those most marginalized communities who are underrepresented across the media landscape and who may lack access to the technologies necessary to participate in networked visibility campaigns (Latina and Docherty, 2014). Systems of inequality structure access to representation in the marketplace, enabling economies of visibility to compound intersecting oppressions by further marginalizing underprivileged survivors, as seen in white women's domination of #MeToo media coverage. When read together with more celebratory takes, this research suggests that hashtag feminists' viral performances may edge popular culture toward more feminist discourse, but their emphasis on *symbolic* power risks leaving *structural* systems of domination untouched.

NETWORKED FEMINIST VISIBILITY: A CASE STUDY OF #METOO

At the heart of the hashtag feminism and #MeToo debates are a number of questions concerning the efficacy of networked visibility and performance as protest tactics. Is the hashtagged performance compelling and convincing? If so, does it go beyond moving its audience to transforming systems of power? Or does it sacrifice structural analyses in favor of poignant sound bites? Which actors are given time in the spotlight and which are ignored? What risks come with making one's experiences of trauma and injustice visible on a globally networked stage? And does the performance proceed smoothly, or is it interrupted or co-opted by others with ulterior motives?

My analysis of #MeToo participants' reflections on the campaign points to hashtag feminism as a type of performance that enables activists to bridge *two* levels of visibility—the individual and the collective—in order to make the personal political and advance new interpretations of everyday experiences of oppression. Within this practice in the politics of visibility, the latter is not possible without the former; for sexual violence to be made visible as a systemic injustice, individuals needed to publicly perform their status as survivors or their allies. The process of building up from an individual to a collective performance of visibility, however, introduces a variety of personal and political vulnerabilities. Grounded in my sample of meta-tweets, I highlight the affordances and limitations #MeToo participants identified as signature to hashtag feminism and the performance maintenance strategies they used to juggle both. Their media practices illustrate not only the strengths and weaknesses of the do-it-ourselves approach to feminist protest; they also underscore the reflexive, processual, and resilient nature of contemporary feminist protest.

The Affordances of Saying "Me Too"

For many #MeToo participants, simply tweeting the two-word phrase was a "brave" and "revolutionary" action akin to protesting in the streets:

> @Spreading_Love: To all of those bravely sharing their stories of sexual assault/harassment using #MeToo: we stand with you and by you. (October 15, 2017, 8:16 p.m.)[7]

> @colecato6: Me too. There shouldn't be so many of us, but there are. Let them hear us, we're silent no more. #MeToo (October 15, 2017, 9:21 p.m.)

> @AVAproject: To all those who are speaking out with #MeToo. Your collective roar is more powerful than you can imagine. Thank you! (October 16, 2017, 8:07 a.m.)

As these tweets make clear, the power of #MeToo stemmed from the sheer volume of people publishing their stories under the hashtag. The hashtag created a platform for hundreds of thousands of survivors, who, through their networked assembly, demanded recognition of sexual violence as a global, systemic injustice.

But before there could be a plural "we," the campaign needed to start with the singular "me," the individual activists who made the personal decision to participate in the campaign. Prior to #MeToo, many participants reported that they had rarely, if ever, spoken about their trauma in public. Some even gave voice to experiences they had repressed for decades; as one participant wrote, "60 years old and I still have trouble saying it out loud. #MeToo (October 15, 2017, 8:02pm)." The hashtag's semantic structure made taking this potentially painful or terrifying step somewhat easier. The phrase, "me too," stands on its own as a complete statement that, when read within the context of the viral hashtag campaign, requires no further explanation. This meant that participants could stand in solidarity with other survivors without necessarily having to detail traumatic experiences. While some tweeted #MeToo and nothing else, others offered reflections on their experiences, participating in the campaign that shed light on the power of its simplicity:

> @LJonasDaughter: #metoo tried to figure out how to explain it with the character restriction. Decided #metoo said enough (October 15, 2017, 8:28 p.m.)

@LieutenantDainty: #MeToo because while I'm not ready to share my story, I can be strong enough to admit that it happened. (October 16, 2017, 7:15 p.m.)

@iamhelene: I don't think I'll ever be comfortable enough to talk about it publicly but #MeToo (October 15, 2017, 8:43 p.m.)

To tweet #MeToo, regardless of the rest of the message, was to perform a public demand for recognition on behalf of the staggering number of sexual violence survivors worldwide.

The relationship between the "me" of #MeToo and the hashtag's "collective roar" indicates that there are two types of visibility at play in the campaign. First, *individuals* needed to make themselves visible as survivors of sexual violence. When aggregated and connected through Twitter's hashtag function, their individual performances became the building blocks for the campaign's *collective* visibility. For U.S. feminists, the hashtag's ability to network *individual* performances into *collective* protest is an especially key political affordance. A hashtag's aggregation of individual expressions under a collectively shared framework parallels the feminist practice of making the *personal political*. Feminist hashtags symbolically index a set of personal experiences that, while varied in their specific details, are rooted in a shared context of oppression. In this way, hashtag feminism engages in a performative politics of visibility, in which one person's narrative, when shared and connected with many others, makes power visible so that it might be deconstructed and challenged. Like the discursive activism of previous generations, hashtag feminists' performative speech popularizes alternative epistemologies for interpreting and responding to injustices.

Tweeting #MeToo, in other words, produces a generative visibility, a performance that, beyond asking for attention, has material effects for the performer and her audience. Much of the activist commentary in my sample argues that, just as #MeToo bridges individual and collective levels of visibility, its performative politics can spark change at both the personal and structural levels of society. At the level of the individual, the sheer volume of #MeToo tweets elicited intense emotional responses from those watching the campaign unfold, suggesting that the hashtag's performance resonated deeply with many audience members. For some, seeing friends, family, and colleagues using the hashtag made the magnitude of the problem hit home, gave sexual violence statistics a human face, and inspired them to take action:

> @JennyS38: #MeToo brings so many emotions right now . . . But one over-whelming emotion is admiration towards the people who have stood up and shared their experiences so that the everyone will realize this problem is real and can't be buried and ignored. (October 16, 2017, 8:08 p.m.)

> @hmetal250: #MeToo as a man I am so shocked this has been happening to so many women. It has to stop. Speak out women and be brave (October 16, 2017, 8:33 p.m.)

> @BolderSpeed: Every #MeToo tweet in my timeline is a kick to my stomach. I have no words. Sad. Angry. Not surprised. Keep speaking out (October 16, 2017, 8:17 a.m.)

For others, seeing their social media feeds filled with survivors' stories, paired with words of support from allies, removed the shame associated with being a sexual violence victim and encouraged them to speak out about their own experiences. The process of retelling their stories, from their perspectives and in their words, enabled survivors to wrest agency over their own narratives away from dominant frameworks for interpreting sexual violence, facilitating a personal transformation:

> @BonnieLMann: I struggled with posting publicly. So, I made myself do it, because that's the point. It isn't my shame. It wasn't my fault. #MeToo (October 15, 2017, 8:17 p.m.)

> @topreject: #MeToo It took me many years to be able to cope. In the end I decided talking about it removed all of its power (15 October 15, 2017, 9:27 p.m.)

Individual male allies used the hashtag to document how #MeToo had changed their perception of sexual harassment and assault and what steps they were going to take to combat misogyny and sexual violence in their everyday lives. When read alongside survivors' reflections, their tweets evidence a shift at the individual level in who carries the burden of shame for sexual violence, from victims to perpetrators and bystanders:

> @oughthere: The #MeToo hashtag is heartbreaking but not surprising. I have definitely harassed women before. I must do better. We must do bet-ter. (October 15, 2017, 8:11 p.m.)

@Tejano2200: Reading stories of sexual harassment makes me feel ashamed of my gender for staying quiet. We need to speak out against injustice. #MeToo (October 15, 2017, 7:20 p.m.)

Survivors' #MeToo stories moved readers to reevaluate their perspectives on sexual violence and take action, either by coming forward with their own experiences or by making a commitment to change their behavior and challenge that of others.

As the campaign grew from individual survivors coming forward to a collective protest that spanned the globe, so, too, did #MeToo's ability to implement change at the structural level of society. Repeatedly throughout my sample, activists identified the hashtag campaign's viral visibility as a powerful tactic for illustrating the pervasiveness of sexual violence and busting victim-blaming myths that have come to dominate discourse surrounding harassment and assault. One sentence frequently copied and pasted throughout the campaign's first few days described the hashtag's power in numbers: "If all who have been sexually harassed or assaulted posted #MeToo, people might understand the magnitude of the issue." The hundreds of thousands of stories compiled under the hashtag implicitly challenge the notion that sexual violence results from a one-off encounter with a "bad guy" or from a victim's irresponsible choices. In a common sentiment shared among activists reflecting on the campaign, one survivor tweeted, "#MeToo, just like most other women" (October 16, 2017, 6:45 a.m.), framing sexual violence as an issue that is deeply rooted in gendered systems of power and that cuts across all industries, sectors, and cultures. While each narrative shared under the hashtag is unique, the "too" in #MeToo's discursive framing explicitly points toward sexual violence as a repeated and systemic, rather than private or personal, issue. The hashtag's ability to network a large variety of sexual violence narratives under a common interpretive framework enabled activists to politicize personal encounters with harassment and assault, contextualizing participants' individual stories against the shared backdrop of the gendered systems of oppression that enable sexual violence to persist. In turn, #MeToo helped survivors to break through the shameful alienation that often comes with sexual violence and mobilize around their shared trauma. One activist described the feeling of collective solidarity and power that #MeToo generated: "My entire feed is filled with survivors say-ing #MeToo. Something powerful is happening. We're everywhere, and together, we're unstoppable" (October 15, 2017, 7:18 p.m.).

The Challenges of Saying "Me Too"

At the same time, relying on visibility as a protest tactic opened #MeToo participants up to a number of vulnerabilities. Repeatedly throughout my sample, #MeToo participants highlighted the personal risks that came with choosing to make oneself visible as a survivor on a globally networked platform like Twitter. Publicly performing the identity of a survivor in a cultural context where sexual violence victims are shamed and doubted leaves one vulnerable to personal attacks. Activists in my sample were quick to remind those commenting on the remarkable reach of the cam-paign that, in one participant's words, "There's so much shame around sexual abuse/assault/harassment. What you see publicly here is just a sliver #metoo" (October 15, 2017, 2:21 p.m.). For many, the difficulty or danger of having friends, family members, the general public, and possibly even their abusers see their #MeToo stories likely outweighed the benefits of participating in the campaign:

> @EzerRising: Too many women are unable to say #MeToo because they are being silenced by abusers and fear being called a liar. (October 15, 2017, 8:31 p.m.)

> @jennyanthro: A reminder—#MeToo might not appear on all your social media feeds because survivors might still be virtually connected to their abusers (October 16, 2017, 2:28 p.m.)

> @bnack: if you see some women not posting #metoo they've probably been harassed but feel silenced by a society that often punishes the woman who was harassed and not the man who harassed her (October 16, 2017, 8:00 a.m.)

Those who chose to engage with the hashtag described a range of nega-tive personal outcomes. While some survivors found comfort in the hashtag, for others, #MeToo was a "triggering" campaign that required survivors to "relive their trauma." One participant found the campaign "brutal" and "overwhelming": "Sometimes, knowing you are not alone isn't inspiring. It's tragic. When the world screams they've all been through the same thing, it can make a survivor feel like there is no safe place and every person they pass, every dark alley or bar, could be the next rape" (@Grace_Durbin, October 15, 2017, 6:34 p.m.). Participants were also subjected to harassment. Perpetrators appropriated #MeToo to launch attacks against the campaign's participants, promulgate rape myths and jokes, accuse participants of lying and "attention seeking," and, in a painfully ironic testament to the campaign's relevance, sexually harass and threaten participants with rape. As one participant put it bluntly, "Twitter is NOT a safe space" (October 15, 2017, 1:13 p.m.). To make matters worse, when participants reported harassment to Twitter Support, the platform often failed to adequately address the problem: "While #MeToo goes viral and everyone is outraged about Weinstein, @TwitterSupport does not consider rape taunts a violation of their Terms of Service" (October 20, 2017, 2:54 p.m.). At the same time Twitter benefitted from the traffic generated by #MeToo, it failed to address sexual violence on its own platform.

Just as individual visibility lays the foundation for collective visibility, these personal vulnerabilities quickly scaled up into political vulnerabilities. Noting the risks that went along with posting #MeToo, many worried that the campaign asked too much of survivors while doing too little to hold their assailants accountable. For these participants, #MeToo joined other campaigns like #WhyIStayed and #YesAllWomen in encouraging sexual violence victims to publicly reflect on their experiences without explicitly pushing perpetrators to examine their own behavior:

> @CatherineShu: #MeToo . . . but I also ask, why is the onus for change once again placed on victims reliving their trauma? (October 15, 2017, 9:05 p.m.)

> @shannonclaire9: I'm sick of seeing hashtags like #MeToo every couple of months. It's yet another effort to get people to believe us. How many hashtags will it take to make people see that sexual violence is a systemic issue? (October 16, 2017, 10:35 a.m.)

> @LinLibrarian: #MeToo and, yes, you, too. But I already knew that since we did #YesAllWomen three years ago. Now I need to know what men are doing to change this. (October 15, 2017, 11:15 p.m.)

Other activists were apprehensive about whether the #MeToo movement provided an inclusive platform for *all* victims of sexual violence. In the days and weeks after #MeToo first took off, feminists of color used the hashtag to call out the campaign's focus on white, economically privileged, heteronormative women:

> @VenkaylaH: A Black woman launched this movement and white women tried to take credit for it until people made it clear that Tarana Burke was the creator. #MeToo is supposed to center the marginalized, not the privileged who have access to adequate resources. (December 6, 2017, 8:13 a.m.)

> @akdwaz: This hashtag is just tip of the iceberg. There are millions without a computer or access to the internet who have experiences abuse on a daily basis (October 16, 2017, 2:59 a.m.)

Similarly, others pointed out that most discourse surrounding the campaign worked from the assumption that sexual violence is an issue that only affects cisgender, heterosexual women:

> @ItsNathanielT: It's interesting that people assume that no men have #MeToo stories. We have also experienced these things. (October 16, 2017, 3:47 a.m.)

> @JinPossible1: I feel uncomfortable adding my #MeToo because I am not a woman, but trans and non-binary people need a voice, too, so here I am. (October 16, 2016, 1:14 a.m.)

> @LindseyManson1: Men are not the only ones who assault. I rarely share my story because of the embarrassment that my attacker was a woman #MeToo (October 15, 2017, 6:38 p.m.)

#MeToo, these activists argued, needed to better center and amplify the experiences of those most marginalized victims in order to address sexual violence and its intersections with racism, classism, heterosexism, and transphobia. Their critiques highlight a major limitation of viral visibility as a political tactic—a hashtag may enable broad participation, but access to mainstream media representation continues to be structured by race, sexuality, and class.

In addition to concern over *who* was included in #MeToo, activists also questioned *what* issues and experiences fell under the hashtag campaign's broad umbrella. The simplicity and flexibility of the phrase, "Me too"—two words that can gloss a wide range of experiences—made the campaign compelling and easy to join, even if sharing the complete details of one's story could be difficult, and especially conducive for success on Twitter, where brevity is key. But the hashtag's ambiguity, combined with the tendency for accounts of more severe instances of sexual violence to gain more retweets, led some participants to feel apprehensive about whether or not their narratives fit within the #MeToo framework:

@MadisonLesc: I have been debating whether or not my experiences were bad enough to warrant a #metoo tweet. (October 15, 2017, 11:07 p.m.)

@ChefTorrie: When you post #metoo & immediately debate taking it down because you feel embarrassed & figure your harassment wasn't bad enough to count. (October 15, 2017, 9:03 p.m.)

@laurphelps: Something messed up about #metoo—I feel like being groped several times is too mundane to mention & not "real" assault (October 16, 2017, 1:32 a.m.)

Combined with conservative critics' charge that the hashtag lacked a clear platform (Peyser, 2017), #MeToo participants' concerns over whether their story "counts" suggest that the same degree of flexibility that enabled the hashtag to go viral may leave the movement's core message somewhat unclear.

Above all, participants feared that the ease with which one could support the campaign would create the illusion that no further work was necessary and lull the public into inaction. If participation in the #MeToo movement was equated with performing solidarity through symbolic actions like sharing a hashtag or dressing in all black for a red-carpet event, anyone could feign support for survivors without actually taking steps to end sexual violence:

@arnajain1: To the "woke men" now expressing their sympathy for #MeToo on social media, I say this—if you consider yourself an ally, you need to do more than just post a hashtag. (October 16, 2017, 11:07 p.m.)

@KellyIceSkates: If you're a male celebrity you should be doing a hell of a lot more than just wearing a black suit you were going to wear anyway. Plus there were known sexual assaulters participating. #MeToo (January 8, 2018, 6:45 p.m.)

@isaakvall: celebs wearing black for #MeToo at the golden globes don't deserve to be celebrated. it's an empty gesture without actual actions and words to back it up. (January 11, 2018, 3:54 p.m.)

For these activists, the media spectacle of a viral hashtag campaign, while an effective tactic for raising awareness and initiating important conversations, was not enough on its own to transform structures of power or hold others accountable for taking action. As several #MeToo participants put it simply, "We must do more."

The Maintenance of #MeToo

Participants who voiced critiques of #MeToo often began by acknowledging the movement's real or potential impact before lamenting its limitations, starting their tweets with a celebratory tone but following quickly with a caveat: "#MeToo is important and powerful *but* I'm getting tired of women having to bare everything for ppl to consider sexual violence a systemic issue" (October 15, 2017, 7:58 p.m.). The challenge, then, for hashtag feminists becomes how to attain collective visibility while circumventing these shortcomings.

#MeToo participants engaged in a number of *performance maintenance practices* to balance the affordances and limitations of hashtag feminism. Participants developed these practices to support #MeToo storytellers, correct erasures in the campaign, maintain narrative control over audience's interpretations of #MeToo, and model actions audiences could take after the hashtag's viral performance came to a close. In other words, performance maintenance practices helped ensure the successful transmission of meaning from actors to audiences, all while caring for those participating in the emotionally taxing performance and proposing actions to extend engagement beyond the performance itself. These strategic correctives mitigated the personal and political vulnerabilities of networked visibility campaigns and moved activists toward a hashtag activism practice that reflected their feminist values.

The most widely practiced strategy involved offering support for those who shared their #MeToo stories as well as those who did not or could not. Often written in the form of direct address, hundreds of tweets in my sample included statements of *recognition* that acknowledged survivors, legitimated their experiences, and expressed solidarity with them:

> @TheJimmyWatson: I see you, I believe you, I stand with you. #MeToo (October 16, 2017, 8:43 a.m.)

> @kejames: My unconditional love, acceptance, and solidarity to everyone tweeting #MeToo and to those who can't yet, or ever. (October 15, 2017, 5:46 p.m.)

> @RachelTGreene: To everyone who has a #MeToo story whether you're able to share it or not—it's not your fault, you're not alone, and you're not "overreacting." (October 16, 2017, 5:37 a.m.)

Participants also frequently reminded #MeToo audience members that they were not obligated to share their story, especially if doing so would be painful or dangerous, and encouraged survivors to practice self-care:

> @petitecaitlin: as awesome as #metoo is PLEASE don't feel obligated to publicly share your trauma if you don't want to, if you aren't ready, or if sharing will be harmful for you (October 17, 2017, 4:47 p.m.)

> @karenkhdesigns: If #MeToo is triggering, it's okay to log off. It's okay to not participate. It's okay to not be okay. Remember to take care of yourself. (October 16, 2017, 10:02 a.m.)

Others offered more tangible forms of support, such as a listening ear, links to resources for survivors online, and phone numbers for sexual assault hotlines. Through this outreach work, campaign participants embodied the original "me too" movement's emphasis on "empowerment through empathy" (Just Be Inc. 2013) and performed emotional care labor for sexual violence survivors. Sharing stories of assault and harassment or reading others' testimonies is often a difficult and even traumatic experience for survivors living in a culture that normalizes sexual violence and shames victims. But participants' interpersonal expressions of support and solidarity represented a collective effort to alleviate at least some of the personal strain that came with posting or reading #MeToo tweets.

In another popular performance maintenance strategy, participants worked to shift #MeToo's attention away from survivors altogether and refocus the campaign on those who commit sexual violence and those who have the power the stop it. A common trend was to suggest new hashtags that called on perpetrators and bystanders, rather than victims, to publicly reflect on their behavior:

@LeenaVonD: "We need more than #MeToo. We need #ididnt: "#ididnt listen," "#ididnt do enough when she asked for help," "#ididnt support her" (October 15, 2017, 10:20 p.m.)

@photografiona: Instead of #MeToo, I want to see #ImSorry, #iUnderstand, #ItWasMe, #IWasWrong, #iChanged, #iBelieveYou #iHelped (October 19, 2017, 4:50 a.m.)

@patlibrarian: In the face of #MeToo, I say #MenWeMust step up, speak up, listen up, and shut up (October 16, 2017, 6:09 a.m.)

Others reframed the purpose of #MeToo in terms that transferred the burden of responsibility to bystanders and allies, with a special focus on men, who are less likely than women to experience sexual violence, but more likely to be in a position to stop it. For these users, the hashtag campaign's most important work was not in creating an outlet for women to express themselves openly, but in demanding that men pause, listen, learn, and take action. In one highly retweeted post, for example, a participant called on "men everywhere to scroll through #MeToo, because ending sexual violence against women is ultimately on you" (October 15, 2017, 8:48 p.m.). Such tactics for recasting the campaign's primary actors as men rather than women added a new element of accountability to #MeToo.

#MeToo participants highlighted and corrected other gaps and exclusions in the hashtag campaign, particularly its emphasis on white women. From the campaign's earliest days, feminists of color amended the record and called out journalists who misattributed the origins of #MeToo to Alyssa Milano rather than Tarana Burke. For these activists, drawing attention to Black women's organizing labor was especially important given their historical marginalization in U.S. feminist movements:

@Blackfeministaa: Journalists who have written pieces on #MeToo—go back and add the correction that Alyssa Milano did NOT start the movement. @TaranaBurke did. (October 17, 2017, 12:24 p.m.)

@Luvvie: White women do not get to take credit for creating #MeToo. Yes, credit matters b/c our work STAYS getting co-opted and our names erased. (October 17, 2017, 12:25 p.m.)

Activists took this intervention a step further by inserting intersectional analysis into #MeToo and articulating the ways in which rape culture has converged with other systems of oppression to produce specific experiences of sexual violence for marginalized communities:

@Karnythia: We're not going to solve the problem of sexual violence by ignoring that some victims are targeted because of their race. Or that racism means they are less likely to get support. We need to address all of rape culture #MeToo (November 19, 2017, 12:39 p.m.)

@monaeltahawy: #MeToo is not about white women. It's about patriarchy—its ubiquity, how it intensifies other oppressions such as racism, ableism, classism, etc. It must not be exclusively about what powerful men do to white women nor which white women say they're ok w/powerful men's "seduction." (January 14, 2018, 11:07 a.m.)

@katypellinger: Women & girls face systemic harassment & violence for simply existing. Add intersectionality & it gets worse. You're queer? Trans? Racialized? Disabled? English isn't your first language? The violence intensifies. #MeToo (October 16, 2017, 5:23 p.m.)

Through performance maintenance practices aimed at broadening #MeToo's scope, participants advanced the intersectional analysis missing from news coverage of the hashtag.

Activists also emphasized that, regardless of the specificities of one's identity or experience, every survivor's story is valid: "#MeToo. Whatever happened to you, whether it was rape or inappropriate jokes or groping, it counts. You count" (October 17, 2017, 7:28 p.m.). These activists viewed the variety of narratives collected under #MeToo as evidence that rape cultural exists along a "continuum of violations" (October 16, 2017, 6:29 a.m.) from verbal harassment to physical assault, all of which are rooted within a common matrix of oppression. Rather than being vague or ambiguous, their intentionally expansive conceptualization of sexual violence productively highlighted the connections between verbal harassment and assault.

In addition to expanding the hashtag's interpretive framework, #MeToo participants developed other strategies to maintain control of the campaign's narrative and correct misinterpretations of its message. A large number of participants anticipated and addressed problematic audience responses to #MeToo, shoring up the movement's message in the process:

@hannahchoreo: To anyone saying #MeToo tweets are attention-seeking, you are the reason women are afraid to speak up after being sexually assaulted. (October 15, 2017, 7:54 p.m.)

@jimmelville: If you are a troll mocking people posting #MeToo as "snowflake liberals," you need to recognize that you are part of the problem. (October 16, 2017, 12:29 a.m.)

Once mainstream news outlets began covering the viral Twitter hashtag, engaging in performance maintenance practices enabled #MeToo participants to keep a firm handle on the movement's framing. This became especially key as commentators on the movement, ensnared in the media frenzy surrounding high-profile victims and perpetrators, lost sight of its original purpose:

@arrenjj: In the wave of accusations against celebrities and politicians, it's easy to forget the point of #metoo: sexual violence is widespread across all industries and walks of life. (December 23, 2017, 9:32 a.m.)

@TaranaBurke: This is a movement for and about survivors. If you let the mainstream media define who the "survivors" are then we will always only hear about famous, white, cis-gendered women. But they don't own this movement—we do. YOU DO. Survivors need to take ownership. #MeTooMVMT (March 21, 2018, 5:47 p.m.)

Unlike highly structured social movements, hashtag campaigns lack the organizational capacity to issue unified, collective responses to critics and commentators. Even so, individual participants can make up for this limitation by using social media platforms to directly respond to and redress backlash and misconceptions about the campaign.

Lastly, #MeToo participants proposed actions individual audience members, especially male allies and bystanders, could take to support survivors and combat sexual violence in their everyday lives:

@EzerRising: Men. Pay attention & follow #MeToo and please spare us the #NotAllMen speech. Just listen & call out your bros who ARE part of the problem. (October 15, 2017, 8:46 p.m.)

@DaniCaprielle: Men, your solidarity w/ #meToo means nothing unless you also call out sexual assault and harassment, refuse to work w/ abusers, believe survivors, demand your female coworkers are paid equally and hold other men accountable. Don't just talk about it, be about it (January 7, 2018, 3:27 p.m.)

@MatthewELouis: Solidarity with everyone out there sharing #MeToo. Men, teach your kids about consent & abuse of power, hold your peers accountable. (October 16, 2017, 2:28 a.m.)

Their suggestions encouraged activism against sexual violence beyond simply sharing or reading the hashtag and laid out a roadmap for long-term engagement after the hashtag's viral media moment had come to an end. There is, of course, no guarantee that audience members will follow through. Participants' proposals, however, offered answers to a much-asked question in the aftermath of #MeToo—*now what?*—and challenged the assumption that posting a hashtag was enough to end sexual violence. Through these maintenance strategies, activists offered an antidote to the performative "slacktivism" of the economy of visibility in the form of action plans that audience members and allies could implement in their day-to-day lives.

#MeToo participants' performance maintenance practices illustrate the creative strategies do-it-ourselves feminists have developed to balance their media practices' affordances and limitations. From the simple act of expressing support for survivors who shared their stories to the more complex work of intersectional analysis, participants drew on a variety of tactics to reduce the personal costs and political shortcomings that came with participating in #MeToo. Their continual efforts to strengthen the campaign shed light on hashtag feminism as a reflexive performative practice, in which actors constantly evaluate and negotiate between their scripts, their audience, their goals, and their social and technical contexts. In the process, these activists pushed #MeToo toward a more inclusive, transformative politics of visibility, even as they wrestled with the pitfalls of performing protest actions on a globally networked platform.

A FLAWED AND MODEL MOVEMENT

Following #MeToo's viral diffusion, commentators rehashed a debate that has haunted hashtag activism since its earliest days—can Twitter create social change? In this chapter, I started with the assumption that those standing on either end of this yes-or-no question may be telling part of a much more complicated story about hashtag feminism in particular and networked activism more generally. Instead of evaluating the effects of the #MeToo campaign, I explored how activists perceive the possibilities and shortcomings of hashtag feminism and what strategies they use to juggle both. Existing scholarship suggests that hashtag feminism is entangled in both liberatory politics and systems of oppression, yet the tactic remains an important one for contemporary feminists. Understanding how they navigate the contradictions of hashtag activism is a key step toward theorizing feminists' digital media practices and building a more feminist approach to networked activism.

Drawing on a large sample of meta-tweets, I mapped, from #MeToo participants' perspectives, the affordances and limitations of hashtag feminism and documented their strategies for taking advantage of the former while coping with the latter. I found that, for feminists, hashtag activism is a contentious *performance*, through which actors collectively articulate their individual experiences with oppression on a global stage. The networking functions of the hashtag bridge the personal and the political, recasting, in the case of #MeToo, sexual violence as a systemic, rather than private, issue and calling for structural changes in response. The activist commentary in my sample suggests that the process of making the personal political and scaling up from individual to collective visibility is transformative. A hashtag can advance new interpretations of and responses to oppressive experiences with material effects for both individuals and society as a whole. By using the hashtag to share their survivor narratives and speak out against sexual violence, #MeToo participants powerfully reclaimed their agency and pushed back against discourses that normalize harassment and assault. Relying on visibility as a protest tactic, however, opened the movement up to a variety of different personal and political vulnerabilities, including re-traumatization, backlash, co-optation, complacency, and the exclusion of those most marginalized victims. #MeToo participants developed *performance maintenance practices* to correct erasures, maintain narrative control, and model actions audiences could take beyond tweeting. Activists developed these remedial strategies to convey their message to broad audiences without sacrificing their personal well-being or feminist values.

The iterative process outlined in this chapter—initiating a hashtag, observing its strengths and limitations, developing strategies to intervene on its shortcomings—suggests that hashtag feminism is an interactional, reflexive process. The performance maintenance practices highlighted in this chapter do not address *all* the ways in which hashtag activism can be politically problematic. Notably, the activist commentary captured in my sample did not address the contradictions of performing feminist protest actions on a corporately owned platform, nor did they grapple with the data and privacy concerns that come with sharing one's trauma on social media. My intention is not to suggest that feminists have developed a politically pure practice of hashtag activism that includes, uplifts, and protects all participants at all times. Rather, my goal is to shed light on hashtag feminists as thoughtful, agentive actors who are just as incisive as their sharpest critics and just as aware of the pitfalls of networked visibility campaigns.

Hashtag feminism epitomizes the do-it-ourselves ethos. Feminists engaging in this tactic often do so with great care and creativity, negotiating among their politics, the Twitter platform, and their audiences. Much existing scholarship in feminist media studies and social movement research focuses on *either* the affordances *or* the limitations of networked visibility campaigns. Consequently, researchers often overlook the complexities of hashtag feminism as a *practice* with both strengths and weaknesses that involves reflection and growth. Illuminating the strategies through which feminists navigate the contradictions of networked activism offers a more holistic view of hashtag feminism.

But more importantly, documenting and naming activists' practices for building a more feminist approach to networked visibility stands to benefit all movements and organizers mobilizing for civil rights and social justice in the digital age. The media-as-practices approach taken in this chapter centers feminist activists' perspectives. Their voices are neglected resources for both academics and activists seeking to identify when and how social media platforms best serve social movements' goals and what strategies might help mitigate their structural constraints. In light of the lack of accessible alternative outlets with comparable reach, the practitioners studied here model a feminist ethics for engaging in networked activism on platforms like Twitter and Facebook with a critical sense of care and accountability. Though #MeToo may fade from news headlines, its participants' organizational labor and knowledge-building work have long-lasting implications for future movements.

4 Networked Feminist Communities

Late one night in August 2015, a young mother published a post in a feminist Facebook group describing a series of events that had unfolded just hours prior. "Posting because i am sick of it and need to vent," she began. Earlier that evening, she needed to make a trip to the supermarket to purchase medicine for her daughter. Her car would not start, so she strapped her daughter into her stroller and walked to the store. On the way there, she was catcalled three separate times. Once she and her daughter arrived at the supermarket, an older man followed her into the store and stalked her while she shopped, all the way through the checkout line. When she made eye contact with him, he winked and licked his lips. She refused to exit the store until he left and waited an additional five minutes afterward to begin her walk home: "I hate that I have to explain what these men are doing to my daughter when she is old enough to understand (she is only 1 and a half). I am however so glad i didn't have to tell her this time why we had to stand awkwardly after we checked out because I was afraid of being raped." In the comments section, about a dozen of the group's more than 850 members offered empathy, expressed support, and shared their own experiences with catcallers. Others suggested strategies for coping with street harassment, ranging from talking back to perpetrators to carrying concealed weapons.

Several members made plans to organize a self-defense class for the group. One member, a mechanic, even offered to fix her car. "Thank you for listening," the mother commented toward the end of the thread, "i am glad im in this group and that I feel safe to talk about things like this here."[1]

On an unbearably hot afternoon in the summer of 2015, approximately fifty zine-makers, or zinesters, and distributers (*distros*) packed into the Rotunda, a university-owned community center in West Philadelphia, for the annual Philly Zine Fest. They spread their handcrafted pamphlets and other homespun goods across a few dozen folding tables. In an age of the ubiquitous internet, the death of print, and the monopolization of commercial media, perusing an exhibitor's photocopied and stapled paper magazines, typically exchanged through barter or trade, feels like a throwback to simpler times for activist life in the United States. The festival's broad selection of feminist-inspired media, for example, harkens back to the Riot Grrrl punk zines of the late 1980s and 1990s, their historical roots stemming forth from the alternative presses of the civil rights era and even reaching as far back as the pamphleteers of the suffrage movement. In fleeting moments, however, these age-old print media tactics converge with contemporary digital media platforms: zinesters use iPhones to snap photos and share their displays on Instagram; distros hand out business cards directing future customers to their websites; organizers update the festival's Facebook event page and Twitter hashtag in hopes of boosting attendance; QR codes, unclickable URLs, and email addresses printed across inside covers direct readers to connect with zinesters online. Later, an exhibitor explains to me that, without this digital outreach work, readers would struggle to get their hands on zines because zinesters often choose not to share electronic copies of their work online for safety reasons: "There are things that you can write about in zines, various hard things, that you don't want Google-able, that you don't want associated with your name." Underlying the zine fest's commitment to alternative print media and the face-to-face encounters they foster are digital networks, whose virtual connective tissue serves as the glue that holds the zine community together.[2]

Kai, an organizer for Permanent Wave Philly (PWP), grabbed the mic after the opening act to speak on behalf of the collective: "Thank you so much to everyone who is here, and who's here to support spaces like this. . . . The DIY community is only as strong as the people who come to support it. So let's continue to support spaces like this—safe, inclusive spaces." About one hundred people had crammed into the Philadelphia Mausoleum of Contemporary Art (or PhilaMOCA for short), an ex-tombstone-business-turned-performance-space, for PWP's first feminist punk show of 2015. The temperature had dipped well below freezing that January night, and while the streets in North Philly were quiet for a Saturday, the collective's handmade flyers, emailed newsletters, and Facebook event page had brought a decently sized crowd to the unconventional venue. Attendees were met at the door with a small poster that outlined the collective's "Safer Spaces Policy": "We aim, to the best of our abilities, to have all participants, organizers, and volunteers feel supported in our events: (1) Do not make assumptions about people's identities. (2) Respect everyone's physical and emotional boundaries. (3) Check in before discussing topics that might be triggering. (4) Respect the venue and its policies." Dee, a PWP organizer who worked the door, admitted anyone willing to follow these guidelines and pay the $7–$10 sliding-scale admission fee, stamping every newcomer's hand with a purple Venus symbol. When the Shondes, a woman-led rock back from Brooklyn and the show's headliner, took the stage, they invited people to dance and kicked off their set with a song about "sexism in the music industry," which the lead singer explained is only appropriate for "this feminist night." The audience shifted into a semicircle, forming a small pit in front of the stage, where a couple dozen women danced together, twirling, jumping, laughing, and holding hands. Rows of people behind the pit swayed side to side, and men in the audience stepped toward the back of the crowd. Looking on from Permanent Wave's merchandise table, I was reminded of the Riot Grrrl mission to uplift punk musicians and fans who were not white men, summed up in the movement's rallying cry, "Girls to the front!"[3] *This*, I thought to myself, *is what a feminist mosh pit looks like.*

These three vignettes—the outpouring of support in a Facebook group, the hustle and bustle of a zine festival, the scene at a DIY punk show—tell the story of a long-standing political quest for feminist activists: the search for community. U.S. feminists have consistently valued community-building as a radical intervention into a sociopolitical context that marginalizes and alienates women, queer people, and people of color. Feminist communities take on a variety of forms and focal points, but they have historically shared a common goal—*safety*, or the ability to speak, act, and move freely, unfettered by repressive ideologies and the material and symbolic violence they enable. In separatist safe spaces, second-wave feminists distanced themselves from both the men in their lives and patriarchal thought to openly discuss shared experiences of gender-based oppression and to begin building platforms for organizing against sexism (Kenney, 2001). The 1960s women's liberation movement grew out of meetings held behind closed doors, where women met to safely explore and deconstruct the ways in which power had shaped their personal lives (Kenney, 2001; Taylor and Whittier, 1992). A network of underground press publications sustained second-wave communities between meetings, helped reach those without access to feminist collectives, and provided supportive outlets for women to formulate the collective identity frameworks that would later function as the bases for public protest actions (Harker and Farr, 2015; Hogan, 2016; Young, 1997). For this generation of feminists, in other words, finding safety in community was a means to an end.

In today's context, where public platforms for launching feminist critiques and actions abound but misogyny continues to shape discourse and policy, safety has become a political end in itself for feminist activists. From digitally mobilized global protest movements like the 2017 Women's March described in chapter 2 to the feminist hashtag campaigns discussed at length in the previous chapter, social media platforms have given rise to an unprecedented degree of visibility for feminist figures, actions, ideas, and rhetoric (Banet-Weiser, 2015b). As described in chapter 1, however, this "popular feminism" has triggered a violent "popular misogyny" (Banet-Weiser and Miltner, 2016). This backlash is especially rampant on social media platforms, where women face high levels of sexual harassment, death and rape threats, and doxing attacks (Duggan, 2017). Just as social media have given feminist activists a new platform from which to broadcast their claims, they have also fed what Banet-Weiser and Miltner (2016) call "networked misogyny," a highly visible form of white male supremacy that works to block marginalized groups' participation in online environments through threats of violence.

Within this culture of popular misogyny, constructing safe feminist communities from the ground up has become an important self-care strategy and a political tactic for do-it-ourselves feminists, who operate without the support of formally structured organizations. Networked misogyny functions as what Cole (2015), drawing on the work of Michel Foucault, calls a "disciplinary rhetoric" (p. 356), a form of power that restricts women's participation in the public sphere through threats of bodily harm. In response to this "silencing practice" (Shaw, 2013, p. 94), contemporary feminists have cultivated enclaved communities, closed off from the disciplinary surveillance of popular misogyny through the privacy settings of a secret Facebook group or the symbolic boundaries of a safer space policy. Their goal is to create empowering communities where members can speak and act freely without facing threats of violence.

"Community," however, is and always has been a politically troublesome project for U.S. feminist movements. Repeatedly throughout history, feminists' attempts to foster a sense of collective identity through shared experiences of gender-based oppression have fallen short when faced with the true complexities of "women" as a category. Critics of the 2017 Women's March, for example, called out the movement's prioritization of white, cisgender women over women of color and transgender women in its logistical execution, imagery, language, and mission (Bates, 2017). Their frustration carried the weight of more than a century of struggles for inclusive feminist communities. They echoed the famous question Sojourner Truth purportedly posed to white suffragists gathered at the 1851 Women's Rights Convention in Akron, Ohio: "Ain't I a woman?"[4] They echoed the Combahee River Collective who, speaking on behalf of Black lesbian feminists in their 1977 statement, argued that "no other ostensibly progressive movement has ever considered our specific oppression as a priority or worked seriously for the ending of that oppression" (qtd. in Smith, 1983, p. 267). And more recently, they echoed feminists of color who shared their stories of exclusion from liberal feminist communities that center white, educated women, often dubbed "white feminism," under the 2013 viral hashtag campaign, #SolidarityIsForWhiteWomen (Loza, 2014). At every turn, U.S. feminist communitybuilders have grappled with the need to both foster unity and account for difference.

The social and technological affordances of digital networks present new possibilities for feminists striving to build their own safe, intersectional communities. But while scholars have shed light on the role the internet plays in mobilizing more inclusive, public-facing protests, (Bennett and Segerberg, 2013; Brown et al., 2017; Daniels, 2016; Kuo, 2016; Tynes, Schuschke, and Noble, 2016), little attention has been paid to the relationship between digital media and feminists' practices for building more private, inward-facing communities. These less visible activist spaces are difficult to access and, in turn, to study. Consequently, scholars analyzing digitally networked feminist "communities" today tend to prioritize public-facing sites for discursive exchange, such as feminist blogs and hashtags, but overlook counterpublic "spaces of withdrawal and regroupment" (Fraser, 1992, p. 124). This overemphasis on highly visible forms of feminist media activism parallels a similar bias in social movement research toward public performances of contentious politics (Melucci, 1989). In both cases, scholars neglect to consider marginalized groups' struggles to attain legitimacy within the public sphere and efforts to develop alternative modes of political engagement. Consequently, contemporary feminists' digital media practices for internal community building remain under-theorized, despite the renewed importance of the enclaved safe space against the contemporary backdrop of networked misogyny. A search for "feminist" on Facebook, for example, reveals dozens of private groups, many with upwards of two thousand members or more, that purport to offer "safe space" for marginalized users.[5]

In this chapter, to address this gap in existing scholarship and to contribute to ongoing activist and academic movements for safer online spaces, I explore feminists' digital media practices for building and maintaining networked communities. Drawing on Nancy Baym's (2000) work on early online communities, I define "communities" as social groupings "maintained through the ongoing practices of their members" (p. 31), who are collectively engaged in some common project. Here, I am interested specifically in internal communities, or purposefully closed-off, inward-facing social groupings, whose members share certain aspects of their identities, experiences and/or politics in common and who use a range of networked media practices to construct and maintain boundaries around the group.

I analyze the practices of three feminist communities: (1) Girl Army, a secret feminist Facebook group; (2) U.S. feminist zinesters, a nationally dispersed network of alternative print media makers, who explore gender justice themes in their work; and (3) Permanent Wave Philly, a Philadelphia-based grassroots feminist arts collective. Each community takes on different networked forms. Girl Army moderators adapt the Facebook group interface to cultivate a separatist feminist enclave. Feminist zinesters use digital platforms to both promote and protect their countercultural community, spreading the word about their work on social media but keeping their zines in print, where they can express themselves freely without fear of online harassment. Permanent Wave Philly members use an email listserv to coordinate meetings and plan underground punk shows that center women, LGBTQ+ people, and people of color. But while their particular tactics vary, all three communities are networked—practitioners use digital media platforms to facilitate connection across a horizontally dispersed group of people—and media-oriented—members participate in each community by engaging with or producing media. All three communities are also partially enclosed, meaning that prospective members must cross certain barriers to entry in order to join these spaces. None of these communities is associated with a formally structured organization. Instead, they emerged from the do-it-ourselves media practices of feminists who saw a need for a particular type of community and decided to make their own. And while historically, feminists have struggled to both define and achieve "community," practitioners across all three sites, use the term to describe their groups and to gesture toward their aspirations for these activist spaces. Above all, each community strives to bring, through a variety of practices, *girls to the front*, centering bodies and voices that, because they are marked by gender, are marginalized in the public sphere. Through participant observations and interviews with practitioners alongside theories of communities (Crenshaw, 1989, 1991; Joseph, 2002; Polletta, 1999), safe spaces (The Roestone Collective, 2014), and counterpublics (Fraser, 1992), I put these three unique case studies into conversation with one another. My goal is to highlight their shared political purposes and reflect on best practices for feminist community building.

Across these three communities, feminist activists engage in a common political project. They endeavor to create what I call networked safe spaces, or carefully bounded, inward-facing communities, closed off from popular misogyny and fostered through the technological and social affordances of digital media. Networked safe spaces do not fit traditional frameworks for understanding activist work, which define political engagement as highly visible, state-targeted, public performances (Tilly and Tarrow, 2015). Drawing on the media-as-practice framework, however, I trace the connections among feminist practitioners' contexts, goals, and digital community-building tactics to illuminate the distinctly political work networked safe spaces perform. In their search for safety, feminists in each community appropriate digital media platforms to enact three particular political interventions. First, they construct community boundaries intended to separate the group from the public at large and protect members from misogyny. Second, inside these bounded spaces, feminists experiment with intersectional organizing strategies to center marginalized voices silenced within more mainstream arenas for political participation. Third and finally, feminists in each community endeavor to foster open expression among members, who often lack other safe outlets for their particular experiences and concerns. Ultimately, for these activists, the objective is not to grow networks that, like the hashtag or blogosphere, extend outward indefinitely in a multitude of directions and broadcast political claims far and wide. Instead, their technological and discursive practices produce counterpublic spheres that draw like-minded activists inward, together, where they develop empowering modes of social engagement and create communities that prefigure the kind of society they seek to bring about. Community members' participation within these networked safe spaces is often transformative at the individual and collective levels, challenging conventional notions of what "counts" as political work.

Certain limitations, however, haunt feminists' networked community-building practices. Networked safe spaces are the product of active negotiations between members' feminist values and digital media platforms. In the push and pull of these negotiations, feminists' efforts to cultivate safe spaces at times fall short. Through the technological and discursive boundaries they draw around the group, members of each community exclude marginalized voices, reify power hierarchies, and silo feminist discourses. Platforms' user interfaces and terms of service restrict feminists' ability to ensure community members' safety and to practice nonhierarchical organizing. Participation within these communities is predicated on digital media access and literacy, suggesting that membership is largely limited to younger, educated, middle-class participants, who are accustomed to using these media forms. Moreover, the diffuse, informal nature of these communities raises concerns about activist burnout and sustainability over time. These shortcomings are due in part to both the structural constraints embedded in social media platforms and the always already incomplete state of all safe spaces. The story of each community illustrates the relational, fluid, partial, and imperfect nature of networked safe spaces and pushes toward a more robust conceptualization of what safety might look like online.

I begin this chapter by contextualizing the networked safe space within a longer history of feminist tactics for cultivating community, online and in person. Then, taking up the three case studies in turn and drawing on participant observations and interview data, I explore how feminists in each community use digital media to create and maintain boundaries, center marginalized voices, and foster open expression, highlighting their successes and struggles in the process. Finally, I conclude with a discussion of the lessons these three feminist communities offer researchers and activists grappling with community building in the digital age.

THE SEARCH FOR FEMINIST COMMUNITY

Contemporary feminists' networked communities are rooted in a long history of activist organizing strategies. Alongside other "new social movements" (Melucci 1989) of the late twentieth century, whose participants prioritized identity politics over material inequalities, second-wave feminists pioneered tactics for cultivating communal safe spaces. These countercultural arenas granted women "a certain license to speak and act freely, form collective strength, and generate strategies for resistance" (Kenney, 2001, p. 24). The archetypal feminist safe space was the separatist, women-only, consciousness-raising group, where the license to speak and act freely was instated not merely for the therapeutic purposes of voicing personal experiences but also "to get to the most radical truths about the situation of women in order to take radical action" (Sarachild, 1978) and to identify the systematic injustices women face in order to collectively organize for change. In this way, civil rights–era feminist safe spaces functioned as what social movement scholars have called free spaces, "small-scale settings within a community or movement that are removed from the direct control of dominant groups, are voluntarily participated in, and generate the cultural challenge that precedes or accompanies political mobilization" (Polletta, 1999, p. 1). Melucci (1989) identifies second-wave feminist safe spaces as "submerged networks," where activists could meet outside the public eye to discuss social issues, develop frameworks for interpreting them, and organize collective action accordingly. While formal and informal impediments curtailed women's participation in the public sphere, as Fraser (1992) argues, feminist safe spaces operated as *subaltern counterpublic spheres*, or "parallel discursive arenas where members of subordinated social groups invent and circulate counterdiscourses, which in turn permit them to formulate oppositional interpretations of their identities, interests, and needs" (p. 67). Second-wave counterpublics required active maintenance; members had to work to expose and remedy obstacles to participatory parity in order to create a space conducive to free expression (Fraser, 1992). As such, Polletta (1999) argues that second-wave feminists cultivated these women-only, counterpublic communities to "prefigure the society the movement is seeking to build by modeling relationships that differ from those characterizing mainstream society" (p. 11). Whether conceptualized as safe spaces, free spaces, submerged networks, or counterpublics, second-wave feminist communities were built on the premise that women share common experiences of injustice and could develop a collective identity that would function as the basis for collective action (Taylor and Whittier, 1992).

The cultivation of safe, communal spaces for free and open expression has remained a key political priority among feminists in the digital age. Early scholarship on computer-mediated communication builds on Howard Rheingold's (1993) groundbreaking work on "virtual communities" to provide rich, ethnographic accounts of how women and other marginalized users adapted some of the first web forums to foster communal bonds across time and space. Baym (2000), for example, demonstrates how the predominantly female members of a Usenet newsgroup for soap opera fans "dynamically appropriate a wide range of resources drawn from the structure of Usenet and the soap opera text and combine them with other resources in unpredictable yet patterned ways, ultimately constructing a social space that feels like community" (p. 24). While the newsgroup community was ostensibly organized around soaps, it also functioned "as a community in which traditional female concerns and values are honored" (p. 16). Others describe women's early struggles to cultivate safe communities online via bulletin board systems and listservs (Fredrick, 1999; Gajjala, 2002) and the tactics these community members performed to keep trolls at bay (Herring, Job-Slider, Scheckler, and Barb, 2002; Phillips, 1996). Like the in-person consciousness-raising groups of the second wave, these "cyberfeminists" (Plant, 1997) hoped to create communal spaces where women could connect with one another and speak openly about personal experiences with gender-based oppression.

While much has changed in the nearly forty years since Usenet first became publicly available, more recent research reflects similar community-building practices as those Baym (2000) describes. Keller (2016), in her ethnographic study of girl feminist bloggers, argues that blogs function as an accessible "discursive space" (p. 14), where young women develop feminist identities through personal reflections and interactions with one another, forming a "networked counterpublic" (p. 80). Drawing on danah boyd's (2008, 2014) theory of networked publics, Keller explains that unlike second-wave counterpublics, the *networked* counterpublics of girl feminist bloggers are persistent, replicable, and searchable, and often, participants can remain invisible to one another. Due to their networked nature, online feminist counterpublics also have a greater capacity for growth, which in turn amplifies their ability to launch interventions on the broader public sphere (Keller, 2016). Feminist counterpublics networked across a variety of online platforms have mobilized highly visible collective action campaigns against online and offline misogyny and have fostered transnational feminist communities. Rentschler (2014) highlights how digital feminist tactics, like hashtag feminism, create "feminist networks of response-ability to rape culture" (p. 68), which foster the capacity for collective responses to sexual violence. In a case study that exemplifies this networked response-ability, Mendes (2015) traces how the networked counterpublic of the feminist blogosphere was crucial for sparking the global SlutWalk movement, described in chapter 2. The same networks later became critical spaces for feminists to debate the inclusivity of the movement's tactics and messages. Another study conducted by Rentschler and Thrift (2015) demonstrates how "networked community building" (p. 330) has unfolded through the viral spread of feminist memes. By constructing and circulating memes, feminists not only engage in collective acts of political critique, but also foster communal ties through shared humor that cut across differences (Rentschler and Thrift, 2015). Keller et al. (2016) refer to communal ties formed via social media among women and girls as "affective solidarities" (p. 29), or connections rooted in emotional responses to shared experiences, such as sexual violence. In her research on the Australian feminist blogosphere, Frances Shaw (2013) highlights the range of strategies feminist bloggers use to successfully defend these communal ties against disruptive trolls and violent harassers, including moderation, exposure, and humor. Collective efforts to develop digital tools for navigating and interrupting online harassment compliment these networked, public-facing, community-building efforts, such as FemTechNet's (2017) Center for Solutions to Online Violence, a digital hub for rapid response and educational resources, and HeartMob (2017), an online tool for documenting and requesting support for harassment.

But, despite their enduring salience for feminist activists and scholars, "safety" and "community" are fraught concepts. "Safe" is a relative term, one whose meaning varies from person to person, from one setting to the next, in relation to its binary opposite, unsafe. Safe space practitioners, however, often overlook the highly contextual nature of safety. As Betty Barrett (2010) laments, the ambiguity of "safe space" has led the term to become "an overused by undertheorized metaphor" (p. 1) in both academic and activist discourses, a shortcut that gestures toward presumably shared attitudes regarding the friendliness of a space for certain identities and ideologies. Groups as varied as educators (Stengel and Weems, 2010), performance artists (Hunter, 2008), climate scientists (Rockström et al., 2009), people with environmental illnesses (Coyle, 2004), doomsday preppers and survivalists (O'Brien, 2012), and even white supremacists (Futrell and Simi, 2004) have adopted the term. Across these cases, "safe space" is often invoked as "code" that "covers rather than clarifies the logic of safe spaces" (Stengel, 2010, p. 524). In both theory and practice, "safe space" has been treated as a closed concept, erasing the context-specific work required to construct and maintain its material and symbolic bound-aries in a particular setting.

Like "safety," "community" eludes precise definition. As Lingel (2017) highlights, "many people have powerful associations attached to being part of a community and yet struggle to define what separates a community from a group, family, neighborhood, or place of employment" (p. 5). Joseph (2002) argues that these powerful associations lead to the romanticization of community "as an unequivocal good" beyond critique, an "indicator of a high quality of life, a life of human understanding, caring, selflessness, belonging" (p. vii) enriched by deep social connections. Consequently, "community," like "safe space," is often treated as a closed concept that can be taken up and transplanted across a variety of contexts, without adapta-tion, specification, or reflection on the work required to cultivate commu-nal bonds (Joseph, 2002; Stengel, 2010). When "community" is invoked in both popular and scholarly discourse to describe a particular set of social relations, the individuals in question are typically presumed to already share some essential identity and concomitant experiences, values, and goals, such that active community-building work is not necessary (Joseph, 2002). This elides important differences among so-called community members and, as Joseph (2002) agues, replicates and reifies existing hier-archies of gender, race, class, and sexuality.

Among feminist activists in the United States, the search for safety in community has historically raised concerns about who feminist social movements fight for and represent, a question that has troubled gender justice projects since at least the nineteenth century. Reflecting on the second-wave era, feminist theorists and activists writing in the 1980s grappled with the strengths and limitations of community-building tactics grounded in identity politics (Joseph, 2002). On the one hand, identity-focused movements throughout the 1960s and 1970s in the United States exposed the exclusions of liberal ideologies, which frame public institutions as rational and objective and all citizens as equal under the law regardless of their private differences (Joseph, 2002; Young, 1997). Second-wave fem-inists, in their efforts to make the personal political, raised consciousness about the ways in which power operates at the level of everyday life through discourses regulating gendered identities, roles, and performances that privilege men and disenfranchise women. Their activism pushed women's concerns, once labeled as "private" and therefore nonpolitical, into public deliberation and won concrete gains in the form of civil rights legislation and social resources (Joseph, 2002; Young, 1997). In the process, second wavers fostered community ties rooted in women's shared experiences and needs, which not only generated positive self-definitions and alternative epistemologies, but also functioned as a foundation for solidary collective action (Collins, 2000; Joseph, 2002; Taylor and Whittier, 1992).

On the other hand, however, the identity-as-community approach to much second-wave organizing often erased politically salient differences among women in the name of unity. As Joseph (2002) argues, "The invocation of a community of women has often served to produce a white women's movement that could not adequately address or account for women who were simultaneously or even primarily faced with oppressions based on race or class or sexuality" (p. xvii), instead reproducing the racism, elitism, and heterosexism of society at large. Critiques launched by feminists of color in the decades following the second wave, such as Cherríe Moraga and Gloria Anzaldúa's (1981) *This Bridge Called My Back*, Audre Lorde's (1984) *Sister Outsider*, and bell hooks's (1981) *Ain't I a Woman: Black Women and Feminism*, among many others, questioned whether communities built around singular identity categories could ever enact revolutionary change. These early "third-wave" theorists, in other words, argued that existing frameworks for community based on some shared, essential identity or experience do more to obfuscate than challenge traditional power relations. They called for a more multifaceted conceptualization of subjectivity, one that recognizes the ways in which gender interacts with race, class, sexuality, and other identity categories, in order to build more inclusive and generative feminist communities. While their critiques were lodged at twentieth-century feminist movements, they reiterated the concerns of nineteenth-century activists like Maria Stewart, Sojourner Truth, and Anna Julia Cooper, who questioned Black women's marginalization in abolitionist and women's suffrage movements, despite their simultaneous oppression along the axes of race and gender (Hancock, 2015; May, 2015).

It is from this history of critique that Crenshaw's (1989, 1991) concept of intersectionality, outlined in chapter 2, emerged. In contrast to the "single-axis framework" (Crenshaw, 1989, p. 139) for interpreting identity built into the second-wave identity-as-community framework, intersectionality calls for a multidimensional theorization of identity and power. It necessitates a feminist community-building practice grounded in what Vivian May (2015) calls "a politics of coalition: to contest shared logics across systems of domination, solidarities need to be forged via mutual commitments, not via principles of homogeneity or sameness" (p. 4). In place of the homogenizing essentialism of the identity-as-community framework, an intersectional approach to community-building prioritizes coalitional solidarity across lines of difference, with an eye toward the utopian goal of dismantling the many overlapping oppressions that constitute the matrix of domination (Collins, 2000; May, 2015).

Intersectionality, in other words, can be understood as what Joseph (2002) calls "an ethical practice of community" (p. 5), a reflexive method of collective organizing that incorporates a critical awareness of the potential erasures and exclusions embedded in communal safe spaces. As the Roestone Collective (2014) argues, scholars and activists aiming to practice intersectional politics should "treat safe space as a living concept, identifying tendencies and variations in its use, and recognizing its situatedness in multiple contexts" (p. 1347). Instead of approaching "safe space" as a prefabricated social structure that can be implemented across different settings, the Roestone Collective reconceptualizes safe space as "relational work" (p. 1348), as constantly unfolding social processes rather than structures that preexist their participants' interactions. By framing safe spaces as constantly in flux and always incomplete, they direct researchers' attention toward the processes through which safe spaces are cultivated and encourage safe space organizers to incorporate reflexivity in their cultivation practices. When practitioners underscore the relational work required to actively maintain safe, communal spaces, they move toward a more reflexive, intersectional community-building practice, one that is conscientious of whose voices and needs are centered, and whose are not.

As discussed in the previous chapters, existing research illustrates the technological affordances of social media platforms for promoting intersectional discourse (Brown et al., 2017; Daniels, 2016; Kuo, 2016; Tynes, Schuschke, and Noble, 2016). The role digital media play in feminists' cultivation of intersectional communities, however, remains understudied. Although scholars have also used the term *community* to describe networks of hashtag users and bloggers (e.g., Keller, 2016; Mendes, Ringrose, and

Keller, 2018), these public, openly accessible, densely populated platforms facilitate a fundamentally different type of sociality than the "submerged networks" (Melucci, 1989) of second-wave feminist consciousness-raising groups. My focus here is on the sociotechnical practices contemporary feminists engage in to foster closed-off, separatist safe spaces, where participants meet, virtually and face-to-face, to find community with like-minded activists outside the public eye. While much research on media and social movements emphasizes how digital networks have altered the shape and reach of public protest actions, I draw on a series of case studies to analyze how digital networks are creating new possibilities and challenges for feminists when it comes to internal community building.

CREATING SAFETY THROUGH COMMUNITY

The three case studies explored in this chapter span the spectrum of contemporary feminist community forms. While Girl Army, a feminist Facebook group, operates primarily in digital space with occasional in-person meetups, the feminist zine community prioritizes material, face-to-face exchanges of print media, with digital media functioning only as a channel for organizing access and logistics. Permanent Wave Philly, a grassroots feminist arts collective, offers a hybrid form, hosting in-person meetings and music shows but relying heavily on digital networks to facilitate internal communications and community outreach. But while they vary in form, all three share an emphasis on networked media practices for creating safety through feminist community.

Girl Army started in 2012, when a small group of Philadelphia-based women connected over a shared desire for sisterhood. Each felt that their social lives were lacking deep friendships with other women, which, in turn, created a lack of access to empathy for their gender-specific experiences and concerns. They decided to make a conscious effort to build a community whose bonds were rooted in womanhood in all of its multiplicities. As the group's official description explains, they dubbed their group "Girl Army" in hopes of fostering a reserve of women who could be rallied at a moment's notice to offer members a "supportive community." In its earliest days, the Girl Army community often took the form of regularly scheduled "night picnics," an effort to reclaim women's right to move through public spaces after dark while enjoying safety in numbers. One member started a secret Girl Army Facebook group to facilitate communication, coordinate logistics, and invite friends to night picnics. As friends and friends of friends joined the group, what started out as a meeting space for a small number of women grew into an active feminist network. By the time I began fieldwork in September 2015, Girl Army, open only to Facebook users invited by current members and approved by one of six moderators, had expanded its ranks to more than 850 members, who identify as trans or cisgender women or nonbinary individuals from the Philadelphia area and beyond.

On any given day, Girl Army members discuss current events, exchange resources, call for backup against online harassment, ask for advice, tell deeply personal stories, share feminist memes, support causes through online petitions and fundraisers, and organize offline meetups. But while posts vary widely, one key feature keeps Girl Army members, most of whom have never met in person, returning to the community day in and day out—the promise of *safety*. Members consistently describe Girl Army as a "safe space," frequently invoking the term in posts as a preface before sharing a personal story, requesting support, or starting a discussion on a controversial issue, reminding readers to be gentle in their responses and signaling toward the danger of discussing these topics elsewhere: "It feels like a safe space to ask . . ."; "I feel sooo foolish for letting this affect me in anyway and even mentioning this out loud, but ya know, safe space . . ."; "I need to talk some shit out in a safe space where advice or opinions or whatever else are welcome and encouraged . . ."; "I don't usually post in here but I have a problem that I'd love to get some advice on/vent about in a safe space." Since its inception, the primary purpose of Girl Army has been to provide members with a digitally networked safe-space community that can be accessed anywhere instantaneously through the Facebook app or website.

In contrast to Girl Army's digital nature, zines are handcrafted, self-published, self-funded physical ephemera, usually resembling a magazine or book, on any topic that interests the author(s) and can be shared with few or many readers. The small booklets have played a big role in the feminist media repertoire since at least the 1980s, when the earliest proponents of the Riot Grrrl movement first began publishing manifestos on sexism in the punk music scene (Duncombe, 2008; Piepmeier, 2009). These young feminists appropriated the zine, which got its start in the 1930s among mostly male science fictions fans before expanding in the 1970s to the male-dominated world of punk rock, as a community-building tool (Duncombe, 2008). Feminist zines opened up productive third spaces for authors who fell outside the boundaries of white, heterosexual masculinity and who, consequently, lacked access to or representation in media outlets (Licona, 2005). The medium offered an accessible venue for these underrepresented voices, unfettered by the restrictive norms encoded into commercial media representations of gendered, racialized, and sexualized bodies (Chidgey, Payne, and Zobl, 2009). Feminist zinesters performed the important work of making those encoded norms visible, cutting and pasting images from commercial print media to critique them and offer alternatives (Zobl, 2009). Through their circulation, zines forged communal bonds that facilitated the collective formation of critical feminist subjectivities (Harris, 2003) and created spaces for the negotiation of complex feminist identities (Guzzetti and Gamboa, 2004; Piepmeier, 2009). Moreover, feminist zinesters' politics extended beyond content to infuse the production and circulation processes, which typically unfolded through alternative economic practices that subverted capitalist marketplace norms and blurred the boundaries between producers and consumers (Chidgey, 2009). The democratic exchange and, more recently, the diligent efforts to archive these feminist ephemera have created a vibrant record of feminist history grounded in the work of grassroots activists and makers, whose extra-institutional voices are typically underprivileged within dominant discourse (Chidgey, 2013; Eichhorn, 2014).

Nearly forty years since the start of the Riot Grrrl movement, print zines are making an unexpected resurgence as a key feminist community-building practice. It is impossible to estimate the number of contemporary zinesters in the United States, whose subversive, hodgepodge texts are not cataloged in the Library of Congress or issued ISSNs, but recent mainstream news headlines have heralded their comeback: "Zines Have a Resurgence among the Web-Savvy" (Wortham, 2011); "Are Zines Making a Comeback, Too?" (Bose, 2014); "How Zines Survive in the Internet Age" (Carville, 2015); "Yes, Zines Still Exist, and They're Not Antiques" (Berube,

2013). Today, there are more than sixty active zine festivals (Stolen Sharpie Revolution, 2016b), dozens of distros and stores (Stolen Sharpie Revolution, 2016a; Stolen Sharpie Revolution, 2016c), and about 120 zine libraries and archives across the United States (Barnard Zine Library, 2016). At the time of writing, a search for zines on Etsy, a popular craft marketplace website where many zinesters sell their wares, returns approximately *sixty-two thousand* listings. Among U.S. feminists, the genre remains an important political tactic; annual feminist zine festivals in Philadelphia, Pittsburgh, and New York attract hundreds of makers and readers every year, and feminist zine collections, like the Barnard Zine Library, are thriving. Though their distribution networks may be geographically dispersed, the zinesters I interviewed repeatedly referred to "the zine community."

Like the feminist zine scene, Permanent Wave Philly emerged from a desire to disrupt male-dominated music and arts spaces. In 2010, feminist writer and musician Amy Klein started a blog to document her band's tour and share her thoughts on gender and the male-dominated punk music scene. Soon after, she began receiving messages from young women who identified with her perspective and wanted to establish feminist connections beyond the blogosphere. Klein, inspired by her readers, took to Twitter and Facebook and called for a gathering of feminists at her Brooklyn apartment in December of that year. About twenty people attended and brainstormed ideas for empowering women in the arts, media, politics, and everyday life. After the meeting, Klein started an email listserv to facilitate communication within the budding feminist community and to begin putting their ideas into action. The group eventually came to be known as Permanent Wave (PW), a playful riff on both the feminist wave metaphor and the chemical hair treatment. A descendent of the Riot Grrrl movement, PW grew into a key player in both the DIY arts scene and the grassroots activist network of New York City, hosting feminist punk shows on some weekends and organizing feminist street protests on others. But PW's most important actions took place outside the public eye. The collective created closed-off spaces, virtual and in-person, where members could safely discuss experiences of oppression and request support. Although Klein founded PW, the group had no formal leaders or structure; if you were a member of the listserv, you were a member of Permanent Wave. And while PW had a loose focus on gender and the arts, members' interests drove the group's particular projects. As the mission statement published on PW's website explained, "PW is YOU! There is no secret organizational code or anything. The organization is simply small groups of people working together and making shit happen" (qtd. in Jen G, 2012).

Over the course of the next year, Permanent Wave grew both its local and online presence and the listserv expanded to include hundreds of members from across the country. Among them was Erin, a seventeen-year-old aspiring punk musician living in Philadelphia and looking to make her own feminist intervention into the city's underground music scene. Erin founded Permanent Wave Philly (PWP) with the help of older women musicians and activists and organized a meeting of Philadelphia-based listserv members in December of 2011. Following Permanent Wave NYC, the Philadelphia chapter's mission, as documented on its official website and social media pages, was to create a *community* where feminists could connect with one another via email and in person, openly discuss issues related to gender, politics, and culture, and work together to organize shows and events that prioritized women, LGBTQ people, and people of color. In pursuit of these goals, PWP met at least once per month, hosted several punk music shows, film screenings, and visual art showcases every year, often as benefits for local feminist organizations, and published an annual zine. Like the original PW, a listserv demarcated membership and facilitated communication within PWP between meetings. But unlike PWNYC, PWP had staying power. After the New York chapter began to dissolve in 2012 due to an organizational dispute over the group's lack of racial diversity, PWP continued to meet and host events until members, suffering from burnout, decided the group should go on "hiatus" in early 2017.

All three of these communities were born out of a desire to reimagine what a social setting could look like without the violent constraints of networked misogyny. Dee, one of PWP's earliest members, captured this sentiment in an interview, when discussing her decision to join the collective:

> The only show organizers I knew existed were white men. Like, they're the only people who book shows. . . . And they do a lot of things based on who they're friends with and who knows who, and it was just like, very, very, exclusive. . . . Everyone has definitions of community, everyone defines what

their community is personally. But I for sure knew that *that* was not *my* community. And I was really excited by Permanent Wave Philly building a community and doing their best, doing *our* best, to help a better community, a better scene, exist. (personal communication, May 24, 2015)

The activists in each feminist community not only share a desire for better and safer community spaces for marginalized groups; they also *act* on that desire, embodying the do-it-ourselves ethos by using networked media to build feminist communities that reflect their values and experiences. In the following sections, I draw on examples from each community to trace how this activist community-building work unfolds through three particular networked media practices: (1) constructing community boundaries, (2) centering marginalized voices, and (3) fostering open expression. Each practice involves careful negotiations with networked media tools, which simultaneously pose new opportunities and challenges for feminist activists in their search for safety in community.

Constructing Community Boundaries

As with other safe spaces, in Girl Army, the search for safety starts with the construction of community boundaries. Members and moderators draw technological and discursive boundaries around the group to separate their safe-space community from the broader rape culture. This boundary maintenance work begins with moderators' strategy for admitting new members into the group. In an interview, Jasmine, Girl Army's founding and primary moderator, explained that, like second-wave safe spaces, the group "is a non-men space" (personal communication, December 9, 2015). Unlike second-wave safe spaces, where membership was controlled through face-to-face encounters, these contemporary feminists use digital media to guard their safe space's boundaries. Girl Army moderators take advantage of Facebook's "secret" group settings to carefully screen users' requests to be added to the group. Only existing members can find Girl Army on Facebook and view posts in their newsfeed. To join the group, new members must first be invited by an existing member and then approved by a moderator. This screening process enables moderators to limit membership to users who, through their profile pictures and names or through communication with moderators outside the group, identify as women or nonbinary individuals. The group's separatism is informed in part by the very practical consideration that perpetrators of sexual violence and harassment are typically men. But Girl Army's gendered boundaries also emerge from a desire to correct the gendered power dynamics of rape culture, which privilege and excuse male perpetrators while casting doubt on victims, most of whom are women (Casteel, Wolfe, and Nguyen, 2017). As Rebecca explained about Girl Army:

> You can have a discussion without immediately being interrupted or trolled about experiences related to gender, sex, and sexuality, and particular types of embodied experiences. You can just not have people saying, "Well, that's not true," or "You're wrong about your own experience," or "Hashtag not all men," or "Why do you hate men?" (personal communication, November 18, 2015)

By filtering the group's membership, moderators aim to foster a culture of respect and validation that counteracts members' everyday experiences of networked misogyny.

Alongside this technical boundary work, members also discursively construct Girl Army as a safe space by sharing personal stories of navigating *unsafe* space, online and in person. Jasmine captured the constant threat of offline physical violence many women experience when moving through public space in a post inviting members to

> talk about the risks of getting from A to B. The risks we experience in just passing through public space to get from one place to another. The things we do or carry, or avoid to try to minimize those risks or defend ourselves. The stress this causes and the toll it takes.

A trans member of color and sex worker described Girl Army as a space that provides respite from the everyday dangers of rape culture's interlocking systems of oppression in an interview:

> As long as patriarchy, and ciscentricism, and racism exist, I am not safe. As long as whorephobia is a thing, I am not safe. As long as NB-phobia is a thing, I am not safe.[6] And I'm very aware of that every day, when I get dressed in the morning . . . I need to pick my wardrobe somewhat more carefully than I would like to because the image that I present to the world

could get me arrested. It could get me killed. (personal communication, November 11, 2015)

In addition to frequent posts describing encounters with either physical violence or the threat of it offline, members post stories detailing encounters with rape culture online. Members often share screen captures of men harassing them through various digital platforms and frequently call for backup fending off bigotry in discussion threads elsewhere online. From deeply disturbing insults to rape threats, members have posted stories detailing the consequences faced for ignoring men's messages or refusing men's sexual advances on dating applications, for sharing feminist viewpoints via social media, or for simply, as one member put it, "internetting while female." Girl Army members' practice of naming the countless digital and in-person manifestations of rape culture they encounter daily not only draws a discursive boundary around Girl Army as a safe space formed in sharp relief to rape culture, but also forges bonds of solidarity through shared experiences and creates opportunities for collective interventions into everyday forms of oppression.

Paradoxically, however, the group's dependence on the notion of unsafe space to construct Girl Army as a safe space risks reifying safe/unsafe spatial binaries that "can enact or reflect masculinist social control to regulate women's use of and movement through public spaces" (The Roestone Collective, 2014). On the one hand, as a "secret" Facebook group, Girl Army provides members with a support base to rally in times of need and to develop responses to oppressive situations in private. In the case of both offline and online violence, Girl Army as a digital object can create material interventions. The group, accessible through Facebook's mobile app, provides a constantly available resource for requesting support for a situation unfolding in the moment or thinking through a repeated experience, such as street harassment, so that members might react differently in the future. On the other hand, Girl Army's technologically enabled insolation from broader publics inadvertently supports the relegation of certain voices to the margins by carving out a specific space for those voices. Fraser (1992) cautions that counterpublics risk becoming "enclaved" unless they take up "a publicist orientation" and, in addition to functioning "as spaces of withdrawal and regroupment," perform "agitational activities directed toward wider publics" (p. 124). One interviewee described Girl Army as a "potential space," a community whose bonds might provide the foundation for collective action directed outside its boundaries, but which has primarily remained a site for intragroup dialogue, which she feared might lead the group to become an "echo chamber." While Girl Army members practice separation to collectively strategize personal practices of resistance and healing outside the public eye, the group's necessary foregrounding of the safe/unsafe binary raises questions about feminist safe spaces' reification of the very dualisms they seek to dismantle and, in turn, their ability to engage with the broader public sphere.

Moreover, the group's digital nature undermines the boundary members draw between Girl Army as safe and broader online and offline publics as unsafe. Facebook's technical settings may afford the group a certain degree of privacy but, given that the majority of members registered accounts under their real names, deeply personal and potentially compromising posts are inextricably linked with members' identities. One member remarked in an interview that the lack of anonymity enables members to hold each other accountable, whereas anonymity elsewhere on the web has enabled users to threaten and harass women and queer and gender-nonconforming people. Even with privacy settings in place, however, the lack of anonymity has also resulted in members with ulterior motives taking screen captures of conversations and publishing them in other contexts. In one particularly egregious example, a member shared her story of having to file a complaint with the police because a man she met through another Facebook group threatened to rape her; another member screen-captured the conversation and sent it to the man in question. While Girl Army moderators removed this member for violating the safe space, it remains impossible to prevent members from publishing potentially compromising information about one another in contexts outside the group. As a former member who left Girl Army precisely for this reason told me in an interview, "It's the internet. Nothing is safe" (personal communication, December 9, 2015). Paradoxically, the same digital accessibility that bolsters Girl Army's reach and influence as a safe space also threatens its safety. While, in interviews, some members said the risks of publishing private information online were negligible in comparison to moving through public space with feminine, trans, or queer bodies or bodies of color (to quote one interviewee, "For me, life is not safe"), social media platforms present new challenges for feminist safe spaces.

The risks involved in sharing personal stories and expressions online have led many contemporary feminists to search for safety within the boundaries of the zine community. Zines have an intrinsically limited distribution. Whereas a blog post's reach can grow exponentially among a limitless number of readers, a zine's circulation is restricted by its print run, or the number of copies its author produces. Even so, a zine's reach is difficult to measure. Bloggers might operationalize their audience's size in terms of subscribers or unique visitors, but zinesters, who typically do not use subscription-based models to circulate their print booklets, cannot be certain how many hands their work passes through; a dozen readers may purchase copies of a zine and share them with friends and family, while a dozen others might peruse an issue in a bookstore. Bloggers and other social media users also typically have a means to engage in dialogue with their followers, such as comments sections. A zinester, on the other hand, stands at the end of a one-way communication flow from zine maker to zine reader. In other words, a zinester's public is often invisible to her, only coming into view at festivals and through Etsy transactions.

Yet my interviewees spoke of the feminist zine network as a community and identified community building as one of their primary motivations for making zines. Some described zine making as a community-building practice that brings people together, face-to-face, to coauthor a zine or to mingle at a zine festival. Moose Lane highlighted this as a significant accomplishment in an increasingly mediated world:

> Even though zines are not a good medium for back-and-forth, I think the actual zine community is stronger than online ones, in part because there is a lot more face-to-face interaction. . . . I have met almost all of my friends on the East Coast through zines in someway. In most online communities, I kind of lurk. I'm not much of an active participant. It's a really good way to be exposed to a wide variety of experiences and views, but at the end of the day I'm still sitting at home behind a computer screen. (personal communication, March 29, 2016)

The face-to-face production and exchange of zines paired with the medium's extra-institutional, do-it-yourself nature makes it ideal for building communities that prefigure their authors' political goals and values. For Kerri Radley, "One of the things that I love about the zine community is that I feel like we can shape it to be what we want to. Through active participation, putting on and attending events, and sharing our zines, we work to create the type of community that we want to belong to" (personal communication, April 19, 2016).

But while these in-person interactions are important, a more abstract sense of connection figures centrally into zinesters' experiences of community. My interviewees frequently described zinesters as sharing, at some fundamental level, a common set of experiences and politics, such that a zine maker can imagine addressing an audience who already understands her perspective: "The zine community, for the most part, is such a welcoming and supportive space, that it makes sense that feminists have been drawn to the medium," Kerri Radley explained, "It's a space that is generally safer, one in which they have a voice and can be heard" (personal communication, April 19, 2016). This sense of safety and camaraderie is grounded in the zine's historical association with countercultural and leftist movements (Duncombe, 2008). A feminist zinester may never meet all of her readers but, by virtue of their interest in zines, she can safely guess that they share at least some of her political goals and values. She cannot make the same assumption on highly public social media platforms like Twitter, where users span the political spectrum. As Moose Lane quipped, "Most of the rabid misogynists, transphobes, homophobes, racists, etcetera, you meet online don't read zines" (personal communication, March 29, 2016). The countercultural roots of the medium form a symbolic boundary around the zine community, creating a space "of withdrawal and regroupment" (Fraser, 1992, p. 124), where likeminded activists can engage exclusively with one another without facing suppression or interruption.

Feminist zinesters, in other words, preach to the choir. For some critics, this makes zines a weak medium for political engagement. Sandoval and Fuchs (2010), for example, argue that "the success of alternative media depends on their ability to gain public visibility for their critical media content. . . . To do more than to 'preach to the converted,' they have to try to increase their public visibility and to attract as many recipients as possible" (p. 148). Reaching a wide audience, however, is not the primary purpose that zines fulfill within feminists' repertoire of media practices.

While a social media platform would undoubtedly offer greater visibility, feminist zinesters prioritize what many of my interviewees referred to as "personal impact" over readership numbers. Christine Stoddard, who runs a popular online magazine that generates ad revenue, also makes zines in small runs, producing no more than one hundred copies of a single title. "I'm not looking to communicate en masse with a zine," Stoddard said, "that's what the internet is for. I'm looking to make that personal impact, to give someone a print artifact to cherish and remember" (personal communication, March 26, 2016). Moose Lane, who publishes work on a Tumblr blog, expressed a similar sentiment:

> I'm on Tumblr, and I post a lot of art there, as well as reblog puns and cat pictures. A lot of what I post isn't all that personal, and the stuff that is feels like shouting into the void. Sometimes, that's what I want—self-expression without examination or response. But I don't use zines in the same way. (personal communication, March 29, 2016)

Regardless of whether or not they ever meet their readers in person, zinesters expressed a feeling of personal connection with their readers, facilitated through the exchange and circulation of zines, that they do not experience online. Several interviewees framed zines as objects of mediation that, in comparison to digital media, foster more authentic relationships between authors and readers. Christine Stoddard explained that

> So much web content is meant to be consumed quickly. People usually are clicking around too much to really focus on any single piece for too long. Zines require a longer time commitment. They engross you in a way that most web content does not. That alone can impact the reader very personally and make your message resonate with them for years to come. (personal communication, March 26, 2016)

While each of my interviewees maintains an active social media presence, they turn toward zines to share personal experiences with a small, supportive audience.

The underground, alternative nature of zines enables this intimate community experience. The degree of countercultural capital required to participate in the zine community, however, can make the accessible DIY practice ironically inaccessible to readers not yet acquainted with the medium. Duncombe (2008) describes early zine scenes as "self-ghettoized" (p. 176), unsustainable, and even "elitist" (p. 174) underground communities, whose members struggled to engage with more mainstream publics or extend a hand to newcomers. This elitism is especially problematic for feminists, given women's historical exclusion from the cultures and movements surrounding zine scenes (Duncombe, 2008). Moreover, zinesters are often not inspired to start making zines until they get their hands on someone else's self-published work (Piepmeier, 2009); repeatedly in interviews, feminist zinesters reported that it was a serendipitous first encounter with zines in an offbeat bookstore, a public library, or a classroom that sparked their zine-making careers.

Contemporary feminist zinesters use digital media platforms to democratize access to zines, a practice that may have much to do with zines' apparent resurgence. Christine Stoddard reported that "the internet has made it so much easier to discover new titles and zine festivals" (personal communication, March 26, 2016). While, true to their roots, interviewees reported selling zines at alternative bookstores, ten out of twelve interviewees also sell their zines online, through their own personal websites or through Etsy shops. Others send their zines to distros, who sell and ship zinesters' work, almost always through an online store, to readers for a portion of the cover price. All interviewees have blogs linked to their zine projects, usually hosted on Tumblr, which has garnered a reputation as a platform for leftist "social justice warriors" (Brandt and Kizer, 2015). Importantly for the zine community as a whole, social media have also facilitated what my interviewees described as the recent surge in zine festivals. While, like all aspects of zine culture, the history of zine fests has not been well documented, interviewees speculated that these exhibits and pop-up shops, often hosted in community centers and open to zinesters who pay small tabling fees, are a recent phenomenon. "I have seen more zine fests pop up in the last half-decade and many more are continuing to go strong," Moose Lane observed, suggesting parallels between the rise of zine fests and the development of Web 2.0 (personal communication, March 29, 2016).

For my interviewees, modern-day zine-making is a material social practice channeled in large part through digital media, mirroring the structure of networked publics, or "spaces and audiences that are bound together through technological networks" (boyd, 2008, p. 125). Feminist zinesters, readers, and newcomers to the zine world use digital media to facilitate interactions online and face-to-face. In contrast to the "self-ghettoized" zine communities of previous generations, to borrow Duncombe's terminology, social media platforms have contributed to what Rauch (2015) calls "a converged media environment" (p. 126), blurring the boundary separating zinesters' alternative discourse from the mainstream. Nonetheless, the boundary remains, and feminist zine communities, while networked, are counterpublics, purposefully formed in juxtaposition to wider publics that marginalize women, trans and queer folks, and people of color. The boundary encompassing feminist zine counterpublics, while made permeable via digital networks, is protected through many zinesters' strict policies against scanning and publishing their zines online. Kerri Radley, for example, never shares digital copies of her zines:

> I'm a firm believer in my zines remaining in physical form and on paper only and I do not allow any of my zines to be digitally archived. . . . Even though I can never truly 100 percent control what happens to my zines or their content, keeping them out of the digital sphere does allow me better control over what happens to my writing—where it's shared, who it's shared with, who it's attributed to, and who makes money off of it. (personal communication, April 19, 2016)

Most of my interviewees only make their zine content available to those who take the steps necessary to acquire physical copies, through online shops or in-person festivals. Anyone interested in a feminist zinester's work is likely to be granted access, as zines are often made available at low prices, on a sliding scale, or for barter or trade, but the reader must first invest energy into obtaining a copy of her work. This practice not only grants zinesters more control over the distribution of their work, but also makes it difficult for readers to harass writers with whom they disagree. While some may view zines' one-way flow of communication as a weakness when it comes to building communities, Adelaide Barton explained that for feminist zinesters, "this is actually a benefit. The internet is rife with trolls, especially ones that are looking to attack a woman voicing her opinion, or anyone challenging the patriarchy" (personal communication, April 6, 2016).

Feminist zinesters merge digital and print media practices to cultivate a distributive communication structure (Rentschler, 2015), forging network ties with new readers, maintaining relationships with existing readers, and connecting with one another, but keeping their zines' content offline. Digital networks, then, constitute a boundary between zine makers and readers, providing entry to the feminist zine community but not immediate access to feminist zines themselves. Feminist zinesters' boundary maintenance work gives shape to a networked safe space, where marginalized media makers can express themselves freely without facing harassment.

While members describe both Girl Army and the zine community as fairly closed off spaces, Permanent Wave Philly, as founding member Callie told me in an interview, is an "open collective," a group whose boundaries are fluid and whose core membership is constantly rotating. "You don't need an application to do it," Dee explained, "We don't require a screening, but I feel like if somebody comes to a meeting, that's the screening of if they fit or not. And we're always going to say, 'Come on back'" (personal communication, May 24, 2015). The group is open to anyone, regardless of gender identity, who wants to join. As a testament to this, the group's mission statement, published on their website and Facebook page, includes an open call for participation:

> Permanent Wave Philly is a network and community of feminist artists and activists. We seek to challenge gender inequality not only in all forms of the arts, but also in politics, our personal lives, and anywhere else it seems necessary. We want to continue what was started generations ago by creating a revolutionary arts movement and community that's relevant to women, LGBTQ-people, people of color, and anyone who has been excluded from subjective mainstream norms. We want you to join, collaborate, and inspire us. (personal communication, May 24, 2015)

Anyone interested in supporting PWP's mission can, Callie told me matter-of-factly, "just walk in and join us" (personal communication, May 24, 2015).

In reality, however, joining the group is not quite so easy. Potential members must cross several community boundaries before they can participate in PWP. First, newcomers must find Permanent Wave, either online or in-person, a task made difficult by the group's countercultural characteristics. Members frequently referred to PWP as part of Philadel-phia's "DIY scene," a network of local bands and amateur bookers who host shows in offbeat venues, typically someone's basement or living room, and operate outside the professional music industry. Like the zine com-munity, the DIY scene provides an outlet for unconventional music and art and, historically, leftist politics and alternative identities, but it lacks the visibility of more mainstream cultural circuits. As such, a certain degree of countercultural capital is required to enter the scene, to know where shows are hosted, and to become an active participant, either as a musician or a booker.[7] The same is true for Permanent Wave Philly. Most of the group's members came to PWP through existing connections to the DIY scene; some played in local bands while others had either booked or attended house shows prior to discovering the group. The group's alter-ity acts as a barrier to entry to those not already "in the know" about the Philly DIY scene, which in turn limits participation to those who share the scene's punk ethos and leftist politics. PWP's underground nature raises concerns about exclusivity and impact; as Jenny lamented in an interview, "We get into our own little bubble" (personal communication, May 24, 2015). The group's purposeful positioning along the margins of the city's arts and culture scene, however, not only grants them a certain creative freedom, but also helps members form counterpublic connections with likeminded artists and activists.

In addition to this symbolic boundary, the PWP listserv, hosted on the free-to-use Google Groups platform, functions as a technological bound-ary around the group. Newcomers, once they encounter PWP through the broader DIY scene, officially "join" the group when they become a mem-ber of the PWP listserv, either by filling out a sign-up form in person at a PWP event or sending a request to the group's email account. Only list-serv members can learn about internal meetings, help coordinate event logistics, and weigh in on organizational issues. PWP members carefully maintain the listserv as a boundary between the group and the broader public. Consistently throughout my fieldwork, there were between ten and twenty active PWP members, who reliably attended meetings, partici-pated in events, and contributed to listserv discussions. But when, in 2015, members realized their at times heated email discussions were reaching more than seventy different people, they decided to cull the listserv down to thirty people to protect the community's privacy. The listserv provides the informal grassroots collective with a formal method for demarcating and maintaining membership boundaries. PWP's social and technological boundaries close the counterpublic collective off from more mainstream publics, creating a space specifically for feminist activists and artists.

The networked affordances of a listserv enabled Permanent Wave Philly's founders to construct their own activist community from the ground up, without the institutional resources or structure of a more conventional organization like a nonprofit. Reflecting the DIY ethos of the punk scene and the do-it-ourselves logic of contemporary feminism, PWP was not built around a bureaucratic system of formal leaders or positions, but a dispersed, participatory communication network, where any member who wants to develop or contribute to a group project can. Through the group's networked structure, PWP members practice a horizontalism that, in theory, counteracts the marginalization of women, LGBTQ+ people, and people of color in the punk scene and beyond.

In practice, however, PWP's listserv-as-community structure often gave rise to informal leaders who dominated the group. In her 1972 study of second-wave feminist collectives, Jo Freeman warns activists about what she calls "the tyranny of structurelessness," the risk of a group's commitment to leaderlessness masking the growth of unchecked hierarchies. In PWP, the horizontally networked nature of the listserv exacerbated this age-old organizing problem. Listserv membership indicates that one belongs to the Permanent Wave community, but it does not clarify what one's role is in the community or how community decisions are made. Members with more time on their hands or a higher level of commitment were more likely to take on tasks like calling for meetings, checking and responding to emails, posting on the group's social media pages, and coordinating event logistics. With the structure of the group and members' expectations of one another left unspoken, individual members could take charge and make unilateral decisions, while the rest of the group was left without a formal mechanism through which to hold these informal leaders accountable.

This issue came to a head in the aftermath of PWP's 2015 show at PhilaMOCA, described in the introduction to this chapter. While, on the surface, the event appeared to have been a success—the turnout was decent, the audience enjoyed themselves, the bands were well paid, and PWP made a profit selling merchandise—behind the scenes, Erin organized the show by herself, booking bands without consulting the rest of the group. The result was a lineup that did not reflect the group's feminist focus on centering the work of marginalized artists. "The opening band was a bunch of cis white dudes," Dee lamented at a meeting following the show, and there were no people of color in any of the other bands. Worse still, the opening band's lead singer was known to post degrading images of and messages about women on his social media accounts. Dee placed the blame on Erin, but other group members acknowledged that they had failed to question Erin's choices or even check in on the progress of her event planning. The show's shortcomings ultimately stemmed from a collective failure to practice community.

The PhilaMOCA show points to a particular challenge for feminist community builders in the digital age, one evidenced throughout each of the three communities' struggles to build boundaries that include some while excluding other. While platforms like email listservs may make it easier than ever for even the youngest, unseasoned activists to give shape to new communities, it is not enough to simply create a listerv and call it a community. In fact, doing so often obfuscates the work required to combat the imbalances of power that inevitably emerge within any social space. This is particularly problematic for feminist activists seeking to create communities that counteract patriarchal systems of oppression. When a community's structure is left unspoken, emergent hierarchies can sideline already marginalized voices. Dee pointed toward the tyranny of structurelessness within PWP at the post-show meeting: "I guess I thought this was a collective, and that 'collective' means a certain thing, and that everyone was on the same page about that. But I guess I was wrong." For a feminist safe space community to prefigure its members' values, steps needed to be taken to articulate the community's structure, cultivate a sense of belonging, and build a system of accountability within a community's boundaries.

Centering Marginalized Voices

In the three communities under study, some of this articulation unfolded through practices enacted to center specific marginalized voices. For Girl

Army members, gender-based marginalization is a key focal point. The Facebook group's diminutively feminine yet militant name stems from the legacy of the Riot Grrrl movement of 1990s, which emerged at the intersection of punk music and U.S. feminism's "third wave" and aimed to reclaim femininity as a source of strength rather than weakness (Marcus, 2010). As one member explained in an interview, Girl Army takes up the Riot Grrrl proclamation that "femininity is worth celebrating . . . it's not a bad thing to, you know, be radically feminine." Girl Army is, in form and content, a space where "girl" is treated, to quote one member, as a "radically inclusive" and fluid term that captures "gender beyond the binary" and imagines "the possibility of a different gender order and one that's better for all of us." Members and moderators understand Girl Army to be a space that provides safety for users who identify as women or whose gender identity transcends the male/female binary, blurs the boundaries imagined to separate the binary's polar extremes, or fluctuates over time. In other words, the group serves users excluded from what Fraser (1992) describes as the "masculinist conception of the public sphere" (p. 117), which limits political participation to the realm of men and political discourse to the concerns of hegemonic masculinity. Girl Army emerged as a counterpublic in response to these exclusions to "help expand discursive space" (Fraser, 1992: 124) and recenter marginalized bodies and issues.

On multiple occasions, Jasmine has described Girl Army's mission as an effort to "fill the void of a 'safe space' for women to speak to other women." Zola, a longtime member, referred to the group as "a sisterhood online" that, in a society where women are encouraged to "constantly compete with each other" rather than forge bonds of solidarity, provides a much-needed source of community (personal communication, November 10, 2015). Another interviewee described the bonds of that sisterhood as a shared struggle: "Women, both trans and cis, usually share a lot of history with aspects of their oppression, with the sources of their oppression." Girl Army is, in theory, meant to unite women and nonbinary individuals who are marginalized and alienated from each other within the public sphere; the group's safety is predicated on its status as an inclusive space for otherwise excluded people.

In practice, however, Girl Army members' technological and social practices privilege cisgender womanhood. While moderators' membership screening practices help center some marginalized voices, they exclude others. Facebook users who do not pass as women in their account names or profile pictures or who do not identify themselves to moderators as genderqueer are excluded from the group. Transgender men, who experience high levels of gender-based violence and harassment (Meicher, 2017), are also barred from Girl Army's "non-men space." One interviewee drew attention to the contradictions between Girl Army's strict drawing of boundaries between femininity and masculinity and its intersectional conceptualization of gender-based oppression:

> I'm interested in whether or not we should include transmasculine or male-identified people in the group because effeminate men face a lot of similar intersections of oppression as cis and trans women. In a patriarchal culture, a lot of people, both men and women, are victims of misogyny. (personal communication, November 11, 2015)

Girl Army's technological boundaries also raise questions about exclusion along the axes of race and class. The strategy moderators use to control access to the group suggests that Girl Army is largely an extended network of mutual "friends," which, in turn, implies that racial and economic hierarchies may be reproduced within the group. Plus, group membership requires digital media access and literacy, which suggests that the group likely privileges young, educated, middle- to upper-class women.

Similar biases are reflected in Girl Army members' social practices. In group conversations, members tend to discursively center cisgender womanhood. When, in August 2015, Jasmine published a post asking members if Girl Army should be open to people who do not identify as women, only a few members said that they think the group should be inclusive of all gender identities. Most others requested that the group continue to bar men and expressed desires to keep the group "safe" for discussing female-specific concerns without feeling guilt for excluding people, particularly transgender women, who may not share these physiological experiences. The vast majority of posts published in the group throughout my fieldwork revolved around female experiences, including reviews of feminine hygiene products, questions about birth control, stories about childbirth, and discussions of issues related to women's reproductive health rights. While the group claims to be open to transgender women and nonbinary individuals, in practice, Girl Army discussions often focus on experiences connected to female physiology and cisgender womanhood.

Girl Army members link safety to inclusion and openness. As one member alluded to in an interview, within the broader public sphere, women, women of color, queer and trans women, and nonbinary individuals are often silenced or discredited on the basis of their identities, adding an extra burden to their presentation of self in everyday life. Girl Army limits membership to these groups in order to recenter marginalized voices within the safe space's boundaries and foster solidarity through coalitional bonds. However, the group's privileging of cisgender womanhood through its technological and discursive practices raises questions about Girl Army's inclusivity. Toward the end of her thread on whether or not to admit people who do not identify as women into the group, Jasmine stated, "I want everyone, EVERYONE to feel good in here." Conversely, in a thread three weeks later, Jasmine, frustrated with a member who criticized moderators' practices for screening new members, stated firmly, "Anyone who doesn't get why restricting membership is important maybe doesn't understand the purpose of a safe space." At the heart of Girl Army lies a tension between creating a space that is inclusive of some marginalized identities and drawing boundaries that are exclusive of others. Girl Army ties safety to open access, but in order to draw protective boundaries around particular identities and experiences, moderators must limit accessibility, demonstrating the partial and incomplete nature of the community as a safe space.

The feminist zine community centers a broader spectrum of marginalized voices, reflecting the accessibility of the genre. The tools and materials zinesters use to practice their craft range in degree of professionalism, from paper, pens, Sharpies, glue sticks, scissors, and stolen time on the office's Xerox machine to cardstock, artist-grade inks and paints, silk screen, lithographs, letterpresses, Photoshop, and professional printers. But while feminist zinesters' creative practices and aesthetics may vary, the community shares a common set of norms, which guide the zine production process. As Moose Lane explained, "What separates zines from other self-publications is a commitment to do-it-yourself ethics (or do-it-together ethics) and the prioritization of the spread of ideas and art over making money" (personal communication, March 29, 2016). My interviewees' zines are often explicitly feminist in content, dealing with questions related to gender-based inequities, but the DIY ethics of the zine-making process itself prefigures feminist ideals in ways that digital media platforms and commercial media outlets simply cannot. Christine Stoddard observed that

> Zines are about as approachable as media-making gets. As long as you have a pen and paper, you can make a zine. If you have access to a copier, you can make multiple copies of it. . . . You can be the writer, artists, and publisher. Because the barrier to entry is low, making zines is very empowering. Anybody can make their voice heard. . . . Traditional media is full of barriers and, historically, those barriers have been less amendable to female creators. Those barriers don't exist in the zine world. (personal communication, March 26, 2016)

Christine's comments point toward what Fraser (1992) describes as the "informal impediments to participatory parity that can persist even after everyone is formally and legally licensed to participate" (p. 119), the every-day systems of power that structure participation in the public sphere. White male producers dominate commercial media industries (Annenberg Inclusion Initiative, 2020), gender-based harassment silences women on social media platforms, and economic privilege restricts access to both, but anyone with a pen and paper can "make their voice heard" through a zine. Although some of my interviewees expressed concerns about an aesthetic shift toward more "slick and professional" zines, to borrow Kerri Radley's description, a zinester can invest as much or as little artistry and resources into her work as she chooses and still participate in the zine community (personal communication, April 19, 2016). Aesthetics may shift, but accessibility remains a key value of the feminist zinesters' DIY ethics. At its core, feminist zine-making constitutes an accessible alternative media practice that eschews marketplace values, subverts the producer/consumer binary, and, in the process, creates outlets for marginalized voices, unrestricted by gendered or class-based barriers to entry.

Just as the zine community opens up new opportunities for otherwise marginalized media makers, it also creates spaces for the representation of bodies and subjectivities excluded from dominant discourse and commercial media. Moose Lane's zine series, Get the Fuck Outside (GTFO), focuses on exploring the great outdoors and represents a diversity of characters in the process: "The illustrations in GTFO are centered around ladyfolk, though the content is for anyone. I do this deliberately because, socially, men tend to have easier access to the outdoors, either due to social expectations growing up, or due to perceived dangers for women of traveling alone in remote places" (personal communication, March 29, 2016). Generating visibility through alternative media representation is especially important to Kerri Radley, whose zine, *Deafula*, shares her experiences navigating the world as a deaf woman:

> *Deafula* has garnered a wider reach than I ever expected or thought possible, reaching into the thousands annually. Given how near and dear the topics I cover in *Deafula* are to my heart, and how important it is to me to increase visibility for deaf and disabled folks, my zine having reach is meaningful to me. (personal communication, April 19, 2016)

Through the representation of underprivileged identities, zinesters critique, explicitly or implicitly, the discourses that relegate those identities to the margins of society and construct counterdiscourses of inclusion and empowerment.

But while some authors, like Kerri, reach an impressive number of readers, cultivated in part through their online promotional work, the enclaved nature of the zine community raises concerns about whether the medium silos already marginalized voices. As is the case with Girl Army, the feminist zine community networks a safe space for bodies and issues that, because they are marked by gender, are often excluded from more mainstream arenas for political discourse and action. In doing so, however, the community risks reifying the hegemonic norms that enable the white male domination of the public sphere by creating a release valve for the oppressed, a counterpublic sphere where women can freely critique systems of power without actually disrupting them. Still, while they acknowledged this critique, my interviewees insisted that zines are not intended to serve as launching pads for public-facing actions and critique; like Christine Stoddard said, "that's what the internet is for" (personal communication, March 26, 2016). Rather, while social media platforms offer spaces for planning and executing broader outreach, the feminist zine community offers a space for uninterrupted engagement with others who share similar experiences of marginalization.

While the inherent materiality of zines lays a foundation for accessible community, Permanent Wave Philly had to work carefully to create a space that centers marginalized voices. Rather than, as Dee commented, assume everyone is on the same page about what the collective's goal are and what it means to participate in the collective, members worked on making the group's mission, structure, and expectations for one another explicit throughout the latter half of PWP's active years. Through trial, error, and reflection on missteps like the PhilaMOCA show, Permanent Wave Philly members developed a set of specific strategies to push toward their goal of centering marginalized voices, not only in their shows and events, but internally, within their own community of organizers. These strategies were developed at meetings and added to an internal document referred to as the collective's "Extended Mission Statement" and made accessible for reading and editing to all members via the group's Google Drive. A key mantra for the group became "acting with intentionality," as members sought to align their events and their organizing methods with their feminist politics. PWP's networked community, closed off from outside influence and driven by its members' interests, offered the ideal space to experiment with intersectional organizing practices and imagine alternatives to existing models of social and political engagement.

For PWP, whose core members were a racially diverse group of women ranging in age and sexual orientation, acting with intentionality meant centering marginalized voices throughout the entire organizing process, from the early stages of planning a show through to its execution. At meetings and in interviews, members frequently described feeling alienated and unrepresented at shows, where male audience members aggressively crowded the pit and "guy punks" took center stage. Permanent Wave Philly, Callie explained, was founded with the intention of creating platforms and spaces that empower artists and fans who are women, queer, and/or of color, a political intervention into the DIY scene that could also spill over into everyday life:

> It seems like a "personal is political" kind of thing, because a lot of us have been going to shows or any kind of event and we just feel excluded. We feel like we're not welcomed and we're discouraged from making our own art or doing our own creative work or intellectual work. And also just didn't feel a sense of community when we go to shows. . . . We don't see ourselves

represented when we do go to shows. . . . I want to go to the shows that I want to see, and I want to feel like I can do this, and I want to see other women and gender-queer people making music and doing really cool stuff. It's not that these people don't exist, that they don't do stuff. But it's like, they're not always recognized. . . . I know I just wanted to be recognized, to be supported. (personal communication, May 24, 2015)

PWP's activism was motivated by the idea that a seemingly personal experience—feeling alienated at shows—was rooted in a systematic imbalance of power—the white, heterosexual, male domination of the punk music scene. The collective took concrete steps to address this imbalance on stage, in the pit, and behind the scenes.

Within Philadelphia's DIY scene, PWP was best known for booking bands that were, in Kai's words, "inclusive of women, of queer folks, trans folks, people of color . . . anyone who isn't represented by, I don't know, the Electric Factory or something." Frequently throughout my fieldwork, local bands or venues would reach out to PWP via email or Facebook message, requesting assistance organizing shows that highlighted "girl punks." The collective filled a gap in both the alternative and mainstream music landscapes by creating a team of show bookers specifically focused on promoting and supporting artists who were not straight, white, cisgender men. As much as possible, PWP also aimed to book diverse bands who, either in their lyrics or in their work off stage, advanced feminist causes. Dee put it simply at a meeting—"We choose bands because they're the kind of people we would like to hang out with." After the PhilaMOCA show, PWP members collaborated on a list of local bands that featured a diverse lineup and aligned with the collective's values and went to work booking shows for those artists and promoting their music across PWP's social media networks. But beyond simply showcasing marginalized artists, the collective helped to sustain them. PWP never took a profit from admissions sales for a show, instead giving all proceeds from the door to the bands and covering its own expenses by selling zines, handmade merchandise like patches and buttons, and baked goods. True to its mission to diversify music and the arts, the collective also created opportunities for people to try playing an instrument for the first time. Every February, PWP hosted its annual "Galentine's Day Show," open only to performers who identified as women, nonbinary, or queer, and featuring cover bands with little or no music experience; collective members provided participants with free music lessons leading up to the show.

Permanent Wave Philly's activist work also extended to the audience, and collective members worked to create an empowering show experience. Here, as with the feminist zine community, accessibility was a key value. Like other DIY shows, PWP charged admission on a pay-what-you-can sliding scale, often between $5 and $10, and never turned away anyone who could not afford entry. In an effort to make their events as accessible as possible, the collective also aimed to host shows exclusively at venues open to people all ages, not just those over twenty-one.

But PWP did more than make their shows accessible to diverse audiences; members actively worked to cultivate safe spaces for audiences at their shows. The collective's "Safer Spaces Policy," outlined in the introduction to this chapter, works from the assumption that no space can ever be truly safe for all people at all times but asks participants to respect one another's physical and emotional boundaries to the best of their abilities. Implementing a safer space policy at a show is, as Jenny explained in an interview, an explicitly political critique of the world outside that show:

> Just by having a safer spaces policy is talking about the fact that this isn't the same state outside of the room. . . . I think just acknowledging that is a huge thing for people. I remember having discussions with my coworkers, who were just like, "Well, why do you need feminism? We've all got jobs." This is so much more complex and we're helping to do what we can to acknowledge what's wrong and try to fix it. (personal communication, May 24, 2015)

Safer space policies implicitly gesture toward the existence of domination throughout everyday life. Like Girl Army, PWP's safer space policy produces a counterpublic sphere, where the obstacles that prevent marginalized groups' full participation are explicitly addressed and an alternative mode of sociality that prioritizes care and validation is modeled.

While PWP's more publicly visible actions—its diverse band line-ups and shows with safer space policies—disrupted the gendered power dynamics of the DIY and punk music scenes, their most important political intervention happened behind the scenes, within their own community of organizers. In an interview, Callie described PWP's intra-organizational work as an opportunity to live out utopian visions for a feminist future on a smaller scale:

> I would like to see patriarchal and oppressive attitudes eliminated. And that's really hard, and I think we're all sort of working toward it in our own ways. But the way I see how we organize our shows, it's kind of like we're making that happen on a smaller level. (personal communication, May 24, 2015)

For Callie and others, organizing a show or event did not just involve coordinating logistics; it offered an important opportunity to prefigure feminist values.

PWP members implemented a number of different strategies for modeling their feminist politics through their organizational practices. To keep meetings accessible, collective members usually gathered in a public space, such as a park or a community center, rather than a commercial space, such as a cafe, where members would have to spend money, or a private space, such as a home, which can feel uncomfortable for newcomers. At the start of meetings, key responsibilities, such as facilitator, note taker, email checker, and social media coordinator, were rotated among volunteers. Members applied a similar approach for organizing events. Anyone interested could take the lead on organizing a particular show or project with support from others who volunteered to perform more minor tasks, such as working the door or handling setup, and always in communication with the rest of the collective. All members were granted access to the collective's email account and a "how-to guide" for booking bands and venues, so that even those members without experience could take the lead on organizing a show. PWP's practice of rotating leadership positions subverted the sociopolitical structures that impede marginalized groups' access to leadership positions in the public sphere.

But while leadership roles rotated among individual members, decision-making was a collective process. Options for bands and venues to book were discussed as a group, ideally in person, and all decisions were made through consensus. Because PWP's active membership was constantly in flux, true consensus was not required. Instead, at least four people present at a meeting and in agreement could make a decision on behalf of the group. Striving for consensus was critical to PWP's status as a feminist counterpublic because it established what Dee in an interview called a system of "checks and balances" that helps ensure that all interested members have a say in a given matter. Still, arriving at consensus was often slow and arduous. As Jenny explained in an interview,

> Consensus is something we take very seriously, but it does take time to arrive at something that everyone feels comfortable with. Because that's so important to us, that's something we're not willing to sacrifice to have a finished product. There are times when it's like, an hour or two-and-a-half hour meeting, and we have something that is still not done. And I want to leave, you know? But it's also a conversation I want to continue. That's something that can be both really great and really hard. (personal communication, May 24, 2015)

At times, consensus only came after hours-long meetings and debates, a source of frustration that led some to leave the collective. But as Callie argued at a meeting, "It's not about efficiency. . . . I mean if anything, slowing down the process is like, the whole point. . . . It's about doing something together as a community." For PWP members, the behind-the-scenes process of collectively organizing a show together as a community mattered more than the product, the show itself. Following the Phila-MOCA show, members even agreed to remove the collective's name from any event they planned if the behind-the-scenes process did not live up to their "Extended Mission."

The PWP listserv presented collective members with both the challenge and the opportunity of structurelessness. The group's email network drew feminist activists and artists together within a bounded space that they could shape to both fulfill their organizing needs and mirror their political values. Although the process could be inefficient and, at times, even fruitless, for Permanent Wave members, the process of constructing and maintaining a safe, empowering community was activist work, in and of itself.

Fostering Open Expression

Each community's efforts to center marginalized voices extended into practices to support free and open expression among members. Throughout my fieldwork, Girl Army's moderators established but one guideline for the group, decreed concisely in the group's description: "This group has one basic rule and that is Real Talk. Silencing or bullying members won't be tolerated. Checking each other's privilege is encouraged, disagreeing is fine, debate is good." Repeatedly in group posts and interviews, members suggested that Real Talk is the most important affordance of a safe space. As Zola explained to me, the ability to speak openly without being silenced or criticized is the signature achievement of safe spaces:

> A safe space is an inclusive spot where it doesn't matter who you are, that if you have any kind of issue, or just want to kind of talk without any judgment, that's a safe space. It doesn't matter whether it's in person, or if it's online, or if it's your mom, or your dad, if you have that safe space where you just feel so, like, all that burden is just gone, and you don't have to put on any kind of mask. That's a safe space. (personal communication, November 10, 2015)

The group, in other words, empowers members to speak freely, unfettered by the "silencing practices" (Shaw, 2013, p. 94) of online or offline misogyny. Like the in-person consciousness-raising meetings of the second wave, Girl Army promises members a safe space for openly sharing experiences they might not feel comfortable sharing elsewhere, such as accounts of sexual violence and harassment, mental health struggles, or relationship issues. In discussion threads, members not only offer one another support and exchange resources; they also identify patterns across their experiences and trace connections between their personal lives and overarching systems of power. To borrow Collins's (2000) term, these open dialogues are the first step in the process of rearticulating personal issues as collective struggles, of developing new frameworks for interpreting and responding to everyday manifestations of oppression. Providing a safe space to engage in Real Talk is perhaps the group's most transformative political intervention.

But, as Zola's definition suggests, safe spaces are not bounded fields located in particular places and times, but interpersonal achievements. Safety requires work. It is not built into the Facebook platform, and "Real Talk" is not guaranteed in a Facebook group with hundreds of members. Instead, the relief from the weight of burdensome masks that Zola describes, the freedom to "talk without any judgment," must be actively cultivated and maintained.

Following Fraser's (1992) theory of subaltern counterpublics, whereas other deliberative spaces might "bracket" inequalities and proceed as if they do not exist, Girl Army members "unbracket " (p. 120) inequalities and address them head-on. While the group's description does not outline explicit rules for encouraging and engaging in Real Talk, in practice, Girl Army members and moderators draw on a variety of sociotechnical strategies to create the conditions necessary for open expression. In the process, the group prefigures a more empowering mode of online sociality informed by a politics of validation and care that honors individuals' right to speak openly about their own experiences, free from threats of violence.

Within Girl Army, fostering open expression begins with fostering respect for individuals' personal authority, so as to counteract the delegitimization of marginalized voices in more mainstream publics. Members occupying dominant sociocultural positions are often asked to step back from discussions concerning the lives of more marginalized groups. For example, when, in November 2015, a member began a thread on cultural appropriation, members of color asked their white counterparts to either cede the floor to members from the culture in question or consult the writing of people of color published elsewhere online. Similarly, in her aforementioned post about street harassment, Jasmine made space specifically for marginalized voices: "Not all harassment is identical. . . . I want to invite everyone to discuss their experiences, but especially want to hear from those who are not white or cis, since your voices are often not heard in this conversation." When privileged members do not share the floor, they are typically kicked out of the group. Moderators have also removed members who, at various points throughout my fieldwork, questioned the validity of survivors' accounts of sexual violence.

Members also maintain open discussion with care for one another's emotional well-being through the use of trigger warnings or cautionary notes that precede potentially distressing content. While the group does not have explicit rules requiring trigger warnings, members use them to mark posts whose content might induce trauma-related stress, especially personal stories related to sexual violence, domestic violence, and self-harm, or add them to posts after moderators instruct them to do so. Moderators also intervene on discussion threads when members "tone police," or derail discussions related to experiences of oppression to ridicule a commenter for using angry or impassioned speech. Girl Army moderators' stance against tone policing creates a safe space where participants have the freedom to fully express emotions that are often invalidated within the broader public sphere. While expectations for behavior within Girl Army become clear only through participation within the group, several interviewees commented that members who misstep are often given second chances. As one interviewee commented, "I genuinely feel like I can say whatever I want on Girl Army and I feel like even if I say something that people disagree with or even something that's wrong, I can at least have an opportunity to learn from it" (personal communication, November 11, 2015). The safe space is meant to be a comfortable one for learning through discussion.

Still, even within this safe space, members sometimes wish to share a story or request anonymously, a challenge given that Facebook requires users to register their accounts under their real names (Facebook, 2018). Girl Army moderators, however, have developed a workaround. Using Facebook Messenger, Members can send a moderator a message to post in the group on their behalf. While the moderator will know the true identity of the author, the rest of the group will not.

And yet, despite the group's combined ideals of accessibility and openness, there are several barriers to entry when it comes to Real Talk in Girl Army. What Jasmine and others have referred to as "101 questions," or questions about the basics of intersectional feminism, are not allowed in Girl Army, which presumes access to engagement with feminist theory prior to joining the group. While this rule, which is not stated in the group's description, prevents women of color, queer and transgender women, and nonbinary members from feeling obligated to educate more privileged members about oppression, nowhere do moderators or members explicitly define intersectionality or provide resources about intersectional feminism. The group description advises members to be open to disagreement, an inevitable by-product of "real talk" among more than eight hundred members, but this appeal to an undefined set of values draws boundaries around what can be discussed.

This discursive boundary making took on a technical dimension when, after the previously mentioned question about cultural appropriation was later deemed offensive, Jasmine banned the member who posed the question and changed the group's privacy settings to require moderators to prescreen all posts prior to their publication. The Facebook group platform does not provide any mechanisms through which members can challenge moderators' choices to censor posts or ban users. Moderators are not democratically elected; rather, a Facebook group's founder becomes the default moderator and she can grant moderator status to any other members of her choosing, who, in turn, may grant moderator status to other members. Once a moderator chooses not to publish a post, it disappears from the Facebook platform altogether. Similarly, once a moderator chooses to remove a member from the group, that member will not be able to find the group through Facebook's search function, cutting her off from a potentially valuable source of support. Banned members can attempt to make amends with moderators via direct messages on Facebook, but these, too, can be blocked. As such, Facebook's group platform is not conducive to the democratic values or horizontal organizing traditionally favored by feminist activists (Freeman, 1972). Each moderator has complete control over the group and members must ultimately rely on moderators to foster safety within the group.

Through their technological and social practices, moderators encourage discussion while also protecting members from certain types of content, making the Girl Army safe space simultaneously open to but limiting of discourse, just as it is both safe but unsafe, inclusive but exclusive. The Girl Army safe space would not exist without the boundaries members establish to guard group access and regulate group interactions, but these boundaries also paradoxically reify the very social inequities Girl Army, as a feminist community, aims to transform. Like all safe spaces, the group is always already incomplete and imperfect, and the structural constraints of the Facebook platform add new challenges to the process of safe-space cultivation. Still, the group's sociotechnical practices for building and maintaining a networked safe space point to the obstacles marginalized users face in more public arenas while also modeling more empowering practices of online discourse and engagement.

My interviewees reported that zines enabled freer expression than digital platforms. As demonstrated by the variety of topics, aesthetics, and forms that characterizes the genre, zines offer creators an outlet for open expression, free of censorship, limitations, and interruptions. "Zines are a medium where it is easy to express ideas without (much) fear of repercussion, or without bending to outside influence," Moose Lane explained, "This makes it a good medium for feminists to express personal experiences, stories, theories, etc." (personal communication, March 29, 2016). With the zinester as author, editor, and producer, she subverts the producer/consumer binary and is not beholden to filter her work through the perspectives and expectations of anyone else. Adelaide Barton's gendered experiences as a woman zinester illustrate that this is an especially important affordance for feminist media-makers: "There's something about the expression of a zine which doesn't allow for interruptions. I feel that as a woman, I've been socialized to tolerate interruptions, even when it results in me not being able to finish articulating my point" (personal communication, April 6, 2016). While, as Moose Lane suggested, sharing personal stories on social media often "feels like shouting into the void," zinesters described feeling as if their audience, however small, actually listened to what they have to say (personal communication, March 29, 2016). As Adelaide Barton explains to the uninitiated in her zine about zines, You Should Know about Zines, "It's not easy to 'spam' zines, so folks are more likely to actually read them and consider what they have to say."

The materiality of zines enables this uninterrupted freedom of expression. Zines, unlike digitally mediated expressions, are not easily traceable back to their authors, granting zinesters the option to publish under true anonymity. As Dee, a member of Permanent Wave Philly, explained, "With zines, you have a little more control than the internet. Google is a helpful tool, and also a very hurtful tool. There are things that you can write about in zines, various hard things, that you don't want Google-able, that you don't want associated with your name" (personal communication, May 24, 2015). Zines, as ephemera, are temporary and potentially anonymous material artifacts, providing zinesters an outlet for deeply personal stories and the freedom to experiment with feminist identities and theories without worrying about damage to their future reputations. The genre's materiality also makes it difficult to troll or harass zinesters. It is precisely zines' intrinsically limited audience that makes the genre so attractive to feminists in an age where reaching large audiences is easier than ever but often comes at the cost of harassment, violent threats, and hate speech. In Adelaide Barton's experience, "Zines don't really provide a platform for abusive comment sections. Anyone who wants to harass a feminist zine-maker must put in more effort to do so, and do so in a way that is not immediately attached to their zine" (personal communication, April 6, 2016).

Zines, as accessible DIY media that operate outside of both market-place logic and sociopolitical constraints, enable the invention and circulation of counterdiscourses that might otherwise find no outlet within commercial media. Almost all of my participants described zines as affording them more authentic, intimate, or personal expressions than other media outlets. According to Moose Lane, for example, the internet "tends to reward short pieces or snippets, where zines can really be as long as you want" (Moose Lane, personal communication, March 29, 2016). Similarly, Kerri Radley observed that "Digital expression is much looser and less controlled, more exhibitionist and a curated expression of the self. Zines are more intimate and truer to the self" (personal communication, April, 19 2016). The medium also grants authors greater flexibility when it comes to incorporating more personal touches into the design of zines. As Candice Johnson, a Permanent Wave Philly member, explained, the materiality of zines offers a degree of personalization not readily accessible through digital platforms: "There's more of a human imprint on a zine, because you can see the way that they chose to type it and design it, whether it's collage or there's doodles and drawings and stuff. It feels personal, and its tangible, so you can have it and refer back to it and keep it in a collection" (personal communication, May 24, 2015). The unfiltered, slow, low-risk, hands-on process of zine production lends itself to personal meditations one might not otherwise share publicly. The topics considered across my interviewees' zines attest to the medium's intimate nature: personal experiences with street harassment, disability, sexism in academia, menstruation, sexual health, gender identity, familial relationships, trauma, and more all find an outlet in their handcrafted booklets.

Free from digital surveillance, online harassment, the capitalist value of fast production and consumption, and the approval or resources of a commercial host, zines offer feminists an unrestricted and unregulated medium for expression. While limited in reach and impact, for feminist community builders, zines offer a safer, more empowering alternative to digital media platforms, where violent threats and hate speech continue to suppress marginalized voices. If, as Couldry (2012) argues, media are practices that emerge in response to users' needs within a particular context, zine-making practices supplement feminists' digital media repertoire with a networked safe space free of the harassment and vitriol that has characterized web 2.0 platforms. Zines' resurgence comes at a time when feminists are seeking alternatives to digital media platforms, where violent threats and hate speech continue to suppress marginalized voices.

While at a smaller scale than both Girl Army and the zine community, Permanent Wave Philly developed a number of thoughtful practices for empowering marginalized voices. When successful, Permanent Wave Philly's tactics for centering marginalized voices throughout their organizational process created platforms for punk music artists and fans sidelined within the broader DIY scene and the public at large. Throughout my fieldwork, bands and audience members frequently thanked PWP for organizing events that highlighted underrepresented voices and that offered freedom of expression, away from the aggression and sexism they had come to expect at more typical DIY shows.

In line PWP's emphasis on process over product, however, the collective's most transformative work happened off stage and outside the public eye, where members worked together to offer one another opportunities for creative control otherwise unavailable within the DIY scene. Members frequently spoke of the empowering experience of coming up with an idea for an event, pitching it to the collective, and bringing it to fruition with, in Jenny's words, "the power of Permanent Wave" on your side. Prior to joining PWP, most members had never planned their own house show before, let alone a public event. In a music scene that offers little room for artists and organizers who are not white men, the ability to flex creative control over a house show was exhilarating:

> Definitely for me in the beginning, that felt really powerful, because I felt that you had to have some kind of magical authority to put together an event and actually have people go to it, oh my God. So, when I first started putting on shows with Permanent Wave, yeah, it definitely felt, I felt, powerful in a situation where I usually feel more powerless in the world. (personal communication, May 24, 2015)

Throughout my fieldwork, I often witnessed PWP's more seasoned bookers encourage novices to take the lead on a show, offering them assistance and advice along the way. Successfully hosting a show with the support of the group gave members a sense of self-confidence that they carried with them into their everyday lives.

Beyond planning shows together, PWP members also cultivated a community where members could openly discuss their experiences with gender-based oppression, especially sexism in the DIY scene. "If I didn't have this group, where we meet every couple weeks to rant after every show, I don't know what I would do," Dee told me in an interview. Members often began meetings sharing stories of frustration from the most recent "guy punk" house show, or outside the scene, their latest run-in with a street harasser or a sexist coworker. The "safer space" policy of PWP's shows applied to its meetings as well; wherever members convened, they offered one another a counterpublic sphere where they could give voice to these experiences and offer one another the reminder that they were not alone in their struggles. When new members attended meetings for the first time, they were welcomed with open arms and treated as friends. Every meeting began with group introductions, which almost always included an icebreaker members refer to as "Rose, Bud, Thorn"; each attendee shared something positive that happened to them recently, something they were looking forward to, and something that had been troubling them. With anywhere from four to ten people at a meeting, the process could take upwards of thirty minutes, but like consensus-based decision-making, this opportunity to share personal stories openly was part of PWP's community-building and maintenance practice. In its ideal form, the PWP collective provided members with a counterpublic safe space, where they found political agency and solidarity among a group of activists and artists who shared a common set of experiences and goals.

But "acting with intentionality" to center marginalized voices and foster open expression requires a great deal of time, energy, and patience, which can become a challenge for activists juggling the work of community-building with a day job and other responsibilities. As Dee told me in an interview, "This is not any of our main thing. It's just not. It's not our job. We're not getting paid to do this." After instituting their "Extended Mission" following the 2015 PhilaMOCA show, Permanent Wave Philly successfully hosted several events, but the effort required to live up to their ideals was often strenuous. Members began drifting back to old habits, allowing those with the most time to take charge without the group's consent, which inevitably led to internal disputes. By the fall of 2016, most members stopped attending meetings altogether. In early 2017, reluctant to officially end the group, PWP members decided to go on "hiatus," ending their listserv correspondence and engagement with the DIY scene.

Permanent Wave Philly's six-year run offers important lessons for feminist community builders in the digital age. While they struggled to live up to their ideals, collective members' efforts to grow a listserv into a feminist community that "acted with intentionality" illustrate the relational work required to cultivate safe spaces, online and off. As Dee told me in an interview, "The important part is that we try. It's not that we always accomplish that, but that's our intention, and that really matters. . . . When we mess up, we want to do better. We try to reevaluate the situation. . . . We try to make sure that if something went wrong, it's better for next time." PWP's resolve to be reflexive, to dissect and improve their organizing tactics until they aligned with their intersectional values, serves as a reminder that safe space communities are not fixed objects, but collective projects that require constant maintenance and tireless commitment.

MOVING TOWARD *SAFER* FEMINIST SPACES

Safe space communities have long played a key role in the tactical repertoire of U.S. feminist movements. But within our contemporary media landscape, where public and openly accessible digital platforms for expression and deliberation abound, the closed-off enclave has taken on new relevance for feminist activists. As I argue in the previous chapter, contemporary U.S. feminists have, with great fervor and success, adapted highly visible networked protest forms like hashtag activism to suit their goals and values. However, the same social media platforms that have launched viral campaigns like #MeToo into global movements for gender justice have also given rise to a largely unchecked culture of networked misogyny, whose proponents subject anyone who is not a conservative, white, cisgender, heterosexual male to backlash, harassment, and violent threats (Banet-Weiser, 2018a; Banet-Weiser & Miltner, 2016). In a 2014 piece for the *Pacific Standard*, feminist journalist Amanda Hess cites sociologist Zygmunt Bauman to argue that while men surf the web as "tourists," freely moving from one site to the next in search of new experiences, harassment displaces users with gendered, racialized, and sexualized bodies as "vagabonds . . . pushed and pulled through mean streets where they could never hope to settle down." The three communities under study in this chapter—a secret feminist Facebook group, the feminist zine network, a grassroots feminist arts collective—provide desperately needed safe spaces where women and other marginalized groups can not only "settle down," but feel protected and uplifted. By bringing, to again borrow the Riot Grrrl mantra, *girls to the front*, these communities cultivate spaces that explicitly recognize the ways in which white male supremacy operates and develop alternative, more empowering ways of being, online and off. While their particular practices vary, each community draws on the social and technical affordances of digital media platforms to construct and maintain boundaries that filter out harassment, prioritize marginalized voices, and encourage free and open expression. Through their example, these communities help us imagine what a feminist internet might look like.

At the same time, however, these three case studies also illustrate that certain paradoxes characterize safe spaces. These paradoxes are magnified for intersectional feminists seeking to build safe, inclusive communities in the digital age. Girl Army, for example, purports to offer safety for women and nonbinary individuals, who often face threats of violence for expressing themselves in public spaces and on the internet, but because the group is hosted on a corporately owned social media platform, moderators cannot completely guarantee the safety and privacy of Girl Army members. Permanent Wave Philly and the feminist zine community both describe themselves as inclusive spaces, where media makers sidelined in mainstream commercial industries can enjoy creative agency, but the amount of countercultural capital and digital media literacy required to know about and enter these spaces renders them somewhat *ex*clusive. Similarly, while each of the three communities under study offers an outlet for open expression that is otherwise unavailable, both their internal principles and external boundaries restrict the flow of free speech. Girl Army moderators, for instance, ban members who ask "feminism 101 questions" and the materiality and limited print run of zines means that feminist zinesters often reach only a small audience. And, while the mission of all three communities is to center marginalized voices, each paradoxically risks contributing to the marginalization of those voices by carving out a siloed space for them.

Safe but unsafe, inclusive but exclusive, open to but limiting of discourse, the three communities I studied in this chapter demonstrate that feminist safe spaces are always incomplete, excluding some to include others, and imperfect, potentially reifying the inequities feminism aims to transform. These paradoxes have haunted feminist safe spaces across their history in the United States, but the digital environment raises new questions for feminist community builders: What does safety look like online? How do social media platforms constrain or enhance activists' ability to cultivate safe space communities online? What impact can enclaved, digitally networked communities have on more visible, mainstream publics? How can we begin reshaping public-facing platforms to reflect the values of safety and inclusion embedded in feminist communities?

The answers to these questions will vary alongside the specific goals, context, forms, and practices of the feminist community in question. Taken together, however, my three case studies suggest that when it comes to cultivating safe space communities, activists should follow Permanent Wave Philly's lead and instead strive for *safer* spaces, always working from the assumption that no space can ever be truly safe for all participants at all times. The comparison implied in the term *"safer* spaces" between the community at hand and the broader public sphere clarifies the relational nature of safe spaces as living concepts that require constant maintenance, rather than closed objects with fixed but unspoken principles. Framing networked feminist communities as ongoing *projects*, conducted in negotiation between activists' values and the digital community-building tools at their disposal, encourages a more reflexive safer space praxis, one that works to account for a community's exclusions and shortcomings. This relational, processual approach to building communities will be integral to the long-term sustainability of do-it-ourselves feminists' extra-institutional activist projects and movements.

As Miranda Joseph (2002) argues, "To invoke community is to immediately raise questions of belonging and power" (p. xxiii). Feminist activists must constantly revisit these questions as they build their own communities while navigating the political affordances and limitations of digital media platforms.

5 Strength in a Feminist Present

I started this book caught between the hopeful swell of editorials heralding 2017 as the "Year of Women" and the harsh reality of President Donald Trump's regressive policy efforts throughout his first year in office. As the years waged on, the disconnect between media declarations of women's time and institutional rollbacks of women's rights grew sharper. In 2016, commentators grappling with Trump's election looked toward 2020 as an inevitable turning point, when the hundreds of thousands of protesters who took to the streets for the Women's March would take to the ballot box. Indeed, their predictions, in some respects, came true. Thanks to record numbers of voters, Trump lost the 2020 election to former vice president Joseph Biden and his running mate, Senator Kamala Harris, who would make history as the first woman and first woman of color to hold the office of the vice presidency.

That said, to call 2020 the "Year of Women," as commentators continued to do throughout the election cycle (e.g., Conroy, 2020; Hais and Winograd, 2020; Kovan, 2020; Seib, 2020; Woodall, 2020; Zillman and Hinchliffe, 2020), would be to overlook the struggles and losses marginalized people suffered that year. As the COVID-19 pandemic tore through communities around the world, women and families of color in the United States, particularly Black families, experienced especially high coronavirus cases and deaths (CDC, 2020). People of color, who are over-represented in essential frontline service industry jobs, faced increased risk of COVID-19 exposure, often without the benefits of medical cover-age or paid sick leave (CDC, 2020). The virus's economic toll compounded its negative health effects. Women across demographics were four times more likely than men to be forced out of their jobs to look after children and family members as schools and care centers closed (Schneider, Hsu, and Horsley, 2020). When businesses shut down and unemployment rates soared, people of color dealt with disproportionately high rates of job loss, with little social net or government aid to support their basic needs (CDC, 2020). On top of the devastation of COVID-19, in 2020, police violence rocked Black communities, continuing a decades-long trend. The May 25, 2020, death of George Floyd after a police officer knelt on his neck for nearly nine minutes sparked a series of protests and uprisings across the country. Meanwhile, Trump refused to condemn white supremacy and his followers staged violent counterprotests in his name (Lang et al., 2020; McCammon, 2020). Adding to feelings of despair and fear on the left, September 2020 brought the death of feminist icon and Supreme Court Justice Ruth Bader Ginsburg, along with the successful nomination of conservative Justice Amy Coney Barrett as her replacement. The court's shift further rightward seemed likely to spell the end of nationwide legal abortion, anti-discrimination laws, voting rights, and more (Cohen, 2020). Even with a Biden/Harris administration on the horizon, by the end of 2020, women's futures, the futures of marginalized communities, and the future of feminist policies felt as bleak as ever.

Despite *all of this*—a Trump presidency, a pandemic, a surge in racial unrest, a recession, an increasingly conservative judicial branch—feminist activists, discourses, and movements remained energized. In fact, femi-nism became more popular than ever. More women ran for Congress in 2020 than in any other election cycle (Conroy and Rakich, 2020), many on explicitly feminist platforms, leading to the most diverse Congress in history (Marcos, 2020). According to a 2020 Pew Research Center study conducted to mark the one-hundredth anniversary of white women's suf-frage, more than six-in-ten U.S. women say the label "feminist" describes them "very" or "somewhat" well (Barroso, 2020), marking an all-time high for women's alignment with the F-word. Meanwhile, the feminist media moment that bubbled to the surface in 2014 outlasted any viral trend to become a pop culture staple. The market for feminist topics and angles continues to grow, with young writers and activists carving out new spaces for their voices in mainstream media (Schlack, 2017).

Social movement research has long suggested that movements are most likely to effectively mobilize and gain supporters during periods with high degrees of "political opportunity," when windows for intervention or advancement open up within state institutions (Meyer and Minkoff, 2004; Tilly and Tarrow, 2015). From this perspective, 2020 and the years leading up to it should have been a period of low opportunity and high burnout for feminist movements, as their foothold within the highest levels of government became increasingly unsteady and as activists struggled against the compounding weight of global health, economic, and social crises. Parallel times of conservative, reactionary politics saw U.S. feminist movements enter periods of "abeyance," adapting to hostile climates by stepping away from the public eye and shifting focus internally to preserve movement communities and values (Rupp and Taylor, 1987). What, then, could explain the popularity, vibrancy, and influence of U.S. feminisms in this difficult moment?

The answer is rooted in a feminist groundswell that has been building steadily for decades in the United States, despite the rise of the new right and antifeminist backlash and an overall decline in collective action. Drawing on an array of media tools and platforms, contemporary feminists have been engaged in a revitalization project, rebuilding feminist actions and spaces for the twenty-first century. The current generation of activists has moved away from the formally structured movements that characterized previous waves of U.S. feminism and toward the *do-it-ourselves* ethos of *networked feminism*. This highly mediated organizing logic enables a diversity of people to join and shape collective actions, free from the gatekeeping functions of formal leaders or the entrenched exclusions of institutionalized politics. At the same time, as the contradictions between "The Year of Women" and the Time of Trump suggests, without the resources of formal organizations, networked feminism faces a wide range of obstacles when it comes to creating lasting social and political transformations. These challenges include, but are not limited to, violent backlash; activist burnout; commercial co-optation; movement sustain-ability; and, consequently, difficulty changing institutions, laws, and poli-cies. At this critical juncture, activists' networked media practices have left feminist movements simultaneously reinvigorated *and* precarious.

Throughout this book, I explored the questions this dilemma raises: how are activists negotiating between the affordances and shortcomings of networked feminism to craft an activist praxis that reflects their values and responds to the challenges of the current context? Why do networked media figure so centrally in contemporary feminists' political visions? And what are the implications of feminists' networked media practices for the long-term shape and reach of feminism, social movements, and political activism? Existing scholarship at the intersections of both gender and media and movements and media presents important insights into the structure of political opportunities and constraints surrounding net-worked feminism and offers detailed case studies of individual feminist media campaigns and their outcomes. Missing, however, is a theoretical framework built around actual activists' agency, perspectives, and expe-riences that sheds light on the relationship between feminists' political visions and their networked media tactics and, in turn, creates space to reflect on activists' shared triumphs and struggles.

In this multimodal qualitative study of networked feminism, I have approached feminist media as *political practices*, informed by activists' goals, contexts, and resources, to better understand what feminists are doing with media and why. Through a practitioner-centered methodology grounded in six case studies, I have explored three key types of networked feminist practices: networked feminist organizing, networked feminist visibility campaigns, and networked feminist community building. An overarching media *praxis*, or embodied relationship between feminists' political goals and media tactics, connects all three types of practices. I call this praxis *do-it-ourselves feminism* (DIOF). Networked feminist practices vary in form and content but they share a common DIY ethos, a collectively held set of normative assumptions that, with a little media savvy, anyone can build their own feminist actions and spaces from the ground up, regardless of previous organizing experience or available resources. Like other DIY projects, DIOF is an accessible, bottom-up, extra-institutional practice whose practitioners tactically "make do" (de Certeau, 1984) with whatever materials are on hand to quickly address a problem or need. But unlike some do-it-*yourself* projects, do-it-*ourselves* feminism is a collective activist praxis, whose campaigns may start with the actions of one person with a social media account and an idea for a protest, but grow to include dozens, hundreds, or, at the global level, thousands or even millions of participants. DIOF represents a paradigm shift in the organizational logic behind U.S. feminism that reverses the typical trajectory of movements. Now, instead of having to build organizational capacity prior to launching a major action, with large audiences only a few keyboard strokes away, the action happens first and the capacity-building may follow later. The result is protest actions that enable the collective articulation of dissent from a diversity of subject positions, rather than a singular, unified message filtered through an individual leader or organization. While a similarly networked mode of activism can be found across other social movements, DIOF represents a distinctly *feminist* praxis, shaped to embody feminist values and respond to the particular political challenges facing feminist activists.

When it comes to organizing feminist protests, the DIOF praxis can be found across actions of different scales. The Women's March on Washington (WMOW) began after one person—a retired grandmother living in Hawaii—created and shared an event on Facebook. Her mediated outreach eventually sparked the wave of global street protests that took place around the world on Trump's Inauguration Day. Similarly, Philadelphia's March to End Rape Culture (MTERC), a local protest event that draws a crowd of about five hundred to one thousand people annually, grew out of the international SlutWalk Movement, which started when two activists used social media accounts to mobilize protesters in Toronto after a police officer blamed rape victims for their own assaults at a university assembly. But the DIOF praxis extends well beyond the initial sparking of a protest event. The same do-it-ourselves sensibility guides the logistical planning and execution of an action. The ad-hoc planning committee behind WMOW, for example, developed and revised the movement's mission statement in response to feedback and critiques dispersed networks of activists circulated through social media. The DIO ethos is deeply embedded in the organizing team behind MTERC, who have purposefully avoided formalizing as a structured organization or nonprofit in order to ensure broad participation and creative freedom. Every year, MTERC organizers start from scratch and, through online outreach and fundraising events, promote the protest and pool the resources necessary to host the march. At both events, protesters rally together under a variety of rallying cries, collectively representing their individual experiences and concerns while also standing in solidarity with one another. Whether mobilized at the global or local level, do-it-ourselves feminism draws on everyday media tools to create openly accessible outlets for personalized protest expressions. In turn, this organizational paradigm produces more inclusive feminist movements and campaigns, free from the structural inequities ingrained in organizational bureaucracies or institutional politics, reflecting DIO feminists' core guiding value of intersectionality.

The same participatory, self-starting logic underpins feminist campaigns to make visible everyday social injustices that, like sexual harassment and assault, are otherwise normalized into invisibility. Through networked visibility tactics like hashtag feminism, activists engage in contentious performances that, following the classic U.S. feminist mantra, "make the personal political" by pushing it into the realm of public deliberation. The networking functions of the hashtag form bridge the individual with the collective; campaign participants can add their own experience or concerns to the hashtag, personalizing their expressions of dissent while also participating in a solidary collective action by virtue of using the same hashtag as others. In the case of #MeToo, for example, hundreds of thousands of sexual violence survivors shared their personal narratives. While each story was unique, activists were connected through their collective participation in the hashtag's overarching narrative frame—the phrase "Me, too"—which explicitly emphasized the widespread nature of sexual violence. Other movements have used hashtag activism and similar networked visibility tactics. But for U.S. feminists, who historically have worked to expose the ways in which power operates in everyday life, the practice helps reframe seemingly private experiences of injustice as public issues that require public responses. Moreover, the open accessibility of a Twitter hashtag, built into a social media platform that many peruse on a daily basis, brings a broader diversity of voices into visibility campaigns, enabling more intersectional feminist actions in the process.

Behind the scenes, in closed-off spaces where activists gather to connect, regroup, and plan actions, feminists also use networked media to build their own communities. Together, my case studies of the Girl Army Facebook group, the national feminist zine network, and the grassroots music and arts collective Permanent Wave Philly speak to the do-it-ourselves logic scaffolding contemporary feminist communities. In each case, feminists use media tools, such as Facebook or email listservs, or engage in collective media-making projects, such as producing a zine or hosting a punk show, to create enclaved safe spaces, purposefully closed off from the "networked misogyny" (Banet-Weiser and Miltner, 2016) that plagues public-facing media sites. Whereas, in previous generations, feminist community spaces were structured through a web of organizations, across these field sites, groups of otherwise unaffiliated activists who shared a common goal or need came together to construct their own communities, using networked media as their building blocks. Within the boundaries of these spaces outside the public eye, feminists can foster communities that prefigure their values, establishing social practices that center marginalized voices and encourage the open expression of experiences silenced or ignored within dominant discourse. While the search for community has long been a goal for U.S. feminists, in both the current digital media landscape and political climate, women, trans and nonbinary people, people of color, and queer people face especially high levels of harassment and violent threats. At precisely the same moment when public platforms for self-expression and political dissent abound, private feminist communities, where members can seek support and talk openly, are more important than ever. The DIO communities studied here suggest that networked media offer feminists new opportunities for community building at both the local and global levels.

For today's activists, DIO feminism updates traditional feminist values, like personal politics and community, while also incorporating more contemporary goals, such as intersectional analysis and inclusion, and responding to current challenges, including the need to revitalize collective politics and circumvent networked misogyny. The do-it-ourselves media praxis, however, also suffers from a number of shortcomings that undermine all three types of networked media practices.

Chief among them is the question of sustainability. Within each type of networked feminist practice, burnout, attention, and co-optation are

major issues. The bottom-up, participatory nature of do-it-ourselves organizing allows a more diverse range of activists to become involved in protest mobilization and enables a greater degree of creative freedom over the
shape a protest takes, producing movements that, in form and content,
embody the feminist value of intersectionality. At the same time, without
the resources of a formal organization, the labor required to mobilize a
protest can wholly consume activists' time and energy. This is the case, for
example, with the MTERC organizing team, which has struggled to maintain a stable membership over the years. These same features of DIOF
also empower feminists to build communities that live out their political
visions, but, as my case study of Permanent Wave Philly illustrates, the
effort required to do so can strain activists and even lead to in-fighting,
both of which threaten the longevity of the group.

Similarly, when it comes to networked visibility campaigns and hashtag
feminism, activists use social media to quickly mobilize protest actions
and invite a broad range of participation, laying the groundwork for viral
waves of dissent like #MeToo. But publicly sharing personal stories on a
globally networked stage can be both risky and traumatic, endangering the
marginalized groups the tactic is meant to uplift. Through their mediated,
personalizable nature and emphasis on visibility, these networked protest
campaigns scale quickly and attain mainstream media attention easily. But
they are also easily coopted by commercial interests, as seen in celebrities'
and corporate entities' use of #MeToo as a branding strategy. Moreover,
while the months-long discourse that unfolded in the wake of #MeToo
stands as an important exception, hashtag networks can disperse just as
quickly as they came together, fading from public discourse before ever
developing the capacity necessary for long-term struggle. The strengths of
the do-it-ourselves praxis ultimately undermine its staying power.

Networked feminists' turn away from formally structured organizations
facilitates more inclusive movements and communities. Their refusal to
engage with institutional politics, however, raises concerns about contemporary feminism's ability to make the policy reforms necessary to push
toward a more equitable future in the United States. MTERC organizers,
for example, frequently use the march's official social media account to
raise awareness about legislative issues or encourage followers to contact
their representatives. But throughout my fieldwork, organizers did not

make formalized efforts to lobby for better sexual violence legislation in the Philadelphia area. In contrast, the WMOW planning committee has formalized into a highly structured "National Team," which has organized and funded efforts to support women candidates for local and national office. Their formalization efforts, however, have led to a less accessible movement structure and have raised criticisms about the activists who turned the global movement into a professional career. Do-it-ourselves practitioners have struggled to strike a balance between the openness of remaining informal and the often-exclusionary business of engaging in institutional politics.

Lastly, the do-it-ourselves praxis is encumbered by the structural constraints of the corporately owned social media platforms its practitioners rely on. Sites like Facebook and Twitter were not engineered with feminists' intersectional values or organizing needs in mind. Instead, they aim to reach the broadest user bases possible, so as to access and monetize the largest sample of user data possible. This disconnect between feminists' social justice goals and platforms' emphasis on extraction and profits raised a number of troubling issues for activists. Throughout my fieldwork, safety emerged as one of the largest. In several of the case studies taken up in this book, activists struggled to protect one another from violent harassment and backlash. Misogynist Twitter trolls harassed WMOW attendees and threatened survivors who posted #MeToo with rape. Both instances serve as a reminder that the same platforms that have raised U.S. feminism's profile have also facilitated the wave of "popular misogyny" (Banet-Weiser, 2015b, 2018b) that carried Trump to the Oval Office. Platform safety issues also plague closed-off feminist communities. In Girl Army, for example, there was little moderators could do to truly keep their safe space "safe," as members with ulterior motives took screen captures of highly personal posts and shared them with others outside the group.

Beyond participants' safety, in several cases, social media platforms exacerbated members' struggle to develop decision-making and accountability practices within otherwise informal groups. Facebook grants group moderators unilateral control over the group, leaving Girl Army members powerless to push back on moderators' choices to delete posts or ban members. In Permanent Wave Philly, where membership is defined through enrollment in the collective's email listserv, activists struggled to develop the group's collective structure and prevent individual members from making decisions on behalf of the group.

DIO feminists' reliance on digital media also raises concerns about the inclusivity of contemporary feminist movements and spaces. Networked feminist activism might allow for a diverse range of voices to shape movement mission statements or join hashtag campaigns, but participation is predicated on access to and literacy in the technologies that facilitate these actions. What's more, as activists' critiques of #MeToo illustrated, despite feminists' tactical appropriation of new participatory media platforms, old media patterns of exclusion often win the day. As the survivors' hashtagged stories went viral, commercial news media outlets focused audience attention almost exclusively on white celebrities and public figures, erasing survivors of color and working-class survivors from view, despite the disproportionate impact sexual violence has on their lives. While do-it-ourselves feminism is characterized by a named commitment to intersectional analysis and organizing practices, in reality, activists who are not white or cisgender are often left to movements' margins. This aspirational intersectionality risks overshadowing networked feminism's ongoing struggles to decenter whiteness in its movements and communities.

The affinity networks of feminist campaigns and communities can also produce echo chambers, silo marginalized voices, and wall movements off from the very audiences activists are seeking to address. While news media coverage of networked visibility campaigns and street protests can help mitigate this shortcoming somewhat, the political uniformity of a feminist hashtag and closed-off nature of a feminist Facebook group can limit feminism's reach. Activists have to find ways to account for limitations of their networked media practices, while also taking advantage of their affordances.

But this book is about more than the affordances and limitations of networked feminist activism. The stories from the field collected here demonstrate that do-it-ourselves feminists are constantly negotiating among their activist values, the challenges engrained in the current context, and the structural constraints embedded in their networked media tools to develop and refine an activist media praxis that puts their political vision into action. This dynamic is perhaps most evident in my case study of

#MeToo, in which participants developed *performance maintenance strategies*, enacting care labor for survivors who chose to share their stories, correcting campaign erasures, and working to maintain narrative control over the hashtag. But a similar emphasis on reflexivity and revision can be found elsewhere. The WMOW planning committee publicly revisited their "Unity Principles" following critiques from activists standing at various intersections of difference. When infighting indicated that the groups' informal nature had led to a failure to articulate shared values, both the MTERC organizing team and Permanent Wave Philly paused to collectively develop mission statements. Feminist zinesters use public-facing social media sites to expand the accessibility and reach of their closed-off community. And in the months after my fieldwork ended and I shared my findings, Girl Army moderators put their heads together to develop a less hierarchical mode of decision-making despite the Facebook platform's shortcomings, reevaluated their exclusion of trans men from the group, and changed the group's name to reflect the inclusive community they aspire to be.

These are just a few examples of the creative tactics contemporary feminists use to push against the structural constraints of both networked activism and social media platforms and strengthen their practices. Their ongoing reflections and efforts demonstrate that while do-it-ourselves feminism may be precarious, it is also a complex, interactional, and recursive praxis, always in progress and constantly evolving, even while activists also juggle the everyday labors of organizing for social justice.

IMPLICATIONS FOR THE STUDY AND THE PRACTICE OF NETWORKED ACTIVISM

The dynamics of do-it-ourselves feminism highlighted throughout this book offer a number of important take-aways for social movement theory, media activism research, new media studies, and feminist media scholarship—four fields that converge through the study of networked feminism.

For social movement theory, the do-it-ourselves feminist media repertoire productively challenges and expands conventional definitions of "politics" and "activism." Much existing social movements scholarship emphasizes state-targeted, public-facing performances of dissent. Networked feminists' collective actions expose the political dynamics of everyday life beyond the walls of state institutions, and their behind-the-scenes community-building work illustrates that the fight for social justice does not begin and end with the protest.

The processual nature of do-it-ourselves feminism points to the need for scholars of movements and media to treat networked activism as a media *practice*, not simply media content, and one with historical precedents and a repertoire of forms that are constantly evolving. Analyses of networked activism as either effective or ineffective overlook crucial components of the much larger picture that is activist media practices. When activist media, digital and otherwise, are framed as practices, a more expansive view of media as complex arenas for political participation becomes possible. The media-as-practice approach helps point toward activists' historical struggles to negotiate between their political values and their media tactics. Similarly, centering contemporary practitioners' voices in the study of emerging media activism forms produces analyses that hold at once both the affordances and limitations of these new modes of protest. Rather than the either/or assumptions of the "techno-optimist" versus "techno-pessimist" debates, this *both/and* approach pushes beyond the overly simplistic narratives of techno-determinism and moves scholarship toward more robust theories of how practitioners navigate the double-edged nature of networked activism.

Do-it-ourselves feminism offers a related set of lessons for the field of new media studies. Attention to the affordances and limitations of networked feminism and the strategies feminists use to juggle both can expand critical analyses of the structural constraints built into social media platforms. In light of the lack of alternatives with comparable reach and accessibility, activists are developing agentive strategies to navigate platforms' shortcomings without compromising their values. Embedded in their media practices are instructive visions of more empowering digital media platforms.

The media-as-practice approach taken here also highlights gaps in the growing body of feminist media studies scholarship focused on networked feminism. With few exceptions, a great deal of existing scholarship on networked tactics like hashtag feminism, feminist blogging, and online feminist communities takes up media content as its object of analysis. This leaves core components of the feminist media repertoire understudied. If I had not taken a multi-sited, ethnographic approach and "followed the people" (Marcus, 1995), I would not have had access to the networked organizing practices behind the March to End Rape Culture or the mediated safe space practices of inward-facing feminist communities. This practitioner-centered approach also pushed me to home in on #MeToo participants' tweeted reflections on the campaign, highlighting a key tactic—performance maintenance strategies—missing from research on hashtag feminism. Future work in the field should continue to document feminist media campaigns while also grounding itself in feminist activists' perspectives to build a stronger theoretical toolkit for the study of networked feminism.

Above all, this study has implications for networked activists embedded in the everyday fight for social justice. If this sounds like you, the most important message to take away from this book is that you are not alone. Across the United States and around the world, there are countless other activists coping with similar obstacles. Like you, they are working to take advantage of internet technologies' many affordances while navigating their shortcomings. They are crafting a digital media praxis that aligns with their communities' values. They are facing the challenges of networked activism described throughout this book head-on and iterating on creative strategies for resistance and resilience. There has never been a more pressing time to use networked media to connect, collaborate, and learn from one another.

And as the case studies in this book suggest, when it comes to networked feminist activism, we still have a lot to learn. There exists a disconnect between the current feminist generation's emphasis on intersectionality as a key guiding value and the feminist organizing, protest, and community-building practices documented throughout the previous chapters. Feminist activism and discourse has reached an unprecedented degree of visibility, but there remains a disparity in whose voices, stories, and experiences are prioritized across the feminist media landscape. Repeatedly throughout my case studies, feminists of color and queer and trans feminists expressed feeling as if they were not included or valued within today's movements for gender justice. White feminists, myself among them, must revisit our understanding of intersectionality as an organizing *practice*, as an ongoing project in centering marginalized voices, following the lead of Black activists and activists of color, passing the mic, and taking a step back so that others may be heard.

There is also a gap between networked feminism's success in gaining widespread visibility and its ability to implement institutional changes. Feminist media activists have made exceptional strides in pushing gender justice issues into mainstream discourse. Where once feminist figures and topics were excluded from commercial media, today, they have firmly cemented their place within popular culture and discourse. It is difficult to understate the significance of feminism's media visibility and the role everyday media practitioners have played in creating this feminist media moment. Issues like sexual violence and reproductive justice are no longer taboo. Public figures and politicians with left-leaning constituents feel compelled to position themselves as feminists. We have new critical lenses that make visible everyday encounters with gender-based oppression, from street harassment to sexism in the workplace. At the same time, in the United States, key pieces of feminist legislation and policy gains, such as legal abortion and anti-discrimination laws, are in jeopardy. We must find ways to carve paths from cultural visibility to institutional impact. Many of the activists studied in this book know that the two go hand in hand—changing laws often requires changing hearts and minds. The current media environment's emphasis on attention and virality, however, puts us at risk of emphasizing the latter over the former.

Feminism's new visibility in U.S. media can also make it easy to avoid or ignore those who oppose feminist values and ideas. With popularity for feminism at an all-time high, it may seem as though we no longer need to engage with those who disagree with our perspectives. Plus, our media landscape makes it easier to stay within our own echo chambers and feedback loops than ever before. The result may be a false sense of security, as if feminism's visibility suggests that feminist politics reign supreme. While Trump's election blew the lid off of this perception, we have much work to do when it comes to reaching across party lines and beyond feminist networks. One statistic makes this painfully clear: in 2020, 55 percent of white women voted for Donald Trump, a two-point increase from 2016.

This suggests that while women's empowerment may be a topic du jour, most white women have a vested interest in disempowering marginalized women to protect their own privilege. Feminists, especially white feminists, must use what we have learned about effective media messaging to call out inequities among women and push opponents to confront their complicity while underscoring our collective struggles.

The trials and triumphs of the practitioners across my field sites suggest that, to sustain long-term struggles, networked activists must develop tactics for building movement capacities. Thanks to the internet, activists may no longer need a great deal of resources to launch global protest actions. They do, however, need to invest time and energy into learning how to best work together for social and political transformations that will uplift all marginalized communities. Inevitably, they fall short of this ideal, but do-it-ourselves feminists are engaged in this project as a work-in-progress. While they strive toward a feminist future, activists across social justice projects can find strength in the networked media practices they have crafted for this present moment. They have worked hard to negotiate between their feminist values and their digital tools and develop networked organizing practices that prefigure the world they seek to bring about. Through their creative and often audacious use of social media, DIO feminists spearhead new forms of protest actions, giving deeply rooted but often ignored issues like sexual violence new visibility and urgency. Their digitally networked communities demonstrate new, more empowering possibilities for social engagement online. Most importantly, they are willing to acknowledge and grapple with failure until their activist practices mirror their principles. The energy DIO feminists devote to, in Permanent Wave members' words, "acting with intentionality" models a feminist approach to collective action in the digital age for activists and advocates everywhere who see a need for social justice and dream of doing it themselves.

Notes

CHAPTER 1. HOPE FOR A FEMINIST FUTURE

1. Here, I am combining Downing's (2008) conceptualization of "media activism" with hooks's (2000) definition of "feminism."

2. Feminist activists and academics have used the wave metaphor to chronicle the history of U.S. feminist movements since the 1960s, with the fight for suffrage labeled as the first, the 1960s women's liberation movement as the second, and the contemporary generation as the third or even the fourth wave. Scholars have argued that the metaphor flattens the multiple trajectories of women's rights activism, whose many histories have unfolded simultaneously in communities across the country. In particular, the wave metaphor often centers white feminists, locating movement peaks only in moments when white feminists were most active and overlooking the work of Black feminists and feminists of color. See Hewitt (2012) for more on the history and debates surrounding the wave metaphor.

3. The 1980s shift within U.S. media culture toward the postfeminist sensibility of empowerment through self-determination was rooted in a parallel turn toward *neoliberalism* (Baer, 2016; Gill, 2007; Gill and Scharff, 2011). Neoliberalism is a political and economic philosophy that rejects the social welfare model of governance, favors free-market capitalism, and pursues policies that deregulate corporations, privatize public goods, and encourage competition in open markets (Harvey, 2007; Marwick, 2013). But neoliberalism extended far beyond specific

economic policies to, in David Harvey's (2007) words, "become hegemonic as a mode of discourse. It has pervasive effects on ways of thought to the point where it has become incorporated into the common-sense way many of us interpret, live in, and understand the world" (p. 3). Neoliberal discourse constructs the myth of the rational and self-interested economic actor with complete control over and, in turn, responsibility for her own life (Phipps, 2014). Neoliberalism, in other words, privileges private solutions to social and structural problems, obfuscating systems of power and, consequently, making social movements seem obsolete. While neoliberal discourse and policies pose major obstacles for any downwardly redistributive social movement, there exists an especially powerful resonance between postfeminism and neoliberalism (Gill and Scharff, 2011). Both emphasize individualism, choice, and agency at the expense of vocabularies for talking about social welfare, structural inequities, and collective politics (Gill, 2007; Gill and Scharff, 2011; Harvey, 2007; Marwick, 2013; McRobbie, 2004, 2008; Phipps, 2014; Tasker and Negra, 2007).

4. Here, I am drawing on Banet-Weiser's (2012) work on the "politics of ambivalence" (p. 211).

5. See Costanza-Chock (2020) for an in-depth look at the tensions between the design of internet platforms and the politics of liberatory social justice movements.

6. Feminist scholars have launched important critiques of the plausibility of feminist ethnographers' egalitarian goals. Judith Stacey's oft-cited 1988 article, "Can There Be a Feminist Ethnography?" questions the method's ability to mitigate the power imbalances between the researcher and the researched, arguing that "the appearance of greater respect for and equality with research participants afforded by feminist ethnography can make the potential for deeper forms of exploitation" (p. 22). In a 1990 article published (unintentionally) under the same title, Lila Abu-Lughod critiqued feminist ethnographers for often assuming the existence of a universal and romanticized women's experience or standpoint, erasing important differences among women, including the researcher and her participants. Other scholars have charged that privileged feminist ethnographers' representations of subaltern groups often exoticize "the Other" or erroneously assume access to more marginalized individuals' subject positions (Borland, 2007; Schlock, 2013). That said, these critiques model the reflexivity built into the feminist ethnographic project in its ideal form. I have striven to incorporate the same throughout my research for this book.

CHAPTER 2. NETWORKED FEMINIST ORGANIZING

1. In addition to critiques of its whiteness, the SlutWalk movement has also faced critiques for its privileging of middle- to upper-class and Western women. See Hunt, 2018 for a detailed overview of intersectional analyses of SlutWalk.

2. Throughout this book, I used pseudonyms to protect participants' identities. Exceptions were made for some zine authors, who wanted to maintain attribution for their work.

3. See INCITE! (2007) for activists' perspectives on the shortcomings of nonprofit organizations when it comes to pursuing revolutionary political agendas.

CHAPTER 3. NETWORKED FEMINIST VISIBILITY

1. Portions of this chapter were previously published as: R. Clark-Parsons, "I See You, I Believe You, I Stand with You": #MeToo and the Performance of Networked Feminist Visibility. *Feminist Media Studies* 21(3), 362–380. They are reprinted here with permission from the publisher, Taylor & Francis Ltd.

2. Contrary to most journalistic coverage of the hashtag, Milano was not the originator of the hashtag component of the "me too" movement. Amy Siskind, president of the women's advocacy organization The New Agenda, started the hashtag campaign, #WomenWhoRoar on the morning of October 15, in response to Twitter suspending the account of actor Rose McGowan, a prominent voice in bringing Harvey Weinstein down. That afternoon, several people, the earliest including author and activist Nancy Gruver and attorney Careen Shannon, began tweeting #MeToo alongside #WomenWhoRoar to signal that they had faced sexual harassment or assault (Busch, 2017). Milano's tweet did not come until later that evening; however, her celebrity status and millions of followers played a pivotal role in amplifying #MeToo and catalyzing its global diffusion.

3. Studies have shown that users on Twitter are more likely to maintain public profiles than users on Facebook, Instagram, and other platforms (Griffith, 2020; Remy, 2019). This suggests a general understanding of Twitter as a platform designed to promote public visibility beyond users' personal social networks.

4. See *Feminist Media Studies* 14(6), 15(1), and 15(2) for essays documenting some of the earliest and most visible feminist hashtag campaigns. See also Bonilla and Rosa (2015) for a thorough overview of Twitter hashtags' forms and functions.

5. See Traister (2018) for an overview of the editorials #MeToo inspired.

6. Also see *Le Monde*, January 9, 2021, for a column produced by a collective of one hundred women protesting the #MeToo movement's concept of sexual aggression. https://www.lemonde.fr/idees/article/2018/01/09/nous-defendons -une-liberte-d-importuner-indispensable-a-la-liberte-sexuelle_5239134_3232 .html.

7. While all of the tweets captured in my sample were publicly available when archived, I recognize that #MeToo participants have not consented to publicizing their tweets and identities within other contexts beyond the Twitter platform. Throughout this chapter, I use pseudonyms in place of Twitter handles or omit

handles altogether. I also made minor alterations to participants' word choices, such that their tweets retain the same meanings but cannot be traced back to the authors through a search engine. Exceptions have been made in the cases of non-profit organizations, celebrities, and public figures.

CHAPTER 4. NETWORKED FEMINIST COMMUNITIES

1. Portions of this chapter were previously published as: R. Clark-Parsons, "Building a Digital Girl Army: The Cultivation of Feminist Safe Spaces Online," *New Media & Society*, 20, no. 6 (2018), 2125–2144. They are reprinted here with permission from the publisher, SAGE Publishing.

2. Portions of this chapter were previously published as: R. Clark-Parsons, "Feminist Ephemera in a Digital World: Theorizing Zines as Networked Feminist Practice," *Communication, Culture & Critique*, 10, no. 4 (2017), 557–573. They are reprinted here with permission from the publisher, Oxford University Press.

3. See Marcus (2010) for a historical overview of the Riot Grrrl movement and what bringing "girls to the front" looked like in practice.

4. Historians and linguists have disputed accounts that Truth said the words "Ain't I a woman?" in her speech at the 1851 Women's Rights Convention. The famous question is included in a transcript of the speech published by abolitionist Frances Gage more than a decade later in 1863. It is not present, however, in a transcript published a month after the convention by Marcus Robinson, a journalist who was present at the convention and who reviewed the transcript with Truth prior to publishing it. Historians have suggested that Gage altered the speech to falsely attribute a southern slave dialect to the Truth. See the Sojourner Truth Project (2021) for a comparison of the two transcripts.

5. This does not include private Facebook groups, which do not appear in Facebook searches, suggesting that the number of online feminist safe spaces hosted on Facebook is much higher.

6. Here, "NB" is an abbreviation for "nonbinary."

7. See Silberling, 2015 for more on Philadelphia's DIY scene and Lingel (2017) on DIY punk scenes as countercultural communities.

References

Alexander, J. C. (2004). Cultural pragmatics: Social performance between ritual and strategy. *Sociological Theory, 22*(4), 527–573.

Almukhtar, S., Gold, M., and Buchanan, L. (2018, February 8). After Weinstein: 71 men accused of sexual misconduct and their fall from power. *New York Times.* https://www.nytimes.com/interactive/2017/11/10/us/men-accused -sexual-misconduct-weinstein.html.

Anduiza, E., Cristancho, C., and Sabucedo, J. M. (2014). Mobilization through online social networks: The political protest of the indignados in Spain. *Information, Communication & Society, 17*(6), 750–764.

Annenberg Inclusion Initiative (2020). Inequality in 1,300 popular films: Examining portrayals of gender, race/ethnicity, LGBTQ and disability from 2007 to 2019. USC Annenberg School for Communication and Journalism. http://assets.uscannenberg.org/docs/aii-inequality_1300_popular_films_09 -08-2020.pdf.

Baer, H. (2016). Redoing feminism: Digital activism, body politics, and neo-liberalism. *Feminist Media Studies, 16*(1), 17–34.

Bail, K. (1996). *DIY feminism.* Crows Nest, NSW, Australia: Allen & Unwin.

Banet-Weiser, S. (2012). *Authentic™: The politics of ambivalence in a brand culture.* New York: New York University Press.

———. (2015a). Keynote Address: Media, Markets, Gender: Economies of Visibility in a Neoliberal Moment. *The Communication Review, 18*(1), 53–70.

———. (2015b, January 21). Popular misogyny: A zeitgeist. *Cultural Digitally.* http://culturedigitally.org/2015/01/popular-misogyny-a-zeitgeist/.

———. (2018a). *Empowered: Popular feminism and popular misogyny.* Durham, NC: Duke University Press.

———. (2018b). *The vision of empowerment: Popular feminism and popular misogyny* [Audio podcast]. https://soundcloud.com/lsepodcasts/the-vision -of-empowerment.

Banet-Weiser, S., and Miltner, K. M. (2016). #MasculinitySoFragile: Culture, structure, and networked misogyny. *Feminist Media Studies, 16*(1), 171–174.

Banet-Weiser, S., and Portwood-Stacer, L. (2017). The traffic in feminism: An introduction to the commentary and criticism on popular feminism. *Feminist Media Studies, 17*(5), 884–888.

Barnard Zine Library. (2016). Zine libraries. https://zines.barnard.edu/zine -libraries#pen.

Barrett, B. J. (2010). Is "safety" danger? A critical examination of the classroom as safe space. *Canadian Journal for the Scholarship of Teaching and Learning, 1*(1), 1–12.

Barroso, A. (2020, July 7). 61% of U.S. women say "feminist" describes them well; many see feminism as empowering, polarizing. Pew Research Center. https:// www.pewresearch.org/fact-tank/2020/07/07/61-of-u-s-women-say-feminist -describes-them-well-many-see-feminism-as-empowering-polarizing/.

Bates, K. G. (2017, January 21). Race and feminism: Women's March recalls the touchy history. NPR. https://www.npr.org/sections/codeswitch/2017/01/21 /510859909/race-and-feminism-womens-march-recalls-the-touchy-history.

Baym, N. K. (2000). *Tune in, log on: Soaps, fandom, and online community.* Thousand Oaks, CA: Sage.

Benkler, Y. (2006). *The wealth of networks: How social production transforms markets and freedom.* New Haven, CT: Yale University Press.

Bennett, J. (2017, November 5). The "click" moment: How the Weinstein scandal unleashed a tsunami. *New York Times.* https://www.nytimes.com/2017/11/05 /us/sexual-harrasment-weinstein-trump.html?mtrref=undefined.

———. (2018, January 17). The #MeToo moment: Parsing the generational divide. *New York Times.* https://www.nytimes.com/2018/01/17/us/the-metoo-moment -parsing-the-generational-divide.html.

Bennett, W. L., and Segerberg, A. (2013). *The logic of connective action: Digital media and the personalization of contentious politics.* Cambridge: Cambridge University Press.

Berents, H. (2016). Hashtagging girlhood: #IAmMalala, #BringBackOurGirls and gendering representations of global politics. *International Feminist Journal of Politics, 18*(4), 513–527.

Berube, C. (2013, April 18). Yes, zines still exist, and they're not antiques. *New York Times.* http://www.nytimes.com/2013/04/19/nyregion/brooklyn-zine -fest-at-public-assembly-in-williamsburg.html.

Bland, B. (2016, November 10). OKAY guys . . . here you go. I think we should build a coalition of ALL marginalized allies + do this. It will be a great tool to build a national infrastructure of organized action for now and the next 4 years [Facebook status update]. https://www.facebook.com/brooklyn royalty/posts/10101532920816587.

Bonilla, Y., and Rosa, J. (2015). #Ferguson: Digital protest, hashtag ethnography, and the racial politics of social media in the United States. *American Ethnologist, 42*, 4–17.

Borland, K. (2007). Decolonizing approaches to feminist research: The case of feminist ethnography. In S. N. Hesse-Biber (Ed.), *Handbook of feminist research: Theory and praxis* (pp. 621–628). Thousand Oaks, CA: Sage.

Bose, L. (2014, January 23). Are zines making a comeback, too? *OC Weekly.* http://www.ocweekly.com/music/are-zines-making-a-comeback-too -6429146.

Boston Globe. (2018, January 21). A timeline of the Year of Women. https://www .bostonglobe.com/metro/2018/01/20/timeline-year-women/WznxKLbZShTp vA7wo59RoL/story.html.

Bowerman, M. (2017, January 21). There's even a Women's March in Antarctica. *USA Today.* https://www.usatoday.com/story/news/politics/onpolitics/2017 /01/21/womens-march-on-washington-antarctica/96882184/.

boyd, d. (2008). Why youth (heart) social network sites: The role of networked publics in teenage social life. In D. Buckingham (Ed.), *Youth, identity, and digital media* (pp. 119–142). The John D. and Catherine T. MacArthur Foundation Series on Digital Media and Learning. Cambridge, MA: The MIT Press,

———. (2011). Social network sites as networked publics: Affordances, dynamics, and implications. In Z. Papacharissi (Ed.), *A networked self: Identity, community, and culture on social network sites* (pp. 39–58). New York: Routledge.

———. (2014). *It's complicated: The social life of networked teens.* New Haven, CT: Yale University Press.

Brandt, J., and Kizer, S. (2015). From street to tweet: Popular culture and feminist activism. In A. Trier-Bieniek (Ed.), *Feminist theory and pop culture* (pp. 115–127). Boston: Sense Publishers.

Brooks, K. (2017, January 31). This artist sent her painting to *The New Yorker* on a whim. Now it's the cover. *Huffington Post.* http://www.huffingtonpost.com /entry/new-yorker-womens-march-cover_us_588fb495e4b0522c7d3c640e.

Brown, D. (2018, October 13). 19 million tweets later: A look at #MeToo a year after the hashtag went viral. *USA Today.* https://www.usatoday.com/story /news/2018/10/13/metoo-impact-hashtag-made-online/1633570002/.

Brown, M., Ray, R., Summers, E., and Fraistat, N. (2017). #SayHerName: A case study of intersectional social media activism. *Ethnic and Racial Studies, 40*(11), 1831–1846.

Buckley, C. (2018, January 1). Powerful Hollywood women unveil anti-harassment action plan. *New York Times*. https://www.nytimes.com/2018/01/01/movies /times-up-hollywood-women-sexual-harassment.html.

Busch, M. (2017, October 17). 36 "Me too" tweets that will shatter you. *Bustle*. https://www.bustle.com/p/36-me-too-tweets-that-will-shatter-you-2920220.

Butler, J. (1988). Performative acts and gender constitution: An essay in phenomenology and feminist theory. *Theatre Journal, 40*(4), 519–531.

———. (1990). *Gender trouble and the subversion of identity*. New York: Routledge.

Carr, J. L. (2013). The SlutWalk movement: A study in transnational feminist activism. *Journal of Feminist Scholarship, 24*(4), 24–38.

Carville, O. (2015, July 29). How zines survive in the internet age. *The Star*. http://www.thestar.com/entertainment/books/2015/07/29/how-zines -survive-in-the-internet-age.html.

Casteel, K., J. Wolfe, J., and Nguyen, M. (2017). What we know about victims of sexual assault in America. *FiveThirtyEight*. https://projects.fivethirtyeight .com/sexual-assault-victims/.

Castells, M. (1996). *The rise of the network society. The information age: economy, society, and culture, volume I*. London: Blackwell.

———. (2011). *The rise of the network society*. Malden, MA: Wiley Blackwell.

———. (2012). *Networks of outrage and hope: Social movements in the internet age*. Cambridge, UK: Polity.

CDC. (2020, April 30). Health equity considerations and racial and ethnic minority groups. https://www.cdc.gov/coronavirus/2019-ncov/community /health-equity/race-ethnicity.html.

Chattopadhyay, P. (2018, January 28). "It concerns me greatly": Have #MeToo and modern feminism gone too far? CBC Radio. http://www.cbc.ca/radio /outintheopen/that-f-word-1.4494880/it-concerns-me-greatly-have-metoo -and-modern-feminism-gone-too-far-1.4494938.

Chen, T. (2017, January 23). People have strong feelings about cops high-fiving people in the Women's March in Atlanta. *Buzzfeed*. https://www.buzzfeed .com/tanyachen/cops-highfived-womens-marchers?utm_term=.amONa EDAEW#.sflRELYdLB.

Chenoweth, E., and Pressman, J. (2017, February 7). This is what we learned by counting the women's marches. *Washington Post*. https://www.washington post.com/news/monkey-cage/wp/2017/02/07/this-is-what-we-learned-by -counting-the-womens-marches/?utm_term=.6a3580bad261.

Chidgey, R. (2009). Free, trade: Distribution economies in feminist zine networks. *Signs, 35*(1), 28–37.

———. (2013). Reassess your weapons: The making of feminist memory in young women's zines. *Women's History Review, 22*(4), 658–672.

Chidgey, R., Payne, J. G., and Zobl, E. (2009). Rumours from around the bloc: Gossip, rhizomatic media, and the Plotki Femzine. *Feminist Media Studies, 9*(4), 477–491.

Chouliaraki, L. (2006). *The spectatorship of suffering.* Thousand Oaks, CA: Sage.

Ciambriello, R. (2014, October 3). How ads that empower women are boosting sales and bettering the industry. *Advertising Week* panel spotlights "femvertising." *Adweek.* http://www.adweek.com/news/advertising-branding/how-ads-empower-women-are-boosting-sales-and-bettering-industry-160539.

Clark, R. (2014). #NotBuyingIt: Hashtag feminists expand the commercial media conversation. *Feminist Media Studies, 14*(6), 1108–1110.

———. (2016). "Hope in a hashtag": The discursive activism of #WhyIStayed. *Feminist Media Studies, 16*(5), 788–804.

Cohen, D. S. (2020, September 19). What the loss of Ruth Bader Ginsburg means for the Supreme Court. *Rolling Stone.* Retrieved from https://www.rollingstone.com/politics/political-commentary/ruth-bader-ginsburg-scotus-trump-justice-appointment-1063402/.

Collins, E. C. (2016, November 8). Pantsuits Nation on fire: Clinton thanks viral Facebook group. *USA Today.* https://www.usatoday.com/story/news/politics/onpolitics/2016/11/08/pantsuits-nation-clinton/93500206/.

Collins, P. H. (2000). *Black feminist thought: Knowledge, consciousness, and the politics of empowerment.* New York: Routledge.

Compton, J. (2017, February 7). Pink "pussyhat" creator addresses criticism. NBC News. http://www.nbcnews.com/feature/nbc-out/pink-pussyhat-creator-addresses-criticism-over-name-n717886.

Conroy, M. (2020, July 8). 2020 could be the new year of the woman . . . for the GOP. *FiveThirtyEight.* https://fivethirtyeight.com/features/2020-could-be-the-new-year-of-the-woman-for-the-gop/.

Conroy, M., and Rakich, N. (2020, September 2). More women than ever are running for office. but are they winning their primaries? *FiveThirtyEight.* https://fivethirtyeight.com/features/more-women-than-ever-are-running-for-office-but-are-they-winning-their-primaries/.

Correa, C. (2018, January 25). The #MeToo moment: For U.S. gymnasts, why did justice take so long? *New York Times.* https://www.nytimes.com/2018/01/25/us/the-metoo-moment-for-us-gymnasts-olympics-nassar-justice.html.

Costanza-Chock, S. (2020). *Design justice: Community-led practices to build the worlds we need.* Cambridge, MA: MIT Press.

Couldry, N. (2010). Theorising media as practice. In B. Bräuchler and J. Postill (Eds.), *Theorising media and practice* (pp. 35–54). Oxford: Berghahn Books.

———. (2012). *Media, society, world: Social theory and digital media practice.* Cambridge, UK: Polity Press.

Coyle, F. (2004). Safe space as counter-space: Women, environmental illness and "corporeal chaos." *Canadian Geographer/Le Géographe canadien, 48*(1), 62–75.

Crenshaw, K. (1989). Demarginalizing the intersection of race and sex: A Black feminist critique of antidiscrimination doctrine, feminist theory, and antiracist politics. *University of Chicago Legal Forum, 139.*

———. (1991). Mapping the margins: intersectionality, identity politics, and violence against women of color. *Stanford Law Review, 43*(6), 1241–1299.

Crowley, P. (2018, January 19). MTV finds that #MeToo movement is causing young men to question their behavior. *Billboard.* https://www.billboard.com /articles/news/8095226/mtv-metoo-movement-survey-results.

Daniels, J. (2016). The trouble with white feminism: Whiteness, digital feminism, and the intersectional internet. In S. U. Noble and B. M. Tynes (Eds.), *The Intersectional internet: Race, class, and culture online.* New York: Peter Lang Publishing.

Dawkins, N. (2011). Do-it-yourself: The precarious work and postfeminist politics of handmaking (in) Detroit. *Utopian Studies, 22*(2), 261–284.

Dean, J. (2005). Communicative capitalism: Circulation and the foreclosure of politics. *Cultural Politics, 1*(1), 51–74.

Dean, J., and Aune, K. Feminism resurgent? Mapping contemporary feminist activisms in Europe. *Social Movement Studies: Journal of Social, Cultural and Political Protest, 14*(4), 375–295.

de Certeau, M. (1984). *The practice of everyday life.* Berkeley: University of California Press.

Dow, B. J., and Wood, J. T. (2014). Repeating history and learning from it: What can SlutWalks teach us about feminism? *Women's Studies in Communication, 37*(1), 22–43.

Downing, J. (2008). Social movement theories and alternative media: An evaluation and critique. *Communication, Culture & Critique, 1*(1), 40–50.

Duggan, M. (2017, July 14). Men, women experience and view online harassment differently. Pew Research Center. http://www.pewresearch.org/fact -tank/2017/07/14/men-women-experience-and-view-online-harassment -differently/.

Duncombe, S. (2008). *Notes from the underground: Zines and the politics of alternative culture.* Bloomington, IN: Microcosm Publishing.

Dupuy, B. (2018, January 20). Some women of color are boycotting the women's march, here's why. *Newsweek.* http://www.newsweek.com/some-women -color-siting-out-womens-march-785861.

Dvorak, P. (2017, December 28). 2017: The unexpected (and inspiring) year of the woman. *Washington Post.* https://www.washingtonpost.com/local/2017 -the-unexpected-and-inspiring-year-of-the-woman/2017/12/28/8e13611a -ebd6-11e7-8a6a-80acf0774e64_story.html.

Dwoskin, E., and McGregor, J. (2018, January 5). Sexual Harassment Inc: How the #MeToo movement is sparking a wave of start-ups. *Washington Post.* https://www.washingtonpost.com/news/on-leadership/wp/2018/01/05/sexual -harassment-inc-how-the-metoo-movement-is-sparking-a-wave-of-startups /?utm_term=.9f2974d68491.

Earl, J., and Kimport, K. (2011). *Digitally enabled social change: Activism in the Internet age.* Cambridge, MA: MIT Press.

Eichhorn, K. (2014). *The archival turn in feminism: Outrage in order.* Philadelphia: Temple University Press.

Epstein, K. (2017, December 29). The year of women, in policy and politics. *Washington Post.* https://www.washingtonpost.com/news/the-fix/wp/2017/12/29/the-year-of-women-in-policy-and-politics/?utm_term=.cfef47929a9d.

Evans, E. (2015). *The politics of third wave feminisms: Neoliberalism, intersectionality, and the state in Britain and the US.* New York: Springer.

Everett, A. (2004). Double click: The Million Woman March on television and the internet. In *Television after TV* (pp. 224–242). Durham, NC: Duke University Press.

Facebook. (2018). What names are allowed on Facebook? https://www.facebook.com/help/112146705538576.

Fahrenthold, D. A. (2016, October 8). Trump recorded having extremely lewd conversation about women in 2005. *Washington Post.* https://www.washingtonpost.com/politics/trump-recorded-having-extremely-lewd-conversation-about-women-in-2005/2016/10/07/3b9ce776-8cb4-11e6-bf8a-3d26847eeed4_story.html?utm_term=.3ee6441c71f2.

Faludi, S. (1991). *Backlash: The undeclared war against women.* New York: Crown Publishers.

———. (2017, December 28). The patriarchs are falling. The patriarchy is stronger than ever. *New York Times.* https://www.nytimes.com/2017/12/28/opinion/sunday/patriarchy-feminism-metoo.html.

Felsenthal, J. (2017, January 10). These are the women organizing the Women's March on Washington. *Vogue.* http://www.vogue.com/article/meet-the-women-of-the-womens-march-on-washington.

FemTechNet. (2017). Center for solutions to online violence. http://femtechnet.org/csov/.

Filipovic, J. (2017, January 13). Ivanka Trump's dangerous fake feminism. *New York Times.* https://www.nytimes.com/2017/01/13/opinion/sunday/ivanka-trumps-dangerous-fake-feminism.html.

Fotopoulou, A. (2016). *Feminist activism and digital networks: Between empowerment and vulnerability.* New York: Springer.

Foucault, M. (1991). *Discipline and punish: The birth of the prison.* New York: Vintage Books.

Fraser, N. (1992). Rethinking the public sphere: A contribution to the critique of actually existing democracy. In: C. Calhoun (Ed.), *Habermas and the public sphere* (pp. 109–142). Cambridge, MA: MIT Press.

———. (1995). Pragmatism, feminism, and the linguistic turn. In S. Benhabib, J. Butler, D. Cornell, and N. Fraser, (Eds.), *Feminist contentions: A philosophical exchange* (pp. 157–172). New York: Routledge.

———. (2013, October 14). How feminism became capitalism's handmaiden—and how to reclaim it. *Guardian.* https://www.theguardian.com/commentisfree/2013/oct/14/feminism-capitalist-handmaiden-neoliberal.

Fredrick, C.A.N. (1999). Feminist rhetoric in cyberspace: The ethos of feminist usenet newsgroups. *The Information Society, 15*(3), 187–197.

Freeman, J. (1972). The tyranny of structurelessness. *Berkeley Journal of Sociology, 17*, 151–164.

Friedland, L. A., Hove, T., and Rojas, H. (2006). The networked public sphere. *Javnost–The Public, 13*(4), 5–26.

Futrell, R., and Simi, P. (2004). Free spaces, collective identity, and the persistence of US white power activism. *Social Problems, 51*(1), 16–42.

Gajjala, R. (2002). An interrupted postcolonial/feminist cyberethnography: Complicity and resistance in the "cyberfield." *Feminist Media Studies, 2*(2), 177–193.

Ganzer, M. (2014). In bed with the trolls. *Feminist Media Studies, 14*(6), 1098–1100.

Garcia, S. E. (2017, October 20). The woman who created #MeToo long before hashtags. *New York Times.* https://www.nytimes.com/2017/10/20/us/me-too-movement-tarana-burke.html.

Gerbaudo, P. (2012). *Tweets and the streets: Social media and contemporary activism.* London: Pluto Press.

Gessen, M. (2017, November 27). Sex, consent, and the dangers of "misplaced scale." *New Yorker.* https://www.newyorker.com/news/our-columnists/sex-consent-dangers-of-misplaced-scale.

Gianino, L. (2017, October 18). I went public with my sexual assault. And then the trolls came for me. *Washington Post.* https://www.washingtonpost.com/news/posteverything/wp/2017/10/18/i-went-public-with-my-sexual-assault-and-then-the-trolls-came-for-me/?utm_term=.55bdfb69e6b0.

Gill, R. (2007). Postfeminist media culture: Elements of a sensibility. *European Journal of Cultural Studies, 10*(2), 147–166.

———. (2016). Post-postfeminism? New feminist visibilities in postfeminist times. *Feminist Media Studies, 16*(4), 1–21.

Gill, R., Scharff, C. (2011). *New femininities: Postfeminism, neoliberalism and subjectivity.* New York: Springer.

Gladwell, M. (2010, October 4). Small change: Why the revolution will not be tweeted. *New Yorker.* https://www.newyorker.com/magazine/2010/10/04/small-change-malcolm-gladwell.

Goldman, R., Heath, D., and Smith, S. L. (1991). Commodity feminism. *Critical Studies in Media Communication, 8*(3), 333–351.

Goodwin, J., and Jasper, J. M. (Eds.). (2015). *The social movements reader: Cases and concepts.* Malden, MA: Wiley Blackwell.

Grady, C. (2017, December 21). 2017 was the year of women's anger, onscreen and off. *Vox.* https://www.vox.com/2017-in-review/2017/12/21/16776708/2017-womens-anger-womens-march-reckoning-handmaids-tale-alias-grace-big-little-lies-three-billboards.

———. (2018, January 11). The "Shitty Media Men" list: How the argument over an anonymous spreadsheet encapsulates the debates of the post-Weinstein era. *Vox*. https://www.vox.com/culture/2018/1/11/16877966/shitty-media -men-list-Explained.

Graham, R. (2017, January 17). Women's March on Washington says no to pro-life feminist group. *Slate*. http://www.slate.com/blogs/xx_factor/2017/01 /17/pro_life_feminist_group_new_wave_feminists_removed_from_women _s_march_partnership.html.

Griffith, E. (2020, June 29). Social privacy is on the rise: Almost half of social media accounts are kept private. *PC Mag*. https://www.pcmag.com/news /social-privacy-is-on-the-rise-almost-half-of-social-media-accounts-are.

Grinberg, E. (2014, September 17). Meredith Vieira explains #WhyIStayed. *CNN*. Retrieved from http://www.cnn.com/2014/09/09/living/rice-video-why-i -stayed/index.html.

Groetzinger, K. (2016, April 5). How feminists took on the mainstream media and won. *Quartz*. https://qz.com/643130/how-grassroots-feminism-is-taking -over-new-media/.

Guzzetti, B. J., and Gamboa, M. (2004). Zines for social justice: Adolescent girls writing on their own. *Reading Research Quarterly, 39*(4), 408–436.

Hais, M. D., and Winograd, M. (2020, August 7). 2020: The year of the woman voter. *Brookings*. https://www.brookings.edu/blog/fixgov/2020/08/07/2020 -the-year-of-the-woman-voter/.

Hall, S., Evans, J., and Nixon, S. (2013). *Representation: Cultural representations and signifying practices* (2nd ed.). London: Sage Publications.

Hampton, R. (2018, January 19). Branding #MeToo might bring more money to charities, but it misses the spirit of the movement. *Slate*. https://slate.com /human-interest/2018/01/turning-metoo-into-a-brand-doesnt-help-the -cause.html.

Hancock, A. M. (2015). *Intersectionality: An intellectual history*. New York: Oxford University Press.

Hanisch, C. (1969). The personal is political. http://www.carolhanisch.org /CHwritings/PIP.html.

Harker, J., and Farr, C. K. (2015). *This book is an action: Feminist print culture and activist aesthetics*. Urbana: University of Illinois Press.

Harris, A. (2003). gURL scenes and grrrl zines: The regulation and resistance of girls in late modernity. *Feminist Review, 75*, 38–56.

Harvard, S. A. (2017, January 19). #RenameMillionWomenMarch proves exactly why we need the Women's March on Washington. *Mic*. https://mic.com /articles/166026/renamemillionwomenmarch-proves-exactly-why-we-need -the-womens-march-on-washington#.nGVueBiMm.

Harvey, D. (2007). *A brief history of neoliberalism*. New York: Oxford University Press.

HeartMob. (2017). About Heartmob. https://iheartmob.org/about.

Herring, S., Job-Slider, K., Scheckler, R., and Barb, S. (2002). Searching for safety online: Managing trolling in a feminist forum. *Information Society*, *18*(5), 371–384.

Hess, A. (2014, January 6). Why women aren't welcome on the internet. *Pacific Standard*. https://psmag.com/social-justice/women-arent-welcome-internet -72170.

———. (2017a, February 7). How a fractious women's movement came to lead the left. *New York Times*. https://www.nytimes.com/2017/02/07/magazine/how-a -fractious-womens-movement-came-to-lead-the-left.html.

———. (2017b, March 17). The Trump resistance will be commercialized. *New York Times*. https://www.nytimes.com/2017/03/17/arts/the-trump-resistance -will-be-commercialized.html.

———. (2018, January 24). Hollywood uses the very women it exploited to change the subject. *New York Times*. https://www.nytimes.com/2018/01/24/arts/can -hollywood-fix-its-harassment-problem-while-celebrating-itself.html.

Hesse-Biber, S.N. (2007). Feminist research: Exploring the interconnections of epistemology, methodology, and method. In S. N. Hesse-Biber (Ed.), *Handbook of feminist research: Theory and praxis* (pp. 1–26). Thousand Oaks, CA: Sage.

Hewitt, N. A. (2012). Feminist frequencies: Regenerating the wave metaphor. *Feminist Studies*, *38*(3), 658–680.

Hill, Z. (2017, October 18). A black woman created the "Me Too" campaign against sexual assault 10 years ago. *Ebony*. http://www.ebony.com/news -views/black-woman-me-too-movement-tarana-burke-alyssa-milano.

Hine, C. (2015). *Ethnography for the internet: Embedded, embodied and everyday*. London: Bloomsbury Publishing.

Hogan, K. (2016). *The feminist bookstore movement: Lesbian antiracism and feminist accountability*. Durham, NC: Duke University Press.

hooks, b. (1981). *Ain't I a woman: Black women and feminism*. Boston: South End Press.

———. (2000). *Feminism is for everybody: Passionate politics*. London: Pluto Press.

Horeck, T. (2014). #AskThicke: "Blurred Lines," rape culture, and the feminist hashtag takeover. *Feminist Media Studies*, *14*(6), 1105–1107.

Howard, P. N., and Hussain, M. M. (2013). *Democracy's fourth wave? Digital media and the Arab Spring*. Oxford: Oxford University Press.

Hunt, T. A. (2018). A movement divided: SlutWalks, protest repertoires and the privilege of nudity. *Social Movement Studies*, *17*(5), 541–557.

Hunter, M. A. (2008). Cultivating the art of safe space. *Research in Drama Education*, *13*(1), 5–21.

INCITE! (2007). *The revolution will not be funded: Beyond the non-profit industrial complex*. Cambridge, MA: South End Press.

Indigenous Action Media. (2014, May 4). Accomplices not allies: Abolishing the ally complex, an indigenous perspective. *IndigenousAction.org*. http://www .indigenousaction.org/accomplices-not-allies-abolishing-the-ally-industrial -complex/.

Jackson, S. J., Bailey, M., and Welles, B. F. *#HashtagActivism: Networks of race and gender justice*. Cambridge, MA: MIT Press, 2020.

Jain, P. (2017, March 8). Why 2017 will be the year of women. *Huffington Post*. Retrieved form https://www.huffingtonpost.com/entry/why-2017-will-be-the -year-of-women_us_58b9c5ece4b02eac8876ce2c.

Jen G. (2012, August 15). Permanent Wave 2012 Music Festival this weekend!!! *Greenpointers.com*. https://greenpointers.com/2012/08/15/permanent-wave -2012-music-festival-this-weekend/.

Joseph, M. (2002). *Against the romance of community*. Minneapolis: University of Minnesota Press.

Just Be Inc. (2013). Just Be Inc. http://justbeinc.wixsite.com/justbeinc/the-me -too-movement-c7cf.

Keller, J. (2016). *Girls' feminist blogging in a postfeminist age*. New York: Routledge.

Keller, J., Mendes, K., and Ringrose, J. (2018). Speaking "unspeakable things": Documenting digital feminist responses to rape culture. *Journal of Gender Studies*, 27(1), 22–36.

Khimm, S. (August 13, 2017). Trump halted Obama's equal pay rule. What it means for working women. NBC. https://www.nbcnews.com/politics/white -house/trump-killed-obama-s-equal-pay-rule-what-it-means-n797941.

Kipnis, L. (2018, January 13). Has #MeToo gone too far, or not far enough? The answer is both. *Guardian*. https://www.theguardian.com/commentisfree /2018/jan/13/has-me-too-catherine-deneuve-laura-kipnis.

Kirby, J. (2018, June 13). Migrant in detention says her child was taken away while she breastfed. *Vox*. https://www.vox.com/2018/6/13/17462088/family -separation-migrants-breastfeeding-mom-border.

Keller, J. (2015). *Girls' feminist blogging in a postfeminist age*. New York: Routledge.

Kendall, M. (2013, August 14). #SolidarityIsForWhiteWomen: Women of color's issue with digital feminism. *Guardian*. https://www.theguardian .com/commentisfree/2013/aug/14/solidarityisforwhitewomen-hashtag -feminism.

Kennedy, T. L. M. (2007). The personal is political: Feminist blogging and virtual consciousness raising. *Scholar and Feminist Online*, 5(2).

Kenney, M. (2001). *Mapping gay L.A.: The intersection of place and politics*. Philadelphia: Temple University Press.

Koerth-Baker, M. (2018, March 18). What it's like to watch #MeToo when it is you, too. *FiveThirtyEight*. https://fivethirtyeight.com/features/what-its-like -to-watch-metoo-when-it-is-you-too/.

Kovan, B. (2020, October 28). Meet the history-making women running for the U.S. House. *Bustle*. https://www.bustle.com/rule-breakers/women-running-for-office-house-of-representatives.

Kuo, R. (2016). Racial justice activist hashtags: Counterpublics and discourse circulation. *New Media & Society*, 20(2), 495–514.

Ladau, E. (2017, January 16). Disability rights are conspicuously absent from the Women's March platform. *The Establishment*. https://theestablishment.co/disability-rights-are-conspicuously-absent-from-the-womens-march-platform-1d61cee62593.

Lake, R. (2018, February 12). Why #MeToo doesn't translate in China. *Ms. Magazine*. http://msmagazine.com/blog/2018/02/12/metoo-doesnt-translate-china/.

Lambert, L. (2018, January 17). #MeToo effect: Calls flood U.S. sexual assault hotlines. *Reuters*. https://www.reuters.com/article/us-usa-harassment-helplines/metoo-effect-calls-flood-u-s-sexual-assault-hotlines-idUSKBN1F6194.

LaMotte, S. (2017, October 19). For some, #MeToo sexual assault stories trigger trauma not empowerment. CNN. https://www.cnn.com/2017/10/19/health/me-too-sexual-assault-stories-trigger-trauma/index.html.

Lang, M. J., Miller, M. E., Jamison, P., Moyer, J. W., Williams, C., Hermann, P., Kunkle, F., and Cox, J. W. (2020, November 15). After thousands of Trump supporters rally in D.C., violence erupts when night falls. *Washington Post*. https://www.washingtonpost.com/dc-md-va/2020/11/14/million-maga-march-dc-protests/.

Latina, D., and Docherty, S. (2014). Trending participation, trending exclusion? *Feminist Media Studies*, 14(6), 1103–1105.

Lee, C. W. (2014). *Do-it-yourself democracy: The rise of the public engagement industry*. Oxford: Oxford University Press.

Lekach, S. (2017, October 19). #MeToo hashtag spreads beyond the U.S. to the rest of the globe. *Mashable*. https://mashable.com/2017/10/19/me-too-global-spread/#vBDByexqOmqA.

Levy, G. (2017, October 22). For the women under Israeli occupation, it's time for #AnaKaman (#MeToo). *Haaretz*. https://www.haaretz.com/opinion/.premium-for-women-under-occupation-it-s-time-for-anakaman-1.5459392.

Lewis, R., and Marine, S. (2015). Weaving a tapestry, compassionately: Toward an understanding of young women's feminisms. *Feminist Formations, 27*(1), 118–140.

Licona, A. C. (2005). (B)orderlands' rhetorics and representations: The transformative potential of feminist third-space scholarship and zines. *NWSA Journal, 17*(2), 104–129.

Lievrouw, L. (2011). *Alternative and activist new media*. Cambridge, UK: Polity.

Lingel, J. (2017). *Digital countercultures and the struggle for community*. Cambridge: MA: MIT Press.

Liptak, A. (2018, June 26). Supreme Court backs anti-abortion pregnancy centers in free speech case. *New York Times.* https://www.nytimes.com /2018/06/26/us/politics/supreme-court-crisis-pregnancy-center-abortion .html.

Liptak, A., and Shear, M. D. (2018, June 26). Trump's travel ban is upheld by the Supreme Court. *New York Times.* https://www.nytimes.com/2018/06/26/us /politics/supreme-court-trump-travel-ban.html.

Litman, H. (2018, July 5). Anthony Kennedy's Supreme Court retirement threatens abortion rights even if Roe survives. *USA Today.* https://www .usatoday.com/story/opinion/2018/07/05/justice-kennedy-retires-supreme -court-threatens-abortion-rights-column/751271002/.

Lockhart, P. R. (2017, December 19). Women of color in low-wage jobs are being overlooked in the #MeToo moment. *Vox.* https://www.vox.com/identities /2017/12/19/16620918/sexual-harassment-low-wages-minority-women.

Loken, M. (2014). #BringBackOurGirls and the invisibility of imperialism. *Feminist Media Studies, 14*(6), 1100–1101.

Lorde, A. (1984). *Sister outsider: Essays and speeches.* Toronto: Crossing Press.

Loza, S. (2014). Hashtag feminism, #SolidarityIsForWhiteWomen, and the other #FemFuture. *Ada: A Journal of Gender, New Media, and Technology, 5.*

Luhby, T. (January 20, 2018). 8 ways Trump hurt Obamacare in his first year. CNN. https://money.cnn.com/2018/01/20/news/economy/obamacare-trump -year-one/index.html.

Luvaas, B. (2013). *DIY style: Fashion, music and global digital cultures.* London: Berg.

Magness, C. (2017, December 12). It's time to stop the sexual witch hunt and take a hard look at ourselves. *The Federalist.* http://thefederalist.com/2017/12 /12/time-stop-sexual-witch-hunt-take-hard-look/.

Main, A. (2017, October 16). Here's just how massive that #MeToo hashtag has gotten. *Mashable.* https://mashable.com/2017/10/16/me-too-hashtag -popularity/#nUVUKo4GYiqZ.

Mann, S. (2014). Maktivism: Authentic making for technology in the service of humanity. In M. Ratto and M. Boler (Eds.), *DIY citizenship: Critical making and social media* (pp. 29–52). Cambridge, MA: MIT Press.

March to End Rape Culture. (2015). About. http://marchtoendrapeculture .tumblr.com/about.

Marcos, C. (2020, November 9). Next Congress expected to have record diversity. *The Hill.* https://thehill.com/homenews/campaign/524889-next-congress-set -for-record-diversity.

Marcus, G. E. (1995). Ethnography in/of the world system: The emergence of multi-sited ethnography. *Annual review of anthropology, 24*(1), 95–117.

Marcus, S. (2010). *Girls to the front: The true story of the Riot Grrrl revolution.* New York: Harper Perennial.

Marwick, A. (2013). *Status update: Celebrity, publicity, and branding in the social media age.* New Haven, CT: Yale University Press.

Maxfield, M. (2016). History retweeting itself: Imperial feminist appropriations of "Bring Back Our Girls." *Feminist Media Studies, 16*(5), 886–900.

May, V. M. (2015). *Pursuing intersectionality, unsettling dominant imaginaries.* New York: Routledge.

McCammon, S. (2017, December 27). In the wake of #MeToo, more victims seek help for repressed trauma. NPR. https://www.npr.org/2017/12/27/573146877 /in-the-wake-of-metoo-more-victims-seek-help-for-repressed-trauma.

———. (2020, September 30). From debate stage, Trump declines to denounce white supremacy. NPR. https://www.npr.org/2020/09/30/918483794/from -debate-stage-trump-declines-to-denounce-white-supremacy.

McRobbie, A. (2004). Post-feminism and popular culture. *Feminist Media Studies, 4*(3), 255–264.

———. (2008). *The aftermath of feminism: Gender, culture and social change.* London: Sage.

Meicher, T. N. (2017, November 2). Twitter has a transgender problem. *New York Times.* https://www.nytimes.com/2017/11/02/opinion/twitter-transgender -harassment-problem.html.

Melucci, A. (1989). *Nomads of the present: Social movements and individual needs in contemporary society.* Philadelphia: Temple University Press.

Mendes, K. (2015). *SlutWalk: Feminism, activism and media.* New York: Palgrave Macmillan.

Mendes, K., Ringrose, J., and Keller, J. (2018). #MeToo and the promise and pitfalls of challenging rape culture through digital feminist activism. *European Journal of Women's Studies, 25*(2), 236–246.

———. (2019). *Digital feminist activism: Girls and women fight back against rape culture.* Oxford: Oxford University Press.

Merkin, D. (2018, January 5). Publicly, we say #MeToo. Privately, we have misgivings. *New York Times.* https://www.nytimes.com/2018/01/05/opinion /golden-globes-metoo.html?_r=1.

Meyer, D. S., and D. C. Minkoff. (2004). Conceptualizing political opportunity. *Social Forces, 82*(4), 1457–1492.

Meyer, M. D. (2014). #Thevagenda's war on headlines: Feminist activism in the information age. *Feminist Media Studies, 14*(6), 1107–1108.

Milan, S. (2014). The ethics of social movement research. In D. della Porta (Ed.), *Methodological practices in social movement research* (pp. 21–42). New York: Oxford University Press.

Moraga, C., and G. Anzaldúa. (1981). *This bridge called my back: Writings by radical women of color.* London: Persephone Press.

Morozov, E. (2011). *The net delusion: How not to liberate the world.* London: Penguin UK.

Munro, E. (2013). Feminism: A fourth wave? *Political Insight, 4*(2), 22–25.

Murtha, T. (2013, September 26). SlutWalk Philly changes protest name to "A March to End Rape Culture." *Rewire*. https://rewire.news/article/2013/09 /26/slutwalk-philly-changes-protest-name-to-a-march-to-end-rape-culture/.

Nash, J. C. (2008). Re-thinking intersectionality. *Feminist Review, 89*(1), 1–15.

Noble, S. U., and Tynes, B. M. (2016). *The intersectional internet: Race, sex, class, and culture Online*. New York: Peter Lang International Academic Publishers.

North, A. (2018, May 5). #MeToo at the 2018 Oscars: The good, the bad, and the in between. *Vox*. https://www.vox.com/2018/3/5/17079702/2018-oscars-me -too-times-up-frances-mcdormand-jimmy-kimmel.

Nyren, E. (2018, February 11). Michael Haneke says #MeToo movement leads to "man-hating puritanism." *Variety*. https://variety.com/2018/biz/news /michael-haneke-metoo-backlash-puritanism-1202694779/.

Obie, B. (2017, January 23). Woman in viral photo from Women's March to white female allies: "Listen to a Black woman." *The Root*. https://www.theroot.com /woman-in-viral-photo-from-women-s-march-to-white-female-1791524613.

O'Brien, K. (2012, November 16). How to survive societal collapse in suburbia. *New York Times*. https://www.nytimes.com/2012/11/18/magazine/how-to -survive-societal-collapse-in-suburbia.html.

Pagano, J. P. (2018, March 8). The Women's March has a Farrakhan problem. *Atlantic*. https://www.theatlantic.com/politics/archive/2018/03/womens -march/555122/.

Park, A. (2017, October 24). #MeToo reaches 85 countries with 1.7M tweets. CBS News. https://www.cbsnews.com/news/metoo-reaches-85-countries-with-1 -7-million-tweets/.

Park, A., and Perrigo, B. (2017, October 18). "It started when I was 13 years old." Olympic gymnast McKayla Maroney says U.S. team doctor molested her. *Time*. http://time.com/4987066/mckayla-maroney-metoo-molested/.

Permanent Wave Philly. (2015). About. http://permanentwavephilly.tumblr.com/.

Peyser, A. (2017, November 17). #MeToo has lumped trivial in with legitimate sexual assault. *New York Post*. https://nypost.com/2017/11/17/metoo-has -lumped-trivial-in-with-legitimate-sexual-assault/.

Phillips, M. (2018, February 5). MeToo feminism is victim culture, not courage. *The Sunday Times*. https://www.thetimes.co.uk/article/metoo-feminism-is -victim-culture-not-courage-lhogmd3pn.

Phipps, A. (2014). *The politics of the body: Gender in a neoliberal and neocon- servative age*. Cambridge, UK: Polity Press.

Piepmeier, A. (2009). *Grrrl zines: Making media, doing feminism*. New York: New York University Press.

Planned Parenthood Action Fund. (2017, April 27). 10 ways Trump has attacked women's health and rights in his first 100 days. https://www.planned

parenthoodaction.org/blog/10-ways-trump-has-attacked-womens-health -and-rights-in-his-first-100-days.

Plant, S. (1997). *Zeroes+ ones: Digital women + the new technoculture*. New York: Doubleday.

Polletta, F. (1999). "Free spaces" in collective action. *Theory and society, 28*(1), 1–38.

Power to the Polls (2018). Women's March presents Power to the Polls. http://www.powertothepolls.com/.

Pruchniewska, U. M. (2017). Branding the self as an "authentic feminist": Negotiating feminist values in post-feminist digital cultural production. *Feminist Media Studies*, 1–15.

Pussyhat Project. (2017). *Get involved!* https://www.pussyhatproject.com/get -involved/.

Ratto, M., and Boler, M. (2014), *DIY citizenship: Critical making and social media*. Cambridge, MA: MIT Press.

Rauch, J. (2015). Exploring the alternative-mainstream dialectic: What "alternative media" means to a hybrid audience. *Communication, Culture & Critique, 8*, 124–143.

Reger, J. (2012). *Everywhere and nowhere: Contemporary feminism in the United States*. New York: Oxford University Press.

Remy, E. (2019, July 15). How public and private Twitter users in the U.S. compare—and why it might matter for your research. *Decoded*, Pew Research Center. https://medium.com/pew-research-center-decoded/how -public-and-private-twitter-users-in-the-u-s-d536ce2a41b3.

Rentschler, C. A. (2015). #Safetytipsforladies: Feminist Twitter takedowns of victim blaming. *Feminist Media Studies, 15*(2), 353–356.

———. (2017). Bystander intervention, feminist hashtag activism, and the anti-carceral politics of care. *Feminist Media Studies, 17*(4), 565–584.

Rentschler, C. A., and Thrift, S. C. (2015). Doing feminism in the network: Networked laughter and the 'Binders Full of Women' meme. *Feminist Theory, 16*(3), 329–359.

Rheingold, H. (1993). *The virtual community: Finding connection in a computerized world*. Boston: Addison-Wesley Longman.

Richardson, B. (2018, January 18). Feminists: "MeToo" has gone too far with Aziz Ansari accusation. *Washington Times*. https://www.washingtontimes.com /news/2018/jan/18/metoo-has-gone-too-far-with-aziz-ansari-accusation/.

Rockström, J., Steffen, W., Noone, K., Persson, Å., Chapin, F. S. III, Lambin, E., ... and Foley, J. (2009). Planetary boundaries: Exploring the safe operating space for humanity. *Ecology and Society, 14*(2).

Rodino-Colocino, M. (2014). #YesAllWomen: Intersectional mobilization against sexual assault is radical (again). *Feminist Media Studies, 14*(6), 1113–1115.

The Roestone Collective. (2014). Safe space: Towards a reconceptualization. *Antipode, 46*(5), 1346–1365.

Roiphe, K. (2018, March). The other whisper network: How Twitter feminism is bad for women. *Harper's Magazine.* https://harpers.org/archive/2018/03/the -other-whisper-network-2/.

Rothenberg, B. (2002). Movement advocates as battered women's storytellers: From varied experiences, one message. In J. E. Davis (Ed.), *Stories of change: Narratives and social movements,* (pp. 203–227). Albany: State University of New York Press.

Rowntree, A. (2017, January 20). The Women's March on Washington needs to better embrace sex workers. *Huffington Post.* http://www.huffingtonpost .com/entry/human-rights-include-sex-workers-rights_us_58806da0e4 b0aa1c47ac287f.

Rubin, G. (1997). The Traffic in Women: Notes on the "Political Economy" of Sex. In L. Nicholson (Ed.), *The second wave: A reader in feminist theory* (pp. 27–62). New York: Routledge.

Rupp, L. J., and Taylor, V. (1987). *Survival in the doldrums.* Oxford: Oxford University Press.

Salo, J. (2017, October 18). Retailers are trying to profit off the #MeToo movement. *New York Post.* https://nypost.com/2017/10/18/retailers-are-trying-to -make-money-on-the-metoo-movement/.

Sandoval, M., and Fuchs, C. (2010). Towards a critical theory of alternative media. *Telematics and Informatics, 27,* 141–150.

Sarachild, K. (1978). Consciousness-raising: A radical weapon. In Redstockings (Eds.), *Feminist revolution* (pp. 144–150). New York: Random House.

Sayej, N. (2017, December 1). Alyssa Milano on the #MeToo movement: "We're not going to stand for it anymore." *Guardian.* https://www.theguardian.com /culture/2017/dec/01/alyssa-milano-mee-too-sexual-harassment-abuse.

Scharff, C. (2016). *Repudiating feminism: Young women in a neoliberal world.* New York: Routledge.

Scher, B. (2017, November 24). Why 2020 will be the Year of the Woman. *Politico.* https://www.politico.com/magazine/story/2017/11/24/2020-year-of -woman-democrats-post-weinstein-kamala-harris-klobuchar-gillibrand -warren-215860.

Schlack, J. W. (2017, February 23). Not your mother's feminism: *Teen Vogue* and the next wave of activism. WBUR. https://www.wbur.org/cognoscenti/2017 /02/23/teen-vogue-activism-julie-wittes-schlack.

Schlock, R. D. (2013). The methodological imperatives of feminist ethnography. *Journal of Feminist Scholarship, 5,* 48–60.

Schnall, M. (2017, December 15). 2018 will be the year of women. CNN. https:// www.cnn.com/2017/12/14/opinions/2018-will-be-the-year-of-women-schnall /index.html.

Schneider, A., Hsu, A., and Horsley, S. (2020, October 2). Multiple demands during pandemic causing women to abandon workforce. NPR. https://www .npr.org/sections/coronavirus-live-updates/2020/10/02/919517914/enough -already-multiple-demands-causing-women-to-abandon-workforce.

Schulte, S. R. (2011). Surfing feminism's online wave: The internet and the future of feminism. *Feminist Histories and Institutional Practices, 37*(3), 727–744.

Seib, G. F. (2020, November 16). The year of the woman really, finally did arrive in 2020. *Wall Street Journal.* https://www.wsj.com/articles/the-year-of-the -woman-really-finally-did-arrive-in-2020-11605539331.

Serfaty, S. (2017, October 27). Congresswoman describes sexual assault in #MeToo video. CNN. https://www.cnn.com/2017/10/27/politics/jackie-speier -me-too-sexual-assault-harassment/index.html.

Shamus, K. J. (2017, December 31). Did you hear her roar? 2017 was unquestionably the year of the woman. *Detroit Free Press.* https://www.freep.com/story /news/2017/12/31/2017-year-woman-feminism/944472001/.

Shaw, F. (2012). "HOTTEST 100 WOMEN" Cross-platform discursive activism in feminist blogging networks. *Australian Feminist Studies, 27*(74), 373–387.

———. (2013). Still "Searching for safety online": Collective strategies and discursive resistance to trolling and harassment in a feminist network. *Fibreculture Journal, 22.*

SheKnows Media. (2018). #Femvertising Awards. https://www.femvertising awards.com/.

Shirky, C. (2008). *Here comes everybody: The power of organizing without organizations.* New York: Penguin.

Silberling, A. (2015, August 3). A brief guide to Philadelphia's DIY scene. *Rock on Philly.* http://rockonphilly.com/2015/08/a-brief-guide-to-philadelphias -d-i-y-scene/.

6abc. (2017, January 22). Women's March on Philly shatters attendance prediction. 6abc WPVI Action News. Retrieved from http://6abc.com/society /womens-march-on-philly-shatters-attendance-prediction/1713873/.

Smith, B. (1983). *Home girls: A black feminist anthology.* New Brunswick, NJ: Rutgers University Press.

The Sojourner Truth Project. (2021). Compare the two speeches. https://www .thesojournertruthproject.com/compare-the-speeches/.

Solomon, D. (2009, November 13). Fourth-wave feminism. *New York Times Magazine.* https://www.nytimes.com/2009/11/15/magazine/15fob-q4-t.html.

Sommers, C. H. (2017, November 26). A panic is not an answer: We're at imminent risk of turning this #MeToo moment into a frenzied rush to blame all men. *New York Daily News.* http://www.nydailynews.com/opinion/panic -not-answer-article-1.3651778.

Stacey, J. (1988). Can there be a feminist ethnography? *Women's Studies International Forum, 11*(1): 21–27.

Steele, C. K. (2016). Siginifyin', bitching, and blogging: Black women and resistance discourse online. In S. U. Noble and B. M. Tynes (Eds.), *The intersectional internet: Race, sex, class, and culture online.* (pp. 73–94). New York: Peter Lang.

Stein, P. (2017, January 31). The woman who started the Women's March with a Facebook post reflects: "It was mind-boggling." *Washington Post.* https://www.washingtonpost.com/news/local/wp/2017/01/31/the-woman-who-started-the-womens-march-with-a-facebook-post-reflects-it-was-mind-boggling/?utm_term=.d1f3ca5d89d7.

Stein, P., and Somashekhar, S. (2017, January 3). It started with a retiree. Now the Women's March could be the biggest inauguration demonstration. *Washington Post.* ttps://www.washingtonpost.com/national/it-started-with-a-grandmother-in-hawaii-now-the-womens-march-on-washington-is-poised-to-be-the-biggest-inauguration-demonstration/2017/01/03/8af61686-c6e2-11e6-bf4b 2c064d32a4bf_story.html?utm_term=.85ecff1de6f7.

Steiner, L. (1992). The history and structure of women's alternative media. In L. F. Rakow (Ed.), *Women making meaning: New feminist directions in communication* (pp. 121–143). New York: Routledge.

Stengel, B. S. (2010). The complex case of fear and safe space. *Studies in philosophy and education, 29*(6), 523–540.

Stengel, B. S., and Weems, L. (2010). Questioning safe space: An introduction. *Studies in Philosophy and Education, 29*(6), 505–507.

Stevenson, A. (2020). From the "Radical women's press" to the digital age: Subversive networks of feminism in the United States. In O. Guntarik and V. Grieve-Williams (Eds.) *From sit-ins to #revolutions: Media and the changing nature of protests* (pp. 51–64). New York: Bloomsbury Academic.

St. Félix, D. (2017, November 30). Matt Lauer's firing and NBC's theatre of accountability. *The New Yorker.* https://www.newyorker.com/culture/culture-desk/matt-lauers-firing-and-nbcs-theatre-of-accountability.

Stockman, Farah. (2017, January 9). Women's March on Washington opens contentious dialogues about race. *New York Times.* https://www.nytimes.com/2017/01/09/us/womens-march-on-washington-opens-contentious-dialogues-about-race.html.

Stolen Sharpie Revolution. (2016a). Stores that sell zines. http://www.stolensharpierevolution.org/stores-that-sell-zines/.

———. (2016b). Zine distros. http://www.stolensharpierevolution.org/zine-distros/.

———. (2016c). Zine events and zine fests. http://www.stolensharpierevolution.org/events/.

Tasker, Y., and Negra, D. (2007). *Interrogating postfeminism: Gender and the politics of popular culture.* Durham, NC: Duke University Press.

Taylor, C. (1997). The politics of recognition. *New Contexts of Canadian Criticism, 98,* 25–73.

Taylor, V., and Whittier, N. (1992). Collective identity in social movement communities: Lesbian feminist mobilization. In P. M. Nardi and B. E. Schneider (Eds.), *Social perspectives in lesbian and gay studies* (pp. 349–365). New York: Routledge.

Theocharis, Y., Lowe, W., Van Deth, J. W., and García-Albacete, G. (2015). Using Twitter to mobilize protest action: Online mobilization patterns and action repertoires in the Occupy Wall Street, Indignados, and Aganaktismenoi movements. *Information, Communication & Society, 18*(2), 202–220.

Thornham, H., and E. Weissmann. (2013). *Renewing feminisms: Radical narratives, fantasies and futures in media studies.* London: I.B. Tauris.

Thrift, S. C. (2014). #YesAllWomen as Feminist Meme Event. *Feminist Media Studies, 14*(6), 1090–1092.

Tilly, C., and Tarrow, S. (2015). *Contentious politics* (2nd ed.). New York: Oxford University Press.

Tolentino, J. (2018, January 24). The rising pressure of the #MeToo backlash. *New Yorker.* https://www.newyorker.com/culture/culture-desk/the-rising -pressure-of-the-metoo-backlash.

Tong, R., and Botts, T. F. (2018). *Feminist thought: A more comprehensive introduction.* New York: Routledge.

Traister, R. (2018, February 6). No one is silencing Katie Roiphe: #MeToo has started a robust, complicated conversation—whether or not she's listening. *The Cut.* https://www.thecut.com/2018/02/rebecca-traister-on-katie-roiphe -harpers-and-metoo.html.

Tufekci, Z. (2017). *Twitter and tear gas: The power and fragility of networked protest.* New Haven, CT: Yale University Press.

Tufekci, Z., and Wilson, C. (2012). Social media and the decision to participate in political protest: Observations from Tahrir Square. *Journal of Communication, 62*(2), 363–379.

Tynes, B. M., Schuschke, J., and Noble, S. U. (2016). Digital intersectionality theory and the #BlackLivesMatter movement. In S. U. Noble and B. M. Tynes (Eds.), *The intersectional internet: Race, class, and culture online.* New York: Peter Lang Publishing.

Valenti, J. (2014a, August 25). Beyoncé's "Flawless" feminist act at the VMAs leads the way for other women. *Guardian.* https://www.theguardian.com /commentisfree/2014/aug/25/beyonce-flawless-feminist-vmas?CMP =twt_gu.

———. (2014b, November 24). When everyone is a feminist, is anyone? *Guardian.* https://www.theguardian.com/commentisfree/2014/nov/24/when-everyone -is-a-feminist.

Walker, R. (2017, January 25). The DIY revolutionaries of the pussyhat project. *New Yorker.* http://www.newyorker.com/culture/culture-desk/the-d-i-y -revolutionaries-of-the-pussyhat-project.

Walsh, D., and Blackwell, N. (2018, January 21). Debate Room: Has #MeToo turned into a witch hunt? *The Journal*. http://www.thejournal.ie/readme /debate-room-me-too-witch-hunt-3803090-Jan2018/.

Weaver, H. (2018, January 7). Golden Globes 2018: Black dresses, Time's Up pins, activist plus-ones, and everything else you need to know. *Vanity Fair*. https:// www.vanityfair.com/style/2018/01/golden-globes-2018-red-carpet-times-up.

Whelehan, I. (2000). *Overloaded: Popular culture and the future of feminism*. London: The Women's Press.

Whittier, N. (1995). *Feminist generations: The persistence of the radical women's movement*. Philadelphia: Temple University Press.

womensmarch. (2017, January 18). The leadership of the Women's March on Washington are not experts on every issue [tweet]. https://twitter.com /womensmarch/status/821879131138826240.

Women's March on Washington. (2016). Women's March on Washington: Origins and inclusion [Facebook post]. https://www.facebook.com/womens marchonwash/posts/1338876609458948.

———. (2017a). *Guiding vision and definition of principles*. https://static1 .squarespace.com/static/584086c7be6594762f5ec56e/t/587ffb20579fb3554 668c111/1484782369253/WMW+Guiding+Vision+%26+Definition+of +Prurthinciples.pdf.

———. (2017b). Sister marches. https://www.womensmarch.com/sisters.

———. (2018a). Sister marches press. https://www.womensmarch.com/sisters -press.

———. (2018b). Women's March board. https://www.womensmarch.com/team/.

Wood, E. A. (2008). Consciousness-raising 2.0: Sex blogging and the creation of a feminist sex commons. *Feminism & Psychology, 18*(4), 480–487.

Woodall, C. (2020, November 3). Year of the woman: How Pa. women are shaping the 2020 election more than previous years. *York Daily Record*. https://www.ydr.com/story/news/politics/elections/2020/11/03/year-woman -how-pa-women-shaping-2020-election/6123243002/.

Woods, H. S. (2014). Anonymous, Steubenville, and the politics of visibility: Questions of virality and exposure in the case of #OPRollRedRoll and #OccupySteubenville. *Feminist Media Studies, 14*(6), 1096–1098.

Wortham, J. (2011, October 22). Zines have a resurgence among the web savvy. *New York Times*. http://www.nytimes.com/2011/10/23/business/media/zines -have-a-resurgence-among-the-web-savvy.html.

Xiao, J. (2017, April 23). Why the white feminism of the Women's March is still on my mind. *The Establishment*. https://medium.com/the-establishment/why-the -white-feminism-of-the-womens-march-is-still-on-my-mind-bbo8d3279f14.

Youmans, W. L., and York, J. C. (2012). Social media and the activist toolkit: User agreements, corporate interests, and the information infrastructure of modern social movements. *Journal of Communication, 62*(2), 315–329.

Young, S. (1997). *Changing the wor(l)d: Discourse, politics, and the feminist movement*. New York: Routledge.

Zacharek, S., Dockterman, E., and Edwards, H. S. (2017). The silence breakers. *Time.* http://www.time.com/time-person-of-the-year-2017-silence-breakers/.

Zeisler, A. (2016). *We were feminists once: From Riot Grrrl to CoverGirl, the buying and selling of a political movement*. New York: Public Affairs.

Zhou, L. (2018, November 2). The striking parallels between 1992's "Year of the Woman" and 2018, explained by a historian. *Vox.* https://www.vox.com/2018/11/2/17983746/year-of-the-woman-1992.

Zillman, C., and Hinchliffe, E. (2020, November 5). 2020 elections mark another "Year of the Woman"—this time for Republicans. *Fortune.* https://fortune.com/2020/11/05/2020-election-results-republican-women-congress/.

Zmuda, N., and Diaz, A.C. (2014, September 2). Empowerment in ads: Soft feminism or soft soap? *AdAge.* http://adage.com/article/cmo-strategy/marketers-soft-feminism/294740/.

Zobl, E. (2009). Cultural production, transnational networks, and critical reflection in feminist zines. *Signs, 35*(1), 1–12.

Index

Founded in 1893,
UNIVERSITY OF CALIFORNIA PRESS
publishes bold, progressive books and journals
on topics in the arts, humanities, social sciences,
and natural sciences—with a focus on social
justice issues—that inspire thought and action
among readers worldwide.

The UC PRESS FOUNDATION
raises funds to uphold the press's vital role
as an independent, nonprofit publisher, and
receives philanthropic support from a wide
range of individuals and institutions—and from
committed readers like you. To learn more, visit
ucpress.edu/supportus.

CPSIA information can be obtained
at www.ICGtesting.com
Printed in the USA
BVHW050750251122
652753BV00004B/386